THE GRAND LIFE

Confessions of an Old School Hotelier in the L

A TRILOGY

PART III : THE GRAND FINALE

1988 - 2011

by

PATRICK L GRIFFIN OAM

with

JULIANA PAYNE

A catalogue record for this book is available from the National Library of Australia

Publisher:
ASPG (Australian Self Publishing Group)
P.O. Box 159, Calwell, ACT Australia 2905
Email: publishaspg@gmail.com
http://www.inspiringpublishers.com

National Library of Australia Cataloguing-in-Publication entry

Author: Patrick L Griffin OAM with Juliana Payne

Series: **THE GRAND LIFE: Confessions of an Old School Hotelier in the Digital Age**

Title: **A TRILOGY – Part III: The Grand Finale 1988-2011**
Patrick L Griffin OAM with Juliana Payne

ISBN: 978-0-6450559-2-4 (Print)
ISBN: 978-0-6450559-3-1 (eBook)

Dedication

There have been three men in my life whom I feel played a significant part in my development, my life and my career. I would like to dedicate Part III to the late James B Sherwood, President and Founder of Orient-Express Hotels, the most visionary businessman and entrepreneur I have ever had the pleasure to know. He said to Elizabeth Grice of the UK *Telegraph,* "I think there is a demand for the best. In life today we are confronted with so much mediocrity. In an age when everyone is deluged with homogeneous brands, I have liked to create the special. There is a real unfulfilled need and desire to experience it."

The Observatory Hotel in Sydney was to be such a hotel. With a dedicated team we lived and breathed his vision and standards. He was proud to include us in the Orient-Express Collection. Along the way he has allowed me to enjoy a life that otherwise I could only have dreamt of, and for that I shall be forever grateful.

James Blair Sherwood
1933 - 2020

Introduction

1954 - 'Patrick is terribly slow and difficult. Very forgetful and lazy. Does not seem to realize that he is growing up. Conduct: Must be more reliable.' *Miss R.C.Bean, Headmistress.*

1992 - 'Patrick you are booked to New Orleans in first class and on the Concorde from New York to London, a suite booked at the Ritz and will board The Orient-Express to Venice the following day' . *Malcolm, The Travel Agent.*

Miss Bean would have been shocked out of her sensible woollen stockings. Mr Bryant, my next headmaster, would have snorted in disbelief, whilst J.M. Merriman, my Housemaster at public school might have mulled over his final sardonic comment of "A smooth and plausible boy this, I am sure he will do well in his chosen *trade.*"

Whilst being treated for a third bout of persistent (but thankfully non-fatal) cancer, I indulged in some inevitable soul-searching. My wonderful haematologist, Dr Julie Crawford, exhorted me - 'don't stress, enjoy life to the full and pray'. I was used to doing the first two, and the third didn't appeal at all, so I concluded that now was the time to write the bucket list.

With the nurse's selection of 1960s music playing in the hospital ward, I realised that my life had already been spectacularly full and privileged. I had family and friends; I had indulged in a luxurious lifestyle in fabulous places, and had met the rich, famous and notorious along the way.

There was very little left to include on the bucket list, but I had a full complement of wonderful memories.

In a hotel career spanning fifty years, I encountered many people of note and notoriety. Some appeared kind and charming but were absolute bastards; others who presented as absolute bastards were, in fact, kind and charming.

In Australia, I opened two hotels that hosted hundreds of public figures, stars of film, theatre, music and society. Most fell into the category of kind and charming, but some were less so. Those of us 'below stairs' were privy to it all, especially their indiscretions. I've recounted a few of these tales, but due to the high cost of defending defamation claims as an impoverished pensioner, I have chosen to err on the side of caution, and many will remain unspoken!

The greatest lessons I had learned had been on the working floors of hotels. I came to appreciate the opportunities that were presented to me every day, and by helping others fulfil their dreams, I was able to fulfil my own.

Recounting my memories (or confessions in some cases) has given me so much fun, pleasure and reward. This is the final part of the trilogy, and I do hope that you also read Parts I and II, and enjoy the story from the beginning.

I am still uncertain as to how I actually achieved what I did, and credit is due to those around me, but one thing I do know is how lucky and fortunate I have been to be able to say, without reservation, that it's been The Grand Life.

Acknowledgements

I have to thank so many who have helped me with this project, my late father, who for reasons only known to himself, kept all my school reports, letters and other documents. My good friend Jonathan Webley, and his PA, June Pockett from The Grand for the copy of their book 'The Grand Hotel' by Peter Pugh, and for photocopying lots of information. Also the many friends from The Observatory Hotel, together with others who reminded me of names and events that I had long forgotten. These memories I have recorded with as much accuracy as I am able. I have mentioned some people by name, hopefully spelt correctly, I have also changed some names, for discretion or simply due to the fact that I really can't put a name to the face. My special thanks and gratitude are extended to all, and my apologies to those that I have inadvertently forgotten to mention. For much of the general information used to elaborate on some issues I must give thanks to the contemporary fountain of knowledge, Wikipedia. Any mistakes in regards to names, places and dates are entirely of my own making and I would be happy to correct any in future editions. The photos are either from my own personal collection or taken from Observations, the hotel's newsletter. I am also grateful for the generosity of the celebrities who so willingly provided many signed photos. I have endeavoured to locate the copyright holders of the very few photos I have downloaded for this book, which has not been straightforward or easy, and I would be happy to correct any omissions or errors.

Most of all my appreciation must go to my dear friend Juliana Payne, who gave me considerable help in reviewing, editing and publishing the books, as without this help, encouragement, and knowhow, I would never have completed this endeavour.

Last but not least, my three sons, Steve, himself an accomplished author*, Tim, a uniquely gifted IT specialist, and Charlie, a hotelier after my own heart. Finally, but far from least, my wonderful wife Gan, for her patience, encouragement and support in times of '*sickness and health*' ... and for supplying the bottomless pot of coffee that has kept me going.

* https://www.steve-griffin.com

EVENTS THAT SHAPED THE ERA 1989 - 2011

1988 - Family arrive in Australia, business class, 200 years after convicts arrive in less comfort - Commence as GM of the Hotel Como, Melbourne. - Company car a Ford LTD complete with my first mobile phone - UK Pubs allowed to open all day now that I have left. Favourite music, *The only way is up,* by Yazz - my Australian theme

1989 - Lose my father to Alzheimer's - Berlin Wall comes down - Pro-democracy rallies followed by tragedy in Beijing's Tiananmen Square - Newcastle, NSW earthquake, 13 die. Favourite music, *Living years,* by Mike and the Mechanics, memories of my father.

1990 - Lose my mother to pancreatic cancer - Tim Berners-Lee invents the World Wide Web - Now Hotel Como has arrived, Melbourne voted world's best city - Paul Keating calls Australia a 'Banana Republic'. Favourite music, *Nothing compares to you,* by Sinead O'Connor.

1991 - Son Charlie is born, the first Aussie born in the family - We become Australian Citizens - Robert Maxwell is found floating in the sea - I join Orient-Express, operator of 14 hotels and am appointed General Manager, of their newest, The Observatory

Hotel, Sydney. Best horror movie since *Psycho: Silence of the Lambs* - Favourite music, *Everything I do,* by Bryan Adams

1992 - Lose my brother Bob to AIDS - Channel Tunnel opens linking England and France - Sydney Harbour Tunnel opens linking North Shore to the City - Fly on Concorde, ride the Orient-Express Train and stay in Italy's top hotels, welcome to the company - Favourite music, *I will always love you,* by Whitney Houston

1993 - Labour wins "unwinnable" election - Juan Antonio Samaranch announces that the winner is...*SYDERNY* for the 2000 Summer Olympics - The Queen opens Buckingham Palace to the public (sadly, I was too busy to join her) - Favourite music NONE - I lose touch and regress to my old favorites while listening to Glenn A Baker's *Reelin' in the Years* as I travel the world with Qantas.

1994 - Apartheid ends in South Africa - Student shoots at Prince Charles - next day we meet - Promoted to Regional Managing Director, Orient-Express Australia.

1995 - Kobe, Japan, earthquake kills 6,433 people - I meet Prime Minister Paul Keating - I meet Liberal Party leader John Howard to show I'm not biased - Bob Carr becomes NSW Premier

1996 - John Howard becomes Prime Minister - Port Arthur massacre, 35 dead, gun laws introduced. I head off to the Atlanta Summer Olympics - AA Milne's son, Christoper Robin, dies.

1997 - Princess Diana dies in a car crash in Paris - Britain hands Hong Kong back to China - The Observatory introduces its own website - Dolly the sheep cloned. I watch *Titanic*.

1998 - Financial Crisis hits South East Asia - we watch MUA industrial action against Patrick Stevedores from The Observatory Hotel - Nominated for 'Independent Hotelier of the World'.

1999 - Australians vote 'NO' in republic referendum - Euro currency introduced – Millennium bug comes to nothing and no planes fall from the sky - The Great South Pacific Express (GSPE) rail service commences in Australia between Kuranda (near Cairns) and Sydney.

2000 - Sydney Olympics - Global stock markets tumble as the dotcom bubble bursts - GST introduced in Australia - OEH purchases Lilianfels Hotel, in the Blue Mountains.

2001 - 9/11, Terrorists crash aircraft into The World Trade Centre - Sir Don Bradman dies - A$ drops below US$.50c - Christopher Skase dies at 53 - Ansett Airlines collapses.

2002 - Bali Bombings, 202 people killed including 38 Indonesians, 88 Australians and 43 from other countries; I lose two friends there. Sydney threatened by bushfires. Best invention - 'Braille Glove'.

2003 - Australia joins US-led attack on Iraq - The final Concorde Flight - Bee Gee Maurice Gibb dies aged 53 - UK Motorcycle Champion Barry Sheen dies of cancer at 52 on the Gold Coast.

2004 - Boxing Day tsunami kills 230,000 in Asia - Facebook launched by Mark Zuckerberg - Qantas launches budget airline Jetstar - Ghan Train travels from Adelaide to Darwin.

2005 - Hurricane Katrina kills 1,836 people in New Orleans, the Windsor Court Hotel is evacuated -YouTube is launched - I am diagnosed with leukemia (CLL), life goes on.

2006 - Execution of Saddam Hussein - Twitter is launched - Commonwealth Games held in Melbourne - Awarded AHA 'Life Member Award' - Racing driver Peter Brock dies aged 61

2007 - Australia avoids recession amidst Global Financial Crisis - John Howard defeated - Labor Kevin Rudd becomes Prime Minister - OEH meet in New Orleans, city still devastated.

2008 - Sydney hosts Catholic World Youth Day which the Pope attends - I buy land in Thailand - I am diagnosed with prostate cancer, life falters a little but I live to fight another day.

2009 - 'Black Saturday' bushfires in Victoria, 173 fatalities - Bitcoin is launched - I am inducted as an inaugural member of Hotel Magazine's 'Hall of Fame'- Awarded a Medal of the Order of Australia (OAM) in the Queen's Birthday Honours List.

2010 - The iPad is introduced - Instagram is launched - I try to figure out what social media is all about, with little success - Attend my last GM's Conference in Charleston, South Carolina.

2011 - Osama bin Laden killed - Wedding of Prince William and Kate Middleton - Doomsday Clock now 23.54 - Orient-Express now has grown from 14 to 52 hotels, trains & cruises - The West African black rhinoceros declared extinct - I retire and might soon follow.

The Story So Far...

On his return from the Hilton Amsterdam, Patrick worked his way up the hotel career ladder from The Castle in Norwich, The Cavendish in Eastbourne, to the De Montfort in Kenilworth as their youngest ever General Manager. He then took on his biggest challenge yet at the De Vere Hotel in Coventry. A holiday in Australia presented a brand new opportunity for him, and he emigrated with his family to a new country, a new challenge and eventually an amazing new phase in his career with Orient-Express Hotels...

Missed out on the beginning? Follow Patrick's early progress in Part I and Part II in the trilogy

PART I : THE GRAND JOURNEY BEGINS
1946 - 1967

PART II : THE GRAND LESSONS LEARNED
1967 - 1988

PART III : THE GRAND FINALE

1988 - 2011

Numbers in superscript throughout the text refer to the photos on pages 364 to 402

Chapter 1

#G'daymelbourne #veniceontheyarra #rubberducks

Having recovered over the weekend from our flight from the UK to Australia and the inevitable jet lag, I was ready to start work as the general manager of The Hotel Como: part of an exciting new project under construction in Melbourne's ritzy South Yarra.[1]

On that sunny June morning in 1988, in what Australians amusingly call winter, I set out for the office: no overcoat, but an umbrella just in case. My new office was a temporary set up next to the hotel during construction. When I arrived at 8.00am, there was already a small team present, a reminder that Aussies are not laid back and lazy. I met the financial controller, an Indian man called Wahid Banihali and the director of sales and marketing, Joy Cartwright, who had been employed before me. They made me very welcome for which I was grateful as I realised I would rely on them.

It was rapidly dawning on me how little I knew of the way things worked in Australia. My strengths had been in my network built up over twenty-five years in English hotels; here, I had none, not a single one. I was nevertheless expected by my new employer AGC, one of Australia's oldest national finance companies, to plan, develop, equip and prepare for a new hotel to open in eight months. I didn't even know where to buy a teaspoon.

Hopefully I could call on John Waring who had been employed by AGC as a consultant for FF&E (Fixtures, Fittings & Equipment). There was also the issue of recruiting and training Aussie staff, whom I had been led to believe were impossible to train and incapable of providing five star service. My earlier confidence was on the wane.

Wahid was a nice guy and a very capable financial controller, however I fell short in his eyes quite early in our relationship when he discovered I did not share his passion for cricket. Joy was a classic Queenslander. She was very experienced in Australian hotels having been on the opening team of another hotel on the Gold Coast. She was not what I would call demure and from a rather conservative Englishman's viewpoint her dress sense was *casual*. She really knew her stuff though, and was very motivated. I liked her as she did not stand on ceremony and if she thought I was wrong she told me so, which was just what I needed to be able to negotiate the cultural minefield I now found myself in.

David Fogarty, who had appointed me to this role on behalf of AGC, proved a great friend. There was an honesty about him; he spoke his mind and he played no political angles. With most relationships, particularly at work, one is always a little guarded, but David really believed in helping those around him. He embodied the saying 'what you see is what you get' and embodied all that was good about the Aussie character. Don Neilson, to whom David reported, was the man in charge of the 'Como Project'. They had taken a controlling share in the troubled multi-million dollar 'Little Venice' development from Jack Chia, a Singaporean magnate. I found Don a difficult man to deal with and David was a blessing to have as an intermediary.

Many of the problems had been due to industrial strife with the unions, something that I was to learn a lot about in the coming weeks. My first encounter erupted sooner than I expected.

Having had a cup of coffee and been updated on the status of the build, I went for a walk to check out my new domain. I entered the unfinished lobby and wandered around. There was not a soul in sight. I headed for the lift, as the hotel rooms started on the third floor. In the lift I found a large armchair that took up most of the space, and a broomstick with no broom head. Very puzzling. I pressed the button for the sixth floor. The doors opened and I stepped out and started to look around. A builder appeared and looked at me in my Savile Row suit with some surprise. "Who are you, mate?"

> "I'm the new GM who is going to run the hotel."
>
> "Not bloody yet you ain't," with which he struck up a chat on a walkie-talkie. In seconds four or five other workers gathered around, all on walkie-talkies. The feeling was not friendly. The group parted and a man appeared in front of me, not in workman's clothes.
>
> "Who are you?" he asked accusingly.
>
> "I'm the guy who is the new general manager of the hotel," thinking now I might get a bit of respect. How naive I was. He ignored my introduction.
>
> "How did you get up here?"
>
> "By the lift."
>
> "What, on yer own?" At first I thought he was just being sarcastic. "Are you a bloody Pom? When did *your* boat get in?"

Yes, I was English and yes I had just arrived. He turned to the others and laughed. "A bloody Pom. Look here mate you have a lot to learn. This is not your hotel, it's a fucking building site, and no one comes on to it without our say so, or without a hard hat.

As far as the lift is concerned, that is only operated by one of our members. OK?" With this it seemed my tour was over and I was somewhat ignominiously frog marched off the premises.

I did get back on site soon afterwards, with an escort and wearing a hard hat, which even had my name on it. I eventually got to know a number of the workers and they were not as unfriendly as it appeared on my first visit. The lift operator and I became good friends. Bill was on what I learned was *workers comp*, being rehabilitated with light duties following a work accident. It was hard to guess what injury he had, as he sat most of the day in his armchair in the lift, broom handle in hand, with which he pressed the buttons. The unions certainly had power.

There was another man I noticed who had a complete broom in his hand, and on occasions actually used it and did a little sweeping and tidying up after the workers. He always gave me a cheery wave. When part of the project was complete, there was a formal cocktail party and we all turned up in our dinner jackets. I noticed the sweeper there, attired in a smart bow tie and dinner jacket, champagne in hand. Curious, I started chatting to him. He was a Seychellois having come to Australia when Albert Rene had taken over the Presidency of the Seychelles from the liberal thinking James Macham in a *coup*. As I had been there and had friends in the Seychelles at the time of the *coup*, I knew all about it. As a result of this conversation he looked on me as a friend. I made a few discreet enquiries as to who this guy was, who on the one hand swept up, and yet on the other hand was on the VIP list for events.

What I learnt made me a little wary of my new friend. It seemed that having had a lot of troubles with union agitators stirring up trouble on the project, the company had employed this man to keep them informed as to any impending problems on site. I couldn't see how it worked; surely everyone knew who he was? He had a reputation for being tough, and had all sorts of contacts both in high places and the underworld. I heard of one case where management were concerned about a man on site. Within twenty four hours his complete police file was on the manager's desk. No one asked questions, we simply called him 'ASIO' after the 'Australian Security Intelligence Organisation'.

I became even more nervous when chatting with him, when he told me how much he hated Rene, the Seychelles president. He told me a grisly story of how Rene had tortured his brother by making him swallow fish-hooks and then pulling them out. He asked if I might be able to help - could I introduce him to wealthy contacts when the hotel opened who may be interested to back another *coup* to overthrow Rene? As a reward I could have any of the hotels on the island. I thought this was a joke, but he was serious.

There had been a *coup* attempt that made the headlines. *Revolvy.com* tells us that "On 25 November 1981, Seychellois security forces put down a coup attempt sponsored by South Africa. 'Mad Mike' Hoare, a well known Anglo-Irish mercenary, and 43 others posed as members of the 'Ancient Order of Froth Blowers' visiting the islands as tourists. Shortly after leaving their aircraft, an airport security guard spotted a Kalashnikov assault rifle in their luggage. The discovery launched a gun battle in which hostages were taken. Most of the mercenaries escaped after hijacking another plane sitting on the runway".

I was no Mad Mike. I had been asked for various forms of support in the past, but none like this. I wanted to maintain my sedate life as the urbane English hotelier. I made sure to distance myself from him. My last encounter with Mr ASIO was after we opened. He wandered into my office and casually sat on my desk. He explained that he wanted the best suite on the weekend to entertain his girlfriend. I was a little nervous about this.

No-one ever said *No* to him. I plucked up the courage to say I could not do it for free, but would give him a good rate.

"No problem. How much? Five hundred bucks?"

I was going to do it for less but he seemed unfazed at the figure, so I agreed.

"Can I use your phone?" He didn't wait for my reply but lent across and started dialing. "I want $500 this afternoon. Cash, OK? I'll be over."

I had no idea who he spoke to, but I knew he was working on the renovation of The Princes Theatre. I assumed he had the same kind of relationship with them as he had with The Como. That afternoon he appeared with a brown paper McDonalds bag out of which he tipped $500 in small bills onto my desk. The money smelt like a Quarter Pounder.

I was also learning the vernacular. 'Smoko', 'this arvo', 'she'll be right mate' and - my favourite - 'get rooted'. I thought this translated to an earthy Aussie equivalent of 'not on your life' or 'get knotted'. I was in a meeting with the board of directors, with a number of women in attendance, explaining how I had got rid of someone who was asking for a ridiculous favour. One of the women asked me what I had said to them. In my best Aussie accent I declared to the room, "I told them to get rooted." I was a little surprised at the reaction. Later, David took me to one side and explained the true meaning, and that it might be better if I maintained my more cultured English expressions in the future. I whole-heartedly agreed.

The hotel edged slowly towards completion. I started to build my team, starting with my PA, Julie, a lovely young woman. She helped to introduce me to what to see and where to go. I started to understand why Australia was known as 'the lucky country'.

One weekend she was off to her summer house up the coast. I was most impressed; this sounded like the stuff that millionaires are made of. "That sounds very nice; does your father live up there?"

"No, mum and dad live here in Melbourne. It's just a weekender and we go up when we can if the weather is good."

"What does your father do?" Expecting him to be a CEO or similar who could afford two homes.

"He's retired now, but used to be a milkman."

It was a simple statement, as if it was the norm to have two homes, although having just purchased my own home with a mortgage rate of 17% I was hard pressed to understand how.

Next was my deputy, Tony May, an immaculately turned out young man, gifted with the experience and style of the international hotelier, who, coincidentally, I had worked with at De Vere Hotels in the UK. One thing I always looked for in a manager was attention to detail. For me there were three types of manager. The first was one who would walk through the lobby and if there was a piece of rubbish on the floor, didn't see it. The second was the one who walked through and on seeing the rubbish, would ask someone to pick it up. Finally, there was the manager who saw it, and picked it up himself. Tony without doubt was number three. He also had the great characteristic that I never understood but appreciated in those early very stressful days. When we were chasing our tails to get everything in place, he maintained an air of calm without a hair out of place. I was pleased that at least one of us could keep calm and carry on.

He was followed by the recruitment of my housekeeper, Marlene Miller. A very tough and thorough woman, ex Navy and gifted with the organisational abilities of a deck officer. Marlene appointed her number two, Dina Angelucci. I soon found my engineer, Graham. Well qualified and for whom nothing was ever a problem. Then came the concierge and the front office and assistant manager, Russell Bullen, a larger than life young man who talked so fast that I had difficulty getting a word in. He and Tony pointed out one of many 'design over practicality' issues we had. A beautifully designed reception front desk had been installed. Wonderful curved glass top with a birds-eye maple base, the signature wood throughout the hotel. With great pride the designer presented it, and Tony asked "Beautiful, but where are the cash drawers?" The desk was meant to serve the cashiers. Red faces on the designers. [2]

"Oh, you need a cash drawer?" Their bewildered response.

We also had magnificent, very deep Japanese baths. They were so high and so deep, we had to provide a little stool for those guests with shorter legs than Elle Macpherson. The rooms were styled to wow the lens of a *Vogue* photographer, with little chairs and a design feature where everything had a five degree angle. It looked great on the glossy magazine pages but I found them most uncomfortable. Apparently this was the price to pay for an innovative, groundbreaking new hotel. We were truly built for style rather than comfort. [3]

We continued recruiting and there seemed to be no shortage of people seeking an opportunity in hospitality. I remembered Don's comment that it would be impossible to get Australians to provide good service, so it was with some trepidation that we started the selection process. I always believed when looking for staff to go for personality and common sense. You can always teach technical skills. In Australia I was finding an abundance of staff with the qualities I sought.

Within a short space of time we had filled most of the positions. The housekeeper set about training her chambermaids, now called 'room attendants'. I focussed on the front of house staff. The first and last contact with any hotel guest is by way of the doorman, porter, and concierge. These were the ones I wanted to ensure truly understood the meaning of personal service.

In my first training session I set out with the mindset I had learned in England. I knew what service was all about and what was required. I would explain that we wanted to be the number one hotel in Melbourne, if not Australia and then I'd explain what I wanted from them.

We all introduced ourselves around the room. The first thing I noticed was that they all used only their first names, and they were calling me 'Patrick'. I couldn't remember when I was last called by that name. My family called me Paddy, at school and as a trainee I was simply called Griffin and then it became Mr. Griffin when I became a manager. But never *Patrick*. I was new, so I chose to go with the flow.

I found this first name basis confusing at first. In England, if someone on the phone called you Patrick, it was someone you actually knew. Otherwise they would call you Mr Griffin. In Australia, everyone on the phone would say 'Hello Patrick' as if they were your oldest friend, so I was never sure whether to use my business-like greeting or my old mates greeting.

Because Australians were not bound by formal etiquette rules, it made for a far more sincere and genuine welcome than ever we had in England. I also found that the young staff were not intimidated by a VIP or company CEO. They had an egalitarian mentality with all the guests and staff alike.

During the training day I started to tell the staff how they should address the guests, how they should open the door and greet them on arrival. I was only minutes into my instruction when I was interrupted. A very Aussie voice piped up with "Why, Patrick?" I wasn't sure I heard him correctly. Was he questioning me? He had no experience in hotels, and he was questioning me? "Why do it like that?" he asked again.

I was about to say, "well that's how it is done and always has been that way" when something stopped me. "Well - have you a better way?" With this, I turned it into a discussion. I suddenly realised that he wasn't being a smartass but genuinely wanted to understand.

What happened in that moment changed my entire thinking on training and dealing with staff in Australia. I took down my planned presentation, the one I would have used in England where staff sit quietly and listen to what they are told, and then hopefully follow the instructions. I turned to a clean sheet of paper on the flip chart and asked the question. "OK, what do you think we should do?"

Their faces changed. No longer blank or bored, but interested and involved. Staff started to call out suggestions that came thick and fast and as they did I wrote them on the flip chart. I put beside them the name of the suggestor. This went on all day and we built up a list of service standards that were all their ideas. They owned these standards. After we opened, I found a porter not maintaining one of the key standards. I took him aside, showed him the standard that was on the flip chart paper stuck up behind the scenes, and pointed to the words we had written up in training, with his name beside it. I said nothing, and he said "I am sorry - how could I forget." He never did again.

I also wanted to bring on board a specialist in hospitality training. The only issue was that he was in the UK. Tom Cosgrove had once been an assistant of mine in Coventry and had left to set up his own training company, in which he had become very successful, having worked with British Airways setting up their First Class cabin service standards. Don agreed to bring him out. I called Tom and he nearly fell off his chair when I asked if he would like to come out from the UK to Australia for a month. He leapt at the opportunity. He was never to return to live in England, as he fell in love with Australia, or rather - an *Australian*. An Australian *man*. I knew nothing about this when we worked together in England.

We developed ideas to add a point of difference to the hotel. Tony, Russell and I had great discussions on 'turn down' gifts and little touches that might make us unique. By now I had stayed in many of Australia's top hotels and was amazed at just how many gifts were showered upon me, chocolates, mints, fruit and all the things that one rather expected. Appreciated, but none had sparked my imagination, there was nothing that stood out, so we had brainstorming sessions about our gifts.

Once, while with the housekeeper and some room attendants, we were discussing what we could do in the bathrooms. How could we display the guest amenities? I was always frustrated when taking a shower in a hotel to find all the soaps and shampoos were displayed very neatly, but far out of reach of the shower. We decided to have another set *in* the shower as well as beside the bath, a small addition but loved by our guests ...and no they weren't all taken home.

With our incredibly deep Japanese baths, we had long chains attached to the plugs. One of the room attendants was playing with the chain and wrote 'COMO' with it. I was impressed - what a great idea. We chatted as to what else we might add to what was already a very special bathroom. [4]

I remembered in Coventry, some years before, we had an Institute of Company Directors conference at the hotel and we gave all these high flying, very conservative bosses a rubber duck in their bathrooms. This idea did not create much of a response amongst my Como team, so I forgot about it. A week later the

Marlene, the housekeeper came into my office with a tray, on which was displayed ten rubber ducks of all shapes, sizes and colours. "Well - which one do you like?"

I was surprised as there had been little enthusiasm shown when I first floated the duck idea. There was one that stood out above the rest. It was the right size, right colour and - with its yellow beak and long eyelashes - cute. Best of all, it was not expensive. After that the duck became part of the hotel, and over time became a celebrity in his own right. I say 'his' as, when we ran a competition to name him, of the several hundred names submitted, we settled on a name in keeping with our art deco design: 'Art Ducko'. [5]

Art even gained some notoriety when he appeared in a cartoon in the Melbourne press. True to Aussie earthy humour, the cartoon depicted a rather voluptuous woman in bed with a man, "The Como" being visible on the pillow. The caption read *"Have you a 'rubber', ducky?"*

In our advertising a small shadow of Art was always present, becoming a 'where's Wally' character, and Art morphed into all sorts of other merchandise, including tshirts, key rings and biscuits. We did hear the occasional complaint, the only one relating to any part of our service. He could never sit upright in the bathwater and kept falling over.

When we had opened and had introduced Art, I was concerned that members of the Board of AGC might not share our little touch of humour, so whenever they stayed we would remove them from their suites. One morning when we had been open for a couple of months, I had a call from the Chairman.

"Patrick, I'm sorry if this sounds strange, but a friend of mine, Lady xxxx, stayed with you and says there was rather a cute rubber duck in her bathroom, which she took with her. The problem is that she has three grandchildren and they now all want one. I explained that it might have been left by a previous guest, as I have never seen one in my suite. She may be getting a little odd in her old age. You don't know of any ducks do you?"

I decided to come clean and tell him about 'Art Ducko'. He loved the idea, and complained that he had not had one, and why not? After that 'Art Ducko' became a fully fledged member of The Hotel Como team, and still is.

The training had gone very well, we had a good team who were ready for anything.

All we needed was the hotel.

I was thankful to learn that we were not responsible for the hotel's restaurant or fine dining kitchen, which were to be outsourced. In the hotel precinct was a restaurant, somewhat presumptuously called Maxim's who had even adopted the Parisian typeface for its name above the restaurant door, run by Vincent, an Italian man and his son Paul. To be fair it had over the years become a Melbourne institution, known for their after-theatre chocolate souffle, and Don had decided this was to be the hotel's official restaurant. They had already signed up, and were to do the room service for the hotel. On going through the contract I discovered that it hadn't been thought through and it became the first bone of contention I had with Don.

The theory was good but the lack of detail made it impossible to see how it would work. Breakfast service was undefined. Room service meals had to fit in with restaurant hours and the service was subject to how busy they were. Dining in the restaurant was actually a very enjoyable experience, as the food was good and the service very traditional and of the style to which I was accustomed, but this was going to be a disaster at the hotel.

Our suppliers drove me mad. They would promise to deliver something, and when they didn't turn up, they never bothered to call to let us know. I would call them and hear that such and such was delayed as the Chinese factory had burned down. I soon realised that everything was imported. When problems arose, the fallback was the Aussie expression 'don't worry, she'll be right mate.' It drove me nuts.

And then the builders. It was a few months to opening. It was late November. I saw, to my horror, all the workers walking off the job, amongst them the guys who were balancing the air conditioning in my office. As they were leaving I asked, "What's happening, why is everyone stopping work?"

"The heat mate. The temperature hit 40°C so we stop working."

"What do you mean it's 40°C? You guys are working in an airconditioned hotel, all you are doing is balancing air conditioning?"

"Tough mate. The union rules are when it gets to 40°C, then the site closes. Can't work in that heat."

The hotel build was behind schedule. We planned to open the first week in February and there was still so much to do. On the 22nd of December, everything stopped at lunchtime. It was the Christmas break, and that was that. They would be back in mid January. The hotel went deathly quiet, and the poem of my childhood came to mind.

'Twas the night before Christmas, when all thro' the house,

Not a creature was stirring, not even a mouse…

Except this was nearly a bloody week before Christmas. No-one was to be found and I walked about the *Mary Celeste*. There were tools and equipment just lying where they appeared to have last been used. On the roof, there was an acetylene bottle, beside it a welding torch and goggles, casually abandoned as if the workman had gone for a 'smoko'. But he hadn't; he had gone off on his Christmas holidays.

They did eventually return and we did get the hotel up and running in time to open the doors in the first week of February 1989: a miracle. Our very first guest to check in was Mr Philip Stern, from Sydney, who worked with McKinsey & Company, a global management consulting firm. I am still in contact with Phil to this day, such were the relationships we formed at The Como.

Chapter 2

#thecup #melbournesociety #gardensinthesky

I had to learn how to handle the Australian press. Most of the time it was relatively easy, although I had my moments. When I was asked "How do you think you will get on not being in the CBD?" I was not familiar with this acronym. CBD? Was it Caterers Benevolent Division something or other? Or some organisation relating to the business?

"Well it is something we will need to think about."

Fortunately I didn't finish my sentence by saying 'and maybe join it'. I got away with it. I always used a bit of humour to get away with things, although not all journalists had a sense of humour. Sometimes I wondered what sense they had at all. On one occasion I was showing a group around the suites and out onto the third floor Japanese rooftop garden. On seeing the Japanese bamboo water feature that rocked back and forth making a knocking sound, one journo asked "What does that do?" [6]

"That is a Japanese deer scarer, the knocking of the bamboo scares them away."

"Does it work?" she enquired, quite seriously.

Being three floors up in the middle of Chapel Street, I simply replied, "I think so, as to date I haven't seen one." She seemed satisfied and we moved on.

Don felt it important that I be introduced to Melbourne society and the sort of clients he believed were most suited to his hotel. He had employed a well recognised social A-lister to help. Our press and our PR activities were to be managed by Barry Everingham, who operated a niche PR consultancy. He had gained some international exposure when, in 1985, he wrote the unofficial biography of the royal renegade, Princess Michael of Kent: *MC. The Adventures of a Maverick Princess*. He had been covering the British royal family since 1979 and had become an acknowledged a "royal watcher", a description he hated.

Barry knew the who's who of Melbourne and, tasked with promoting the Hotel Como and introducing me to the city's movers and shakers, he set about arranging events. He set up a couple of dinners at Maxim's, our official restaurant. [7]

The first of these dinners was to introduce this 'member of the English gentry', as I had been billed by Barry, to the local A-listers of Melbourne. Amongst them were Sir Rupert and Lady Kathleen Clarke, he being a well respected pastoralist and, as chairman of King Ranch properties in Australia was worth around $100 million. There was Lady Sonia McMahon, the wife of one of Australia's least-admired Prime Ministers, remembered for the high cut dress with which she scandalised Nixon's White House in 1971. The daring dress was split up both sides to the armpits, held together by rhinestones leaving an inch of skin visible all the way down. Of course Lillian Frank was invited, a well-known socialite and charity fundraiser, famous for her spectacular hats at the Melbourne races. These notables of local society were joined by many others who all 'knew who they were'. But my social acceptance into the Melbourne glitterati nearly ended before it began.

At the first dinner they were all charming, as we laughed and chatted about my background and my family. They found my little anecdotes of my mother's insistence on 'correct' upbringing very amusing, until I reached a tale about my marriage prospects. I recounted my mother's warning, "Paddy, if you keep behaving as you are, God forbid, you will grow up and marry a hairdresser."

A sudden silence fell. Where was the laughter? There was just shock and horror. It was palpable, and there were glances across the table to Lillian Frank. What had I said? Barry took up the conversation and the chatting continued but not quite as light-heartedly as before. Later Barry took me to one side and quietly explained that Lillian Frank, apart from being a leading socialite and respected fundraiser, was a very high-profile Toorak *hairdresser*. I needed to learn about the new social order in egalitarian Australia.

I was never invited to one of her soirees.

Barry took me to events all over town, culminating of course in The Melbourne Cup. A horse race like no other, not even Epsom and Ascot, and it truly 'stopped the nation'. The race day has its own public holiday, Parliament rises for the race, and it is one of the most prestigious events on the social calendar. Everyone turns out in their finest hats and fashions. On the day the most prestigious invitations were to The Bird Cage at Flemington and to the pre-Cup event at Lynch's. [8]

Lynch's was an ultra-fashionable restaurant, a landmark in South Yarra, and not too far from The Como. This lunch was always sold out and unless you were connected you had no chance. I arrived with Barry, the place was already packed, tables were crammed together, and you needed to breathe in to squeeze through. We had a privileged table near the window. I was surrounded by women who were trying to out-DAAARLING each other. There was a cacophony of chatter and it was impossible to hear anything else.

Our table had one chair vacant as we started the first course. Even with food being eaten the volume of shrill voices had not abated. A sudden scream pierced through, with a very Australian accent, "My daaarlings there you are..."

"The bloody plane was delayed and then the car was stuck in traffic..." She continued. She was a rather short, bubbly woman, dressed to the nines, with red hair and not a care in the world.

"Red, darling let me introduce you to Patrick ..."

'Red', I discovered was Eileen Bond, wife of Alan Bond, the man behind Australia's historic America's Cup victory about whom I had heard so much in Perth. She acknowledged me with a cursory air kiss and turned to the table. She pulled her hair back to reveal her round earrings that she shook about, and in a loud voice asked, "Like them? They're my 'condom earrings', specially for the Melbourne Cup! What do you think?"

Eileen was indeed an interesting society 'lady'. She had a complete disregard for the stiff social customs of England. Everyone laughed, and no one seemed the tiniest bit shocked. This was certainly not the reaction that one might have seen from guests at a lunch at The Ritz. I was growing fond of Australia.

The cultural learning curve was nowhere near as steep as that of my introduction to the world of finance. AGC, our owner, was a subdivision of Westpac, one of Australia's largest banks, so we were run with an accountant's mentality. This was not an approach I enjoyed very much, but it was a learning curve for me that was long overdue.

I found myself having to do financial reports. Any ideas I had, that I thought were visionary, required budgets that estimated the profit the idea would generate. The first time this was asked of me at a meeting, I said that I was uncertain. Don stood up and drew an arrow on a flip chart and drew rings around it. "Patrick, you are firing an arrow at nothing, and then drawing the target around the arrow to show you have hit the bullseye. Business isn't like that."

I confess he was right. It was a belated eye-opening moment of my career. In the past I had come up with ideas and then just run with them. They usually made a profit, sometimes modest, sometimes more. So without a crystal ball, how was one expected to estimate how many guests would take up an idea? In my experience to that time, without all the marketing data and research starting to be used, we went on instinct and gut feeling.

I knew that profits were essential to a successful business, but I thought there needed to be a balance. That was a radical thought when the accountants were in control. They wanted uniform systems and accurate forecasts, which unfortunately does not encourage creativity and individuality and instead suffocates it. I watched the industry change as more hotels were run in this way, to become uniform and indistinguishable from each other. Managers ceased to manage in the old individualistic style and eventually had their styles dictated to them by a central office, often on the other side of the world, with little or no knowledge of the culture or character of the local country. Hotels were becoming bland and I fought against this trend for the next twenty years.

I had been on a tour of Australia in 1988/89 to review the latest hotels and the standards they offered. I had been amazed at just how many five star hotels were being built, offering high quality luxury. I asked many people where they were going to get the customers to fill all these hotels. The reply was *"Well we now have more than two million international visitors to Australia and it is certain to grow, we're forecasting at least five million by 1995"*. In reality it was not until the new millennium that this figure was reached. I could not believe this optimism - where were the accountants' forecasts when these hotels were being planned? More importantly, the oversupply of rooms meant low rates for their room tariffs. We were faced with an uphill battle to make The Como, with its level of investment, its style, size and location, successful in a limited market. How on earth were we to make the profits that would be expected? We'd need a local attraction like Shakespeare's birthplace that attracted a million visitors a year back then in Stratford.

I discussed it with David, who understood the problem we faced, and he tended to agree that some of the decisions Don had taken were 'somewhat lavish'. Don was expecting the hotel to become a leading statement in quality and style and to be of the 'World Standard' to which he often referred.

So my simple question to David was that it would be hard to have both financial success and this level of quality and style, so which was it to be?

> "Go for 'world class' and win awards. Make Don look good and the hotel famous. We will worry about the profits when his enthusiasm has waned for the high life he's now enjoying."

Within the first year we had become the most talked about 'new kid on the block'. We won the prestigious award of Australia's Top Boutique Hotel, shortly followed by Newspoll's Number One Business Hotel in Australia. [9, 11]

The journalist Ben Sandilands wrote,

> *The Hotel Como in South Yarra Melbourne, is too large to be a boutique hotel, too small to be a big city hotel and too discreet to attract the attention associated with either. It is probably the first of a new genre of Australian hotel, the corporate club hotel,*

and guests almost need a guide to find the front door, as there is nothing neon about its appearance lest that attract the riff raff. 'Australian Business' readers are different, however, and those who found and passed through its portal put it straight to the top of the 'Roy Morgan Research Centre' survey commissioned by this journal.

This was manna from heaven to Don: *It is without doubt the finest Australian expression yet of contemporary world hotel design.* We had arrived on the Australian hotel scene, thanks to my team.

Don bathed in the glory and in what he had achieved. His directors at AGC appeared pleased with the results. So far. His joy was clearly apparent at 'The Hotel Awards Night' which he attended with the team in our first year of operation. We'd achieved some 'fame', but fortune would be a long way off. Fame, however, helped us attract the 'rich and famous'. [10]

The Hotel Como was brand spanking new, not only with style, but a high level of security, discretion and personal service. This combination set us apart from other hotels, especially those that had rested on their past glory. We became the favourite of the music and entertainment world in the late 80s and early 90s.

Due to concern about stalkers and overzealous fans, many guests used pseudonyms, which created some amusement amongst the staff trying to decipher who was actually booked to stay in the VIP Suites. My favourite was 'Willy Savive'. That guest was none other than the very lovely Whoopi Goldberg. The name reflected her hatred of flying.

She was anything but a diva and had a great sense of humour. Every morning she would come down and chat at the front desk before heading out to the shopping mall where she would buy 20 lottery scratchies. She stood there scratching each one, letting out a whoop every time she won. It was always two dollars.

Few people recognised her, but those who did and asked her for an autograph were always successful. Of all the female stars I have encountered, she is without a doubt the least demanding and the warmest of them all.

As we became known as the hotel where the stars stayed, so we started to attract the fans, creating a nightmare for crowd control. I was amazed at the fans' efforts to meet their idols. Some people were just starstruck over any famous person, and after a while I got to know the regulars. One guy in particular was always polite, and caused the least problems. He turned up at any time of the day or night, whatever the weather, for any notable star. He was a professional fan with the ability of a *paparazzo*. One day I got chatting to him. What did he do for a living? How could he turn up here so often? Turned out he worked for the Tax Office, so I thought it best not to upset him. He was a very likeable guy, and was respected by the other fans. I struck a deal with him. I would give him the tip off as to the best time to be outside and he, in return, would control the others as best he could. This arrangement ended up working very well: he would alert us about major fan movements, so that we could prepare fences and hire security guards. I called him *'The Mole'*. I never knew his real name.

When I left the hotel in 1991, The Mole kindly sent me a set of the photos he had taken outside The Como, with a very nice thank you note. To my regret I cannot be found in any of them, but I've included some in this book.

Screen legend Shirley MacLaine stayed with us. I had admired her for many years, starting with one of my favourite films, *The Yellow Rolls Royce*, where she played the gangster's moll opposite George C Scott, with the famous French heart throb, Alain Delon. She rated up there with the top stars of her day and therefore we were wary of how best to treat her. [12]

When I greeted her it was obvious that she expected the formalities to be observed and, although not unfriendly, she did not exude the warmth of Whoopi Goldberg. She was elegant and charming. Word was that she could be a little kooky, believing in UFOs, spirituality and reincarnation. She claimed to have slept with Charlemagne when she was a Moorish peasant girl in a past life. I liked her brother, *You're so Vain* Warren Beatty in the 1967 iconic film *Bonnie and Clyde* with Faye Dunaway.

What I was not aware of was the alleged relationship she had with Andrew Peacock, until a member of my team mentioned it when he came to call on Ms MacLaine during her stay. Mr Peacock had been chairman of the Liberal Party and leader of the Opposition, Ambassador in Washington, and at one time was Minister for Foreign Affairs in the Australian Parliament. Shirley MacLaine revealed all in her book that - apart from the Charlemagne dalliance - in this life her affair with Andrew Peacock began when she was touring Australia and continued as both travelled the world, with assignations in Canada, France, Cambodia, Thailand, England, the US and Mexico.

One star I had always admired as a young man, when I owned my own red Ferrari, was of course Tom Selleck, who played Thomas Magnum in the hit TV series of the 80s, *Magnum PI.* I confess that I had even had my hair permed to give it that same wavy look that he sported at the time. A sad face emoji would fit here. He - along with James Bond - was my youthful *alter ego.* Both were noted for raising one eyebrow, which I too practised diligently. [13]

He booked into the hotel for a month while he was in Australia filming *Quigley Down Under*. The Como Suite was his base. It was on two levels connected by a spiral staircase, popular with the stars but not so popular with the producers, who were scared their star might fall down them. Neither was it popular with the porters, particularly in the case of Tom Selleck. He had a huge amount of luggage and his Louis Vuitton cabin trunk weighed a ton. It took three porters to get it up the spiral staircase to his bedroom. We were all curious as to what it contained. It was too heavy to be just clothes and even too heavy for a corpse. Eventually a room attendant solved the mystery when cleaning the suite and finding the lid open, had a quick peek. We were all rather disappointed to find out it was full of video tapes; he was an avid video watcher, as this helped him fill in time between takes.

I got to know him quite well and one evening he invited me to join him at the Ivy nightclub with another colleague. I was very excited and my wife joined us. Whilst at the club, apart from all the envious looks from the women, I was approached by a couple I knew who asked if it was possible to get his autograph, and I said I would if the opportunity arose. As I returned to my group, the chap's wife was hot on my heels. Not content with my offer, she ran past me. "Tom, I'm a friend of Patrick's and a great fan - I love you!"

She threw her arms around him and kissed him. I was mortally embarrassed; it must have looked like I'd set this up. It took a crowbar to prise her off. Where the hell was her husband? Eventually with the help of club staff I got her away.

"What the bloody hell are you doing?" I was furious. "Are you mad?"

"I don't care, I love him, he's fantastic and whatever happens I will be able to say I kissed Magnum!"

The following day I wrote a letter of apology to Tom Selleck. Regrettably, the damage was done, and I was not invited out again.

Tom was a true gentleman. I have seen many male celebrities who invite their 'nieces' to visit them in their suites. Life is what it is and people do what they do. In Tom's case, even with all his charm and good looks, never did he organise for a 'niece' to visit him in the entire month he was with us. He really was a lovely guy.

In the last week he was with us, he was joined by his wife and baby daughter Hannah. He was newly married, having met his wife Jillie Mack in London, who at the time was the high-energy dancer who played Rumpleteazer in the musical *Cats*. They were a delightful couple and at the time of writing they are still happily together after thirty years. In Hollywood that is something special and rare.

Starring with Tom in this production was Alan Rickman, having recently finished *Die Hard* with Bruce Willis, but who was not yet a household name. The other star was Laura San Giacomo. I had not heard of her, but she had just made a movie called *Sex, Lies and Videotape*. Tom Selleck asked me to make sure she was well looked after. "She's a beautiful girl and a great actress, heading for the top."

I was looking forward to meeting her, so when I was called to the desk, I admit I was rather looking forward to greeting the beautiful young star who I assumed must be like those tall statuesque beauties one sees on the red carpet at the Oscars. Instead I met a petite girl in ripped jeans, wearing the thickest, largest pair of glasses I had ever seen. She was indeed lovely, and very photogenic. I looked out for her when she appeared with Julia Roberts in *Pretty Woman.*

Another group of actors who took up residence with us was the cast of *Mission Impossible*. Not the Tom Cruise version, but the slapstick spoof. The actors included an original cast member, Peter Graves. I remembered him from *Flying High (Airplane* in the US and UK), one of my all-time comedy favourites. I'm sure readers will recall him as the mad pilot, playing his character completely straight. Who can forget him asking the young boy: *"Do you like wrestling? Have you ever been in a Turkish prison? Ever seen a grown man naked?"* I suspect they wouldn't get away with that scene today. [14] Greg Morris was there, known for his role in the even earlier series *Twilight Zone*. Another member of the cast was Thaao Penghlis, a local Sydney boy.

Barry Humphries was a regular; an Australian icon - comedian, actor, satirist, artist, and author, but probably best known for his *alter egos* Dame Edna Everage and Sir Les Patterson. He arrived on a number of occasions with his son, Oscar, who was charming but not a 'chip off the old block'. I wondered what it might have been like growing up with so many personalities in the house. Barry Humphries had a gentlemanly air so far removed from Sir Les and a character so different from Dame Edna, it was hard to imagine him playing those parts. [15]

I had a copy of his book *Dame Edna Everage, My Gorgeous Life*, and as he was walking through the lobby I took the chance of asking if he would kindly sign a copy, for my wife. He looked at it and in a serious tone, said,

> "I am sure Dame Edna would be happy to; I'm going up to the suite now and if she is there I will ask if she could sign it for you."

At first I wasn't sure if this was him just being playful but as he walked off I realised that he was serious. Later that day I met him and he handed me back the book duly noted and signed to my wife, *'For My Gorgeous Bina with the Author's Love & Best Wishes'.* When I thanked him, he said, [16]

> "I will pass your thanks on to her. She was delighted to sign it for you and asked if you had read it as yet?"

I said yes, the diplomatic answer, and with a smile, he left.

Other actors came and went, including Franco Nero, ex-husband of Vanessa Redgrave. He was a blue-eyed and well-built Italian actor discovered by director John Huston, who appeared in more than two hundred movies. Heather Thomas had appeared in *The Fall Guy* with Lee *Six Million Dollar Man* Majors, and was half of the infamous battle of the blonde Heathers with TV star Heather Locklear, who stayed at the hotel at a different time thankfully.

Gary Busey is a prolific character actor who has appeared in over a hundred and fifty films, including *Lethal Weapon* and *Predator 2*. He had a toothy grin and an unsettling glint in his eyes, which suited the nasty people he often played. Turns out he's a nice guy. He slept odd hours and was often found in the lobby strumming a guitar, serenading the staff.

We all loved Sigrid Thornton, star of so many Australian classics including *The Man From Snowy River* and *The Lighthorsemen*. She was friendly to all and very down to earth.

Then came the rock stars.

Motley Crew was an early arrival. The name gave me concern as to whether we really wanted 'these sorts of people' crashing our hotel. So while their dress sense was not what I felt appropriate for a five star hotel, they were actually polite, charming and no trouble whatsoever. Prior to their arrival we had been requested to remove all alcohol from their suites. We started to learn how to handle 'the fans'.

From the other end of the musical spectrum came the Bee Gees, who grew up in Australia. Rather unusually, they brought their mother with them, which we all felt was rather nice and certainly fitted their clean-cut image. They were no trouble, although there was an incident when one of the brothers somehow managed to get something in his eye which resulted in the doctor being called. This developed into a crisis of brain surgery proportions for his manager. [17]

In most cases was not the stars, but their staff who created the crises. They were utterly sycophantic and panicked at the drop of a hat. An off-hand comment was an imperative demand, to be delivered immediately or the world would end. A pop star in the hotel lobby was heard to murmur, "I could murder a Crunchie Bar!" With which, the assistant started screaming at the receptionist,

> "Where are the Crunchies? What sort of hotel are you? No Crunchies? I want a box in his suite in five minutes!"

The Bee Gees were great guys and gave us tickets for their concert. We had the best seats in the house and loved the show.

Simon Le Bon and Nick Rhodes of Duran Duran were nice chaps, who had been used to screaming fans in the 1980s but by the time they stayed with us at the Como they evinced hardly a yelp.[18]

Then Lulu arrived, who had been married to Maurice Gibb from 1969 until 1975. She shot to fame at the age of fifteen with her version of *Shout*, and went on to become a household name in Britain after winning the Eurovision Song Contest in 1969. She later sang the theme songs for *The Man with The Golden Gun* and *To Sir With Love*, as well as appearing in the latter film with Sidney Poitier.

I loved her music as a teenager, being just a couple of years older, so I was quite excited about meeting her. I got to know her quite well. She had become interested in Eastern mysticism and Siddha Yoga Meditation. In Melbourne there was a swami conducting meditation gatherings and Lulu was keen to attend. She asked if I wanted to go with her, and to bring my family. Rather nervously, I agreed.

Lulu, with my wife, Tim and me in tow, headed off to a function centre. I was amazed to see several hundred people there. The seats faced a raised dais decked in silk drapes, flowers and Indian mystical symbols. It looked very exotic, boosted by the scent of joss sticks wafting through the air. I was polite, keeping an open mind; my wife settled in with a little uncertainty. Sitting between us was Tim, eight years old and buying none of it. Being with Lulu, we had VIP seats. The lights dimmed and a slow monotone chant began, repeated over and over. Tim was restless. "Where is she? There's no one there."

"Hush, she'll appear soon." A few minutes passed and I sat with eyes shut trying to meditate and chant the mantra.

"Oh, she's coming Dad. She was hiding behind the curtain," Tim reassured us.

"Hush."

"She's here!"

Finally the lights came up, the chanting stopped, we were greeted, we responded and the evening got underway.

I cannot recall what was said, but everyone seemed to like it and all nodded sagely. Tim looked bored. Afterwards, Lulu took us in for a private meeting and blessing. With heads bowed, we received a chant and were tapped with a long stick with peacock feathers at one end. As we wandered out, an unimpressed Tim grumbled in a stage whisper, "If she had hit me on the head once more with that feather thing, I was going to grab it and take it away from her."

Lulu left a couple of days later. I have no doubt that any feeling of peace she had was due to our hotel's comfort and service rather than the swami. [19]

Legendary Grammy-award winning band Fleetwood Mac stayed in 1990. I was a long-time fan and thought Stevie Nicks was gorgeous. I loved the way she sang, swaying in her hippy clothes, reminding me of long gone days in Amsterdam.

Imagine my disappointment when she turned out short, and so pale I thought she might be unwell. She was not a fan of daylight and moved to the darkest suite we could provide. She was rarely seen or heard before late afternoon. I had been looking forward to their concert, but was surrounded by shouting, screaming fans who continually emitted deafening whistles that completely drowned out the music. I left annoyed and vowed to restrict my listening to Fleetwood Mac at home. [20, 21]

Michael Hutchence was a founding member, lead singer and lyricist of rock band INXS, the latest Aussie rock star to be in the news daily. No one knew he was staying with us, and they were not on tour, so we assumed he was having some *me time* and a break from the fans and the publicity. He went to his suite, and that was the last we saw of him during his stay. He did, however, have an endless stream of well known young women of the music and theatre world drop in. They never stayed for long, and I remember thinking 'how nice' that he had mates who could drop in for a coffee, like the rest of us mere mortals. He was an ordinary guy, as far as rock stars go, and it was therefore very sad to learn the details of his death years later from a friend at the Ritz Carlton. The coroner's verdict was that Hutchence's death was a suicide while depressed and under the influence of alcohol and other drugs. Apparently room 524 at the hotel is regularly asked for by fans who wish to stay in the same room where their idol spent his last night. I find this rather morbid - not at all like the fans who ask for suite 702 at the Amsterdam Hilton where John and Yoko had their sleep-in for peace.

A number of touring female artists stayed with us in 1989 and 1990. Belinda Carlisle, Suzi Quatro, and Melissa Etheridge arrived, all of whom The Mole managed to get photographed with. I was starting to believe he had given up work at the Tax Office and become a full-time paparazzo, but he still honoured our understanding. [22]

In February 1991, Billy Joel came to Melbourne. His very beautiful wife Christie Brinkley, the inspiration for his song *Uptown Girl*, joined him for a few days. They were a charming couple, very undemanding and easy going. At that time, coincidentally, I was starting to feel a little overweight from the good life I was enjoying. I had never been one for strenuous exercise but had got into a little routine at the rooftop gym in the hotel each morning. One day I'd done five minutes on the bike and was ready to finish up, when a soft American voice said, "Hello, mind if I join you?"

The voice came from a stunning blonde woman in a yellow leotard, the sort you only see in aerobics videos: Christie Brinkley. All I could gulp was "Sure."

With limited space in the gym, the bikes were only a few inches apart, so it was rather difficult to pretend there was no one there. We chatted a little, she said all the right things. Normally I hated exercise, but for some reason, on this occasion, my usual hasty five minute routine extended to over thirty minutes. My stomach muscles were screaming at being held in. It was the most physical workout I had done in years. I enjoyed it.

The following day, she left the hotel, leaving Billy Joel to do the final concert. Billy's crew relaxed and partied after the last gig. The night log that was completed by the duty night manager recorded a number of comings and goings from Billy's suite during the party. Next day the staff were buzzing with gossip. The words of my old boss came to mind from many years ago: "Nothing is greater than a man who can face temptation and have the maturity to say 'This isn't worth losing what I have'." We all saw the news three years later in 1994 that Christie had divorced Billy. I started to make private bets with myself as to how long relationships might last after a celebrity stint in the hotel.

The big change I witnessed in rock star culture over the years was in the type of guests they would bring back to the hotel. In the early days of rock and roll, the bands would bring back adoring fans to join the party. As the fans got more media savvy, this led to all sorts of repercussions when the adoring fans sold their party stories to the tabloids and gossip magazines. Managers took note of this and set down a new rule for their unruly clients: no more 'fans' were to be brought back to the hotel parties. If needs must, then the services of *professionals* would need to be enlisted.

Bon Jovi were nice lads but the mass of fans who congregated outside really tested the hotel's security. Some fans managed to get on the roof whilst others made it into the fire stairwells. It was a never ending battle; we would catch one fan where they shouldn't be, and another would pop up on the other side of the hotel.

Band member Richie Sambora was in the newspapers over his relationship with Cher. Not that I was aware of this at the time. One afternoon I had a call from the switchboard, "Mr Griffin, I have Cher on the line wanting to speak with you."

"Cher? Who do you mean, Cher?"

"You know, *Cher* - the singer."

This caused a protocol problem; how did I address someone with only one name? Ms Cher? Madame Cher? Eventually

I answered the phone with "Good afternoon, Patrick Griffin, how may I help you?"

At the other end was her unmistakable voice. "Hello Mr Griffin, it's Cher here. You have Mr. Richie Sambora staying with you in suite *X*?" The fact that she knew exactly which suite he was in - and the voice - gave me confidence it was really her. Often fans would try such things to get put through to their idols. Cher continued, "As you may know Richie and I are friends and I would like your help. I have ordered some flowers that I want delivered to his suite at exactly 6.00pm your time. It is important that it is exactly 6.00pm. Can you see to it yourself? I would be most grateful if you could."

Later that afternoon the flowers arrived. The largest bunch of long stemmed red roses I had ever seen. The porter could hardly get his arms around them. At exactly 6.00pm a dozen staff were lined up outside Richie Sambora's suite door and I rang his doorbell. A voice shouted 'come in'. To his surprise, they paraded in carrying the roses as the phone rang. He picked it up. "Hi honey, yes, yes [...] just arrived [...] looks fantastic [...] yes [...] yes [...] call you later [...] yes, love you [...] yes it's 6.00pm here, what time is it with you?"

We placed the roses around the suite and departed, closing the door on a very affectionate transpacific telephone call. It was the night of the last performance in Melbourne.

I was in the lobby the following morning farewelling a few of our guests, when a tall, very attractive young woman walked out of the lift in a slinky, expensive, low cut black evening dress. I suspected it was the same dress she had arrived in late the night before. It wasn't so much what she was wearing that caught my eye, but what she was carrying. A massive bunch of long stemmed red roses.

She saw me looking and approached me a little nervously. "He gave them to me. He was very nice. Is it all right?"

"If you were given them that's fine. They certainly are lovely roses."

I wondered if she had any idea of where they came from and who had sent them. What would Cher think? For my part I took the view that the roses were at least going to someone who could enjoy them rather than being abandoned in the suite.

A little later in the morning the very same young woman appeared back in the lobby dressed in a fashionably smart track-suit and Gucci trainers. I looked at her with what she must have felt was a look of disapproval, so she came over to me.

"I hope it's alright, but Richie said if I came back and waited that he would get the autographs of all the band - my young son is a great fan. I'll keep out of the way."

She looked smart and seemed to be a nice girl, so I thought, what could be the harm?

"Thank you so much. If I may say you are a very nice hotel manager, some would have thrown me out."

I thought of Julia Roberts in *Pretty Woman,* with me as the hotel manager at the Beverly Wilshire Hotel. "Do take a seat and relax. I don't think they will be down for about half an hour."

I noticed she had a pager clipped onto her waist. "All the mod cons I see?"

"Oh yes. I need to keep in touch with the office just in case I'm needed."

I was amazed at just how business-like she was. Not at all what I would have expected from a woman of the oldest profession. We started to chat; she told me she had a science degree, had been married, had a son who she wanted to go to private school, and the sort of salary on offer for a job with her degree qualifications just wasn't enough. She was very organised and pragmatic about her situation. "You really do have a lovely hotel here, your bedrooms are by far the best in Melbourne."

I paused for a second, and realised what a compliment she had just paid us. If a person in her position didn't know of the best bedrooms in the city, then who would? "If only I could use that endorsement in my advertising," I quipped. We both chuckled.

The group then came down. The guest got her autographs, and I got to shake the band's hands and bid them farewell. As I turned to go back to my office she called after me. "Just wanted to say thank you again; have one of our VIP key rings." With which she smiled and departed. I looked at the key ring. It was good quality and very well made. It bore an inscription: *These keys belong to a VIP Client - if found please return them to...*", and a post box address.

I placed the keyring in my drawer and made a mental note: *not* to be used for my car keys. My wife did on occasion use my car, and may not be too understanding of the gift.

As far as the roses were concerned, Bon Jovi kept up their hard partying, womanising and drinking and Cher was unable to tame Sambora. They split after she actually caught him with a groupie in a Madrid hotel room.

Not all the bands lived up to their image of hard living, hard drinking rockers. I mentioned earlier that Motley Crew requested that all the mini bars be emptied of alcohol. So no surprises that their stay with us was one of the most uneventful. Tommy Lee was at the time married to Heather Locklear, who played Sammy Jo Carrington in *Dynasty*. Heather had stayed at the hotel and was not quite as well behaved. I was called to her room by the housekeeper one morning and was greeted by a bed full of her last night's dinner, plates and all. How she had slept in that bed is a mystery. This rather troubled woman then married Richie Sambora in 1994, and filed for divorce in February 2006. So it goes on.

Eric Clapton stayed in November 1990, a rock hero of mine ever since, fifteen years before, I had sat on the terrace of Richard McKevett's home in the Seychelles, overlooking the Indian Ocean, gin and tonic in hand, on a warm tropical evening listening to *Layla*. Richard cranked up the volume so much on that unforgettable opening riff, I expected the coconuts to fall off the trees.

I met Eric Clapton as he sat quietly in the lobby, the quint-essential nice guy. As people passed him, very few recognised who he was, which I think he preferred. He was not driven by ego but by the love of his music. He is one of the greatest guitar-ists alive. He was named "Slowhand" by the Yardbirds' manager, Giorgio Gomelsky, in 1964. The Yardbirds rhythm guitarist, Chris Dreja, recalled that whenever Eric Clapton broke a guitar string during a concert, Eric would stay on stage and replace it rather than storm off.[23]

Another great guitarist stayed with us. Riley B. King, better known as BB King, was playing support with U2. He also was simply devoted to the music he played. His biography describes him as King of the Blues. He began in Memphis and found fame as one of the blues' best performers. He picked up a Grammy for Best Traditional Blues Album in 2006, and found commercial success with many collaborations over the years, including with Eric Clapton. [24]

U2 was not a band I particularly liked, but I was obviously the only non-fan. They were being heralded as one of the world's top bands and, according to *New Musical Express,* it seemed that *the most profound impact was not the sound, but rather the underlying philosophy that U2 represented. It's the polar opposite of punk rock* - which I didn't like either by the way.

The Mole had tipped me off that the fans would be arriving by the busload so we'd better get prepared. I had barriers brought in that ran the entire width of the hotel forecourt. My office window looked out on the forecourt, a great position to view the coming and going of our guests, allowing me time as they pulled up in their limos, to be at the front door to greet them. This would be my sentry post for monitoring the ebb and flow of fans as well.

We managed things well until the day of U2's departure when there must have been a thousand fans out there all cheering and calling for their idols. Apart from the noise they were reasonably well behaved. My concierge called them 'private school punks'.

My acceptance turned to anger as the morning went on. More and more soft drink cans and plastic bags were being discarded over the barrier onto the forecourt. Eventually I spat the dummy, not something I often did. I went out into the lobby muttering under my breath. I was stopped by the concierge, "Where are you going Mr Griffin, it's getting crazy out there, every time we open the door to let a guest out they start screaming and shouting thinking it's the band."

"Have you seen the rubbish out there that they're dropping on the ground? Bloody yobs. You know you will have to clean it up when they go. I think they should bloody well do it themselves."

"I'd love to see who will tell them to do that; they'd get lynched."

The gauntlet being thrown down, I was going to have to do something. I headed out to the barriers, towards a group of girls and least threatening looking boys.

"Look at the mess you lot are making! Someone will have to clear this up! Do you know U2 are into conservation and cleaning up the planet? Do you think they will come over to you lot seeing the rubbish you have thrown about?"

I had no idea if U2 were into that sort of thing, but thought that they wouldn't know either. As yet I hadn't been lynched, so I thought I would go a step further. "OK, I want five of you to clean the place up now and after the band leaves; who will volunteer?"

To my surprise two of the girls put up their hand, then another one, then a couple of boys, not wanting to be shown up, put their hands up as well. "Right, see me afterwards and I will give you brushes and some bags."

Buoyed by my success, and without thinking it through, I added, "As you volunteered, once they've left and you have finished cleaning up, I will take you up to the suites and you can see where they stayed."

I suddenly found myself mobbed by volunteer cleaners. "I'll help! Let me clean up! I'll volunteer!" The chorus grew louder, they were all starting to shout. One of the young women quite shocked me with what she would do if included.

"No - only those who volunteered first. No more. You should have been first." With that, I returned to the safety of the hotel and the concierge.

"What did you say? Are they really going to clean up?"

"Yes I think they will."

As I returned to my office, I heard the fans' chants change from 'Bono' and 'Edge' to 'we want Patrick'. The concierge and a receptionist came into my office. "Have you heard them out there, Mr Griffin? What did you tell them?" I explained to them what I had agreed. They looked horrified. "Are you serious, do you think that's wise?" It probably wasn't.

"Look, I've offered it now. If I went back on my promise we probably really would get lynched."

"Well, maybe it's better if *you* don't actually take them up. I'll get a couple of staff together and we'll do it."

Relieved at the dignified way out they'd given me, I readily agreed.

U2 eventually appeared and waved and smiled their way into the waiting limousines, crowds of fans crying and screaming. I wondered, were they now happy? Having stood outside for several hours to simply get a smile and a wave? Then I remembered twenty-five years ago it was no different with the Beatles. I think it was as much about the fun of just being there, the camaraderie of being with the crowd who shared the same interest, and the screaming was part of the fun. No doubt there will be those, now in their fifties with kids of their own, saying *'I was there! I saw U2! Bono waved at me!'* [25, 26]

The fans honoured their part of the bargain and having collected twelve bags of cans, bottles and chip packets, presented themselves at the door for their due reward. Another twenty turned up who felt that they should be rewarded as well. I came out and identified the original volunteers. The unhappy ones departed, mumbling *not fair*. The chief concierge, the housekeeper, the engineer and a receptionist had agreed to act as the 'tour guides' and the very happy and excited group headed to the lifts, all looking rather in awe of the palatial surroundings that had accommodated their idols.

An hour later there was a knock on my door and in tumbled four very unhappy tour guides. I had never faced such a situation before. The scene resembled something out of *Mutiny on*

The Bounty. I was Captain Bligh, my chief concierge was Fletcher Christian, holding a coat hanger instead of a cutlass, and he looked as if he was ready to use it. The other mutineers looked rather nervously to their leader. "Mr Griffin, if ever you do something like that again, we will all resign." By the look in the eyes of each I knew they were not bluffing.

"What on earth happened? Surely they were just kids who only wanted to see where the group had slept?"

"Kids! They were animals! As soon as they entered, they were like locusts! They went through the bins taking out anything they could find, dirty tissue, cotton buds, nothing was too gross for them. Then they wanted to buy the sheets and one even tried to steal this coat hanger. Worst of all, one of the girls went into the bathroom and pulled some hair out of the plug hole for a souvenir. The other girl took the soap. I have never seen anything like it. *Please* Mr G. *Never* again."

Hardly believing what I had heard, I agreed.

I had spent a lot of time wooing Patti Mostyn, the Australian publicist of a particular superstar who I really wanted to stay with us at The Como. When I spoke to Patti, she explained, rather apologetically, "Patrick I really did try, I got him in the car to come and see you, but as we drew near the building, he took one look and declared *I could never stay in a place that looks like a toilet block.*"

Sir Elton John, I do feel that you were a little harsh.

We had another infallible being who *did* deign to visit us. I had always thought that there was only one Pope, The Bishop of Rome, the leader of the Catholic Church but there is another person with this title: The Pope of the Coptic Orthodox Church of Alexandria and leader of a faith with ancient Christian roots in Egypt. In Melbourne there is a large community of Egyptian Christians and their leaders excitedly asked us if we might be able to look after him during his visit. Of course we were more than happy to help.

Pope Shenouda III was the 117th Pope of this kind, and had begun his Papacy in 1971. He was accompanied by a number of his Bishops. They had few demands and did not require anything special. He was a devout and humble man. Although we respected his wishes for nothing opulent, we felt that it would be best to put The Pope and his entourage on the top floor in the main suites, which seemed appropriate for the purpose of having their meals together and any meetings or prayers they may wish to have.

Most of the time they ate away from the hotel as guests of their local community, with only breakfast being consumed at the hotel. They had a simple menu, comprising mainly fruit. One morning I went to the suite just to ensure they had everything they wanted. They were most welcoming and invited me to join them, however I felt it better to decline, as they were all seated on the floor. They seemed very happy, and with some of them almost in hysterics, I asked what was so funny. They pointed to the carpet, a very expensive hand woven Tai Ping carpet, especially designed for us with a pink and gray border and little black dots in a pink centre. One of the bishops was kneeling down, scraping at the black dots on the carpet. He had very poor eyesight and they explained between chuckles that they had told him not to drop his watermelon seeds on the carpet and to pick them up. Hilarious! I was touched to see that even this Pope and his bishops had a sense of humour.

The only problem we had during his stay was that many of his flock would wait in the lobby for hours, on the off chance they would meet him. Often they did, as he was happy to come down from time to time and give them a blessing. Not a problem in itself, but their well polished shoes caused us a headache. As one after another went down on one knee to kiss The Pope's ring, their toe caps rubbed on the light gray lobby carpet. It was soon starting to resemble the tyre marks on the race track at the start of a motorcycle Grand Prix. The housekeeper spent hours after each visit cleaning black Cherry Blossom shoe polish off the carpet.

When it was time for The Pope to depart, one of his bishops asked if I could be there as he wished to thank me personally. I waited in the lobby and as the flowing black robes approached. I gave him a courteous bow and he held out his hand. Having seen so many kiss it, I felt it would be the correct thing to do. I think this surprised him a little, but he said a few words of blessing and then thanked me for looking after him so well. A bishop appeared at his side and handed me a small box. The Pope added, "A very little gift to remember us by."

They departed with his adoring flock in hot pursuit. As I returned to my office I reflected on what a lovely man he was, and I guess you'd think that a Pope should not be anything else. I sat down at my desk and opened the little box. Inside was a beautifully inscribed carving of The Pope, on a silver key ring. I smiled as I recalled the other keyring I had received in the hotel lobby a few weeks earlier after the *Pretty Woman* incident. Everyone, from popes to prostitutes, understood the importance of marketing.

With our next guest, I was uncertain as to why they'd want a suite with a window that could open. I have always prided myself in meeting the needs of a guest, however demanding they might be, and this was no exception, especially when I discovered the guest was Reg Grundy and his wife Joy Chambers-Grundy. They were a wonderful couple, warm, friendly and approachable. It was hard to believe this down-to-earth man was the doyen of Aussie TV, an entrepreneur who, as reported in *The Sydney Morning Herald*, had with his wife, *built a vast global empire with TV stars, exquisite artworks, super yachts and private jumbo jets, an extraordinary fiefdom, ruled from a private tropical palace in Bermuda*.

We had lovely suites, but being in a tall building we had sealed windows. I could sympathise with Mr Grundy as I also hated to be in an air-conditioned space that was hermetically sealed. I took on the challenge.

I explained to Don, the boss, that Reg Grundy wanted to stay with us but required a suite with an openable window. I had prepared a list of arguments to persuade him to try to accommodate his wishes, and as I started on my list, he interrupted with. "Yes Patrick, good idea." With that he was on the phone to the architects who had designed the building, asking them to come and see me and to discuss how it might be done. End of conversation.

I left wondering if he had really understood, but then I remembered Don's desire to attract the 'who's who' of Australia to the hotel. Who better than Reg Grundy? A media mogul, a pioneer and known for his numerous television productions. He had created local hits of *Blankety Blanks, Wheel of Fortune, Prisoner, Sons and Daughters, The Young Doctors* and the worldwide phenomenon of *Neighbours*. Yes indeed he would get his window.

Reg and Joy, as they insisted on being called, checked in a few days after the window was installed, along with their cook and helper Di Ayres who was never far away. One would have thought I was a longstanding friend. I have written about the behaviour of some of our guests and their casual attitude to their relationships. Reg and Joy displayed the antithesis of this type of behaviour.

In the morning Reg would go to meetings. His car would come to the front entrance and the chauffeur would wait for him as we called his suite. When he came down, Joy would always be at his side and she would go out to the car, give him a kiss and see him off with a wave. It was very touching to see, and brought back memories of my old boss Johnny Johnson at The Cavendish Hotel in Eastbourne, who would wait lovingly for his wife to come down to dinner every evening. Reg and Joy were similarly devoted. They became regulars at The Como.

We had many CEOs, captains of industry and members of Australia's A-List stay with us in those early years. We had also accumulated a long list of awards, both within Australia and internationally. We had indeed established ourselves as a '*World Class Hotel*'. As with most things, this was now taken for granted. What now followed was what I was most dreading: a call for the profits to reflect the substantial investment. I knew we were unlikely to be able to meet these expectations.

Many of the new hotels that had sprouted up around Australia had been over capitalised, and The Como was going to prove no different. It seemed to me that these hotels had not been conceived with a view to making a financial return, but were vanity projects. It was a common saying that *it is never the first owner who can make the returns, it is unlikely to be the second, but the third might stand a slight chance.* When this same conclusion was reached by the powers that be for The Como, the management changed and a new more aggressive head took over. Naturally he was followed by the inevitable consultants.

Being somewhat regarded as the originator of this potential luxury white elephant, I could see the writing on the wall. I rejuvenated my CV to be ready for whatever might eventuate.

Chapter 3

#gettingmobile #outbackjackaroo #sadtimes

As I started work at The Como, my wife Bina, Tim and I realised that we had much to learn about the country we now called home. We had found a nice house, twice the size of what we had left behind in England. It was in Glen Waverley, which to me seemed ideally placed for my commute. With a twenty-five minute drive, people seemed to think we were out in the sticks. They should have seen the traffic and long daily commutes I suffered in England.

My car was a Ford LTD, a big beast, but I was excited to have a car phone, a chunky 1990s brick, as yet in an early stage of development. I sat beside a lake outside Melbourne and called my parents from the car. They were most impressed.

Melbourne turned out to be a lovely city, and a wonderful place in which to enter the Australian way of life. I quickly made new friends, and even got the gist of the unique game of Aussie Rules football. I found this title somewhat contradictory, as I saw little evidence of rules. I was kindly once taken to the VFL Grand Final of The Hawks v The Demons. I guess someone must have known the rules, as apparently the Hawks won.

I found everyone so kind and welcoming. I decided to host a small barbecue at home, as it was so luxurious to be able to count on good weather. It was a far cry from the hit and miss weather we experienced back in England. In summer, it was rare to wear a T-shirt and shorts; likely it would be a sheepskin coat instead.

And the weather was not the only difference. I invited a few friends, a lawyer I had got to know, my friendly bank manager, a couple of friends from the hotel including David and his wife Lesley, and also a lovely Italian man, and his wife, who had helped by painting our new home.

Had this crew been brought together in England, the lawyer's wife would have enquired of the painter's wife, "Hello and what does your husband do?"

And when answered, "He's a painter, he painted Patrick's house," there would have been at best, "Oh really, how nice," and nothing further said, just an awkward silence. Such was the English class system.

At my Melbourne soiree, nobody cared less what anyone did, what accent they spoke with, or for that matter who their family was. They just got on together, over sausages, or snags I should say, which I burned. Glasses of wine I hope made up for it. Invariably they would talk sport, the subject that was the great leveler in Australia.

One day my financial controller, Howard Dinerstein, who had taken over from Wahid, asked if as yet I had seen the outback. Of course I hadn't; at that point the only kangaroo I had seen was at Healesville Sanctuary, outside Melbourne, where I had taken the family on a Sunday outing. He asked if I would care to go on a trip with him and his father to a place called Yunta.

"Where the hell is Yunta?"

"It's about a thousand k's west of us, about halfway between Adelaide and Broken Hill. Dad has some friends who run a sheep station up there."

"How long will that take?"

"Not that long; Dad has a plane."

What great people - and what an invitation!

We flew out of Essendon Airport early on a Saturday, loaded up with all sorts of things, importantly including half a dozen lobsters and a box of prawns. I looked down and watched the land slowly slide by beneath us. Soon the lush green of the Victorian landscape turned brown, with nothing for miles. We said little until we passed over a thin line that I could make out, stretching across the landscape. Howard's father, seeing my interest said, "That's a fence meant to keep out the dingos and rabbits, but I doubt it works."

Australia's dingo fence was nearly six thousand kilometres long, making it not only the longest fence in the world, but also undoubtedly the planet's largest agricultural pest deterrent. It was originally built in the 1880s as a rabbit-proof fence and ran from Jandowae in Queensland all the way down to South Australia. It was extraordinary. My education about the world's largest and flattest island continued.

As we drew close to Yunta, the plane banked and we circled. Where was the runway? I saw nothing except a few dirt roads. To my horror one of those dirt roads was the runway we were to land on. We did a low pass and I saw a pick-up, or ute as I was learning to call them, at the end of the dirt runway. A man by the ute, waved his hat, and we made the approach. I watched with admiration as Howard's father flicked a few switches, adjusted the flaps and throttled back on the levers. The plane seemed to hang mid-air for a few seconds before the wheels touched down. Suddenly we were hurtling along, bumping up and down as the engine roared loudly. As we slowed to a stop - thank God - my grip on my seat relaxed and we taxied back to the ute. The man greeted us with a cheery *G'day*, the first bit of outback Aussie speak I had heard. His face was weather-beaten and looked as tough as the land around us. Howard filled me in on local history as we off-loaded the prawns, lobsters and luggage.

Yunta township was established in the 1880s after the discovery of gold at the nearby diggings at Teetulpa and Waukaringa, when more than five thousand miners came here. It was a busy railway town on the Adelaide to Broken Hill line. From the 1930s, Yunta was the base for the famed outback trucking and mail contractor Harry Ding. Today Yunta is a small service centre for travellers and the surrounding properties, and provides an alternate route to the Flinders Ranges and beyond. The town's facilities include a hotel, two roadhouses, two fuel stations, a post office, police station, and a primary school. To cater for tourists there was a rest area with public toilets located opposite the hotel; if I needed to go, I'd best go now as it was another 40km to the sheep station.

I was curious as to how they had found this place, and Howard explained, "Well Dad often goes off flying and when he sees an airstrip he would fly lower, take a look and if it looked interesting he would land and explore." As I looked around I was puzzled as to what he had found interesting about Yunta.

I used Yunta's 'facilities', and we started our drive to the sheep station in silence. Our host was not very chatty and so I just gazed out, watching the bush go by. I noticed a kangaroo and was about to point him out, but thankfully I thought better of it, as then I saw another and another; dozens of them were keeping pace beside us along with some emus. The one thing I didn't see, which I found strange considering where we were headed, was a sheep.

We eventually arrived at the station, a weatherboard and corrugated iron homestead with a few outhouses, aged by the harsh conditions of the outback. We were greeted by the chap's wife who had collected us from the landing strip, and the welcome was warm and sincere. I felt I had entered a time warp and was in the 1960s film *The Sundowners:* at any moment Robert Mitchum, Deborah Kerr and Peter Ustinov would appear from one of the shearing sheds, greeting me with that terrible Aussie accent that somehow the Americans just could not master.

Our hosts were wonderful. Although the husband said little, his wife made up for it with her conversation, as no doubt she enjoyed a chat when rare guests dropped in. This was truly the real Australia, and the life was hard. My admiration and respect for these people grew with every minute I spent with them. They were very happy as they had for the first time got their own telephone. This was 1990 and they'd only just got a telephone? What did they do before?

> "Well it wasn't that bad. We had a phone, but it was a party line that went to the local exchange in town. Molly was very good, but the only problem was that she only manned the switchboard from 8.00am to 5.00pm and then she had her lunch break between 12.00pm and 1.00pm."

We had a wonderful dinner, augmented by the lobsters and prawns we had brought with us. In Melbourne, with markets overflowing, we took it for granted, yet out here it was a rare delicacy. They were so modest and friendly; the smallest gift or word of appreciation from us was received with a degree of embarrassment. The life out here on the land was tough and those that worked it were tougher still. I couldn't help but recall the words of my new national anthem that I was starting to understand:

Australians all let us rejoice,
For we are young and free,
We've golden soil and wealth for toil,
Our home is girt by sea,
Our land abounds in nature's gifts,
Of beauty rich and rare,
In history's page, let every stage
Advance Australia Fair!

The lyrics were written in 1878 by the Scottish-born composer Peter Dodds McCormick. I felt they did not truly reflect the reality of the sheep farmers' survival in these harsh arid conditions. I am not sure just how much *wealth for toil* came to this couple, or from what I had seen so far, how the *land abounds in nature's gifts.* I would agree, as I looked out over the bush at sunset, beer in hand, that the outback did indeed have *beauty rich and rare.*

Well-fed, I got ready to sleep. I heard the occasional bark of a dog in answer to a dingo's howl, but the rhythmic creak from the blades of the wind pump that was well past its time helped me drift off to sleep. My last conscious thought was that I still hadn't seen any sheep to count.

The pale light of dawn seemed to come very quickly, and I was woken by movement and the smell of breakfast already underway. We all ate a hearty meal, before the four of us piled into the ute and headed off down a dirt road. Our task for the day was to check on the water holes, a job I learned would take all day due to the size of the station. I cannot recall just how many acres it was but it had a lot of zeroes at the end of the number. Having been used to England where you would see a hundred or so sheep in a small field, it was hard to imagine that out here, the land could only support one sheep per acre.

I had never seen so many kangaroos; hundreds of them, all grazing on the sparse vegetation. It was hardly surprising that the farmers saw them as vermin. There were also emus running around in all directions, a strange looking bird. We drove for about two hours in one direction, still with little sign of the sheep. In the cab with our host, I attempted several times to start up a conversation. I was after all a hotelier who liked to chat with people. The only response I ever got was a grunt and the odd word that I could not understand. I followed his lead after a while and just grunted.

We reached the first watering hole and at last I saw some sheep. As we headed back to the ute, Howard asked if I would like to ride on the back with him and get a better view of things. I was relieved and willingly accepted, as I had exhausted all my conversational grunts with my host.

We reached the second hole where there were hundreds of sheep drinking the precious water. I noticed a lonely lamb bleating, whose mother had been caught in a thicket and was dead. As I walked over it looked up and ran to me. It was like a woolly puppy dog, and it looked so helpless. I picked it up, and it just relaxed in my arms; I felt good that I was able to help this little lamb. I took him over to the farmer.

"Looks as if this lamb has lost his mother, do we take him back"

He looked at me and the look said it all. "Nah just put 'im down, can't take 'im with us."

I looked at him in disbelief. How could he be so cruel and callous to this little creature? "What will happen to him, as his mother can't feed him?"

The farmer turned and with no emotion simply said, "Dingoes 'll get 'im tonight."

I realised how impossible my expectations were. This was the reality of life on the land. As we drove away the little lamb ran after me; I felt a lump in my throat at the thought of what lay ahead. I watched him as we pulled away and he was lost in the dust behind us.

Just how the laws of the land worked soon became apparent yet again when we saw a mob of kangaroos (my outback education: the males are called bucks or boomers, and females are does or flyers). As we pulled up the farmer stepped out and before I could even take in what was happening, he raised a rifle and there were two shots. In an instant two of the largest bucks fell over. The others just hopped a few metres out of the way and then just sat there staring as if nothing had happened. They didn't seem to notice that they had just lost two of their own. We drove up to where the kangaroos lay and with a casual but deft motion, the farmer removed the heads with his knife. The last time I had seen anything like it was Crocodile Dundee saying "You call that a knife?" The heads were discarded; the carcasses, without a word, were unceremoniously tossed in the back of the ute.

As we moved off again, with our two new 'companions' I asked Howard, "What are we going to do with them, is this dinner for tonight?"

"Good God no! They are for his dogs." I was rather relieved, and we drove on.

We later stopped and Howard asked if I was interested in shooting a few rabbits. Why not? I had done so as a boy, and at least they offered a challenge by running rather than just sitting there like the roos. When asked if I had handled a gun, I rather proudly announced that I had been in the school shooting eight and a qualified marksman in the school cadets.

A colony of rabbits were spotted and I was handed the rifle. As I brought it up to my shoulder the farmer rasped in my ear, "Only 'it 'em in the head, they're no bloody use otherwise."

Having flaunted my qualifications I was faced with the fact that my *alma mater's* reputation (and mine) was on the line. The pressure was on.

I lined a large buck up in my sights, paused, held my breath and gently squeezed the trigger. *Crack*, and a small thump to my shoulder. I looked down the barrel and saw the rabbit jump and then lie still. Got it. The farmer looked at 'the towny' with surprise. "Nice shot." We started the long drive back. In silence.

I was happy to arrive back to the station and be greeted by the loquacious farmer's wife; well, loquacious when compared to her husband. Again that night we had a lovely meal: lamb, which was delicious and ravenously I scoffed it down. Although it was difficult to put out of my mind the look of those big brown eyes of my little friend left behind earlier in the day, the appetite I had built up over the day helped me to forget. I was starting to appreciate the realities of life on a sheep station.

Our flight back was uneventful, and I pondered my amazing experience. It was truly Australia in the raw, not a contrived experience for a tourist. It was real, tough, and truly unique. If I wasn't before, I was now committed to becoming a 'true blue' Aussie, albeit from the comfort of my luxury five star hotel. These were good times.

Sadly, we cannot expect only to live in good times. There were times when dark shadows fell across the sunny days, bringing grief and regret. Such is life.

Not long after the Yunta visit I heard from Howard that both his parents had died in a plane crash, whilst coming in to land. It was very upsetting news, as I knew how good a flyer he was, and found it hard to believe.

I also had news that my father was gravely ill, so, for the first time since our arrival in Australia, I returned to England. Tragically, I arrived in London to learn that Dad had died a few hours earlier. As I drove up to Warwickshire, how poignant it was to hear on the radio Mike and the Mechanics singing *The Living Years*. It resonated all too powerfully.

I know that I'm a prisoner
To all my Father held so dear
I know that I'm a hostage
To all his hopes and fears
I just wish I could have told him in the living years

My father was not the most demonstrative person and rarely showed his affection, but he was a kind and gentle man whom I loved. At the time I had not appreciated the sacrifices made by my parents to give us all a wonderful home and a good education. The family gathered to lay Dad to rest: my mother, brothers Chris and Bob, and Ginny, my little sister from Perth, on a cold and blustery day in January 1989, at the hillside graveyard of his beloved Saxon St Nicholas Church in the village of Loxley in Warwickshire. We took a photo that day, and I could not have known that this was to be the last photo we were to have together as a family.[27]

Just a year later, in March 1990, I had a call from my brother Chris that my mother was gravely ill with pancreatic cancer. If I wanted to be with her, now was the time. I boarded my flight from Melbourne and headed back to England, to join Chris, Bob and Ginny at her bedside. The last words I had with mum were when I left the evening before I was due to return, and realised I had left the car keys on her bedside table. I returned to her room, "Sorry, I left my bloody keys behind."

She looked at me with a smile, I gave her a kiss, and as I left I heard, "Oh Paddy you will forget your head one day. I love you."

She was buried next to dad in Loxley Churchyard in the spot that looked over the fields to our old home on top of the hill; the home she had loved so much. That afternoon I returned to London, where I was staying at the Ritz, courtesy of my good friend and charismatic hotelier, Terry Holmes, who attempted to cheer me up with a glass of Champagne and his unique humour.[28]

The following day I awoke early to catch my flight back to Australia, and as I ate my breakfast I looked out of the window, down onto Piccadilly. As I stared over my cup of Earl Grey, I felt I could reach out and touch the grey, low-hanging clouds; the street below was wet and grey; the people walking by in bowler hats with raised umbrellas, trying to quickly reach their warm offices, were grey. I was watching a London street scene from an old black and white movie; it was miserable.

Back in Melbourne, the summer warmth hit me as I stepped off the plane. The sun was shining, people were strolling around in coloured shirts and boardshorts. My wife and Tim were there to greet me. There was colour all around. It was at that moment that I felt *'no matter how far or wide I roam',* I would now always call Australia home.

It was early the following year that I had another call from Chris. This time our brother Bob had been taken into hospital. Bob always erred on the side of drama, so we weren't too surprised when he said that he was unlikely to come out this time. Both Chris and I rather took it with a pinch of salt, but I sent wishes for a speedy recovery. A few days later Chris called again. "Hi Pad, I saw Bob today and his doctor. I am sorry to say that what he said may be the case, as apparently he has AIDS."

I was flabbergasted. I could not believe it. Bob with AIDS?

Bob had lived in Africa for many years and had been the general manager of The Hotel Edinburgh, in Kitwe, Zambia. I recalled on one of his visits home he asked me to take him to the infectious diseases hospital in Coventry, where he was to have some tests. When I picked him up he was rather quiet, I had asked him if anything was wrong. "No, just some fever or other that I think I picked up in Zambia."

He said nothing further, so I left it at that. He returned to Zambia for a short time before coming back to England with his new Zambian wife, Kate, a lovely girl, but rather a surprise as no one was aware he had remarried. Bob seemed different. He told us he had had enough of hotels and was just happy *to stack shelves* at the supermarket. Bob at times had been impetuous, and we just put it down to having a new wife and wanting to avoid the stress of his job in Zambia.

I was desperately sorry that he felt he could not tell us, so that we could understand and give him support. At that time, AIDS was regarded as a horrific, incurable disease, more feared than cancer. Even at the hotel in Coventry, the staff were scared that they might contract it from changing the bed linen or cleaning the bathrooms. I cannot fathom the emotional suffering he must have been experiencing in those last years. Within three years of arriving in Australia, I had lost half my family. There was now my sister Ginny in Perth and brother Chris in Warwickshire, and all of us so far apart. I had lost the close family we had grown up in. It was a very, very sad period.

There was another type of shadow that intruded into our happy lives from time to time. There is an unfortunate and ugly racist element in some Australians. It is the proverbial elephant in society's room. I had seen and heard things in Australia that in England would be seen as racist, but here were laughed off. This joviality hides the deeper more harmful stream of racism that still exists in Australia.

Of course being an Anglo Saxon, C of E, educated Englishman, I was never faced with anything even bordering on racism towards myself. I was however, as a father and husband, very sensitive to any hint of insult against my young Asian son and his mother. Readers of an earlier chapter will know I had already had a rude awakening to this attitude in the Australian Consular office in Manchester. The first occurrence in Australia was a minor issue that may well have been overlooked, but I was very much affected by it.

Taking my son to school one morning in 1989, I asked what classes he had today. He said they were doing a special class on *how to speak and read English.* I didn't think much of this other than a concern that he might have dyslexia or something, so I called the headmaster. I explained what my son had said and my concerns, and he assured me he would look into it and call me back.

> "Hi Patrick, nothing to worry about, his English reading and writing is fine, it appears that the teacher sent him off to an English as a second language class thinking as a new arrival to Australia he may need extra tuition, but there's no problem."

I could not understand how this could happen. Tim did not speak any other language, having been educated in England. Obviously they'd lumped him in with the class as he was Asian in appearance, no questions asked.

One afternoon he came home in his white school shirt, and I was horrified to see the word 'CHINK' written on his sleeve. I immediately phoned the school. Their response blew my mind. "Patrick, I am so sorry. What I would suggest is that you try to wash it out and if you can't remove it, I will speak to the boy's parents and ask them to buy you another shirt."

I found it difficult to believe my ears. The headmaster had totally missed the point of my concern and anger. He just didn't get it, even when I tried again to explain that it was the offensive word that had been written; he could only think I was worried about washing the wretched shirt.

The following term I enrolled Tim in the private school Caulfield Grammar, a short distance from our home.

In May of 1991, we were notified that we were to become Australian citizens. I had the zeal of the convert. With the death of my parents, the last deep emotional ties to England were gone. In my own mind I had already made the decision that England was no longer my home. I even questioned those patriotic values that had been instilled in me from birth, *that there was nothing better in this world than to be born British*. We had been in Australia for two years, so now was the time.

We were to attend the ceremony at Glen Waverley Town Hall, conducted by the Lord Mayor on Monday 24th June 1991. We were all dressed up to the nines for this special event. As we entered the Town Hall, I couldn't help but notice that we were one of only two English families. The other ones were resplendent in tshirts, boardies and thongs, somewhat overdoing the Australian fancy dress theme. Rather letting the side down, I thought, for such a special event, but then again this was the relaxed Aussie lifestyle we were about to embrace. Everyone else, however, was in a suit or smart dress for the occasion.

The Mayor arrived and the ceremony began. We all read the cards we had been given. Rather amusing in my case to read the Oath of Allegiance to Her Majesty the Queen of Australia. The ceremony over, we had tea, and the Mayor came around to welcome us all as Australians and to give us a small tree to mark the occasion. A nice touch. He approached me and asked, "Where do you come from? I assume England?"

"Yes, Warwickshire."

"I know it well, my family originally came from Leicestershire, next door." He then looked up and down at my wife and son without any acknowledgement and turned back to me and said, "So - where did you find these two?"

I was absolutely dumbstruck; I simply had no words to answer to such a question. He walked off. I was so angry, I wanted to punch him.

When I got home I decided to write and vent my anger to the local paper, *The Waverley Gazette*. I calmed down, slightly, and wrote that I felt the Mayor's comments, although maybe not *intentionally* racist, were - at the very least - entirely inappropriate for such a solemn occasion.

The following day I had a call from the paper's editor, asking if he could come and see me. He explained that the Mayor allegedly had a reputation for appearing to be somewhat racist. Shortly afterwards, the editor, who happened to be Sri Lankan, and his photographer came to the door. We had a very amiable chat and he spoke of some of the other issues he had reported on. He asked to take a photo of the family, but I suggested we stick to just a photo of me.

When the phone rang again, it was the Mayor, who had been contacted by the newspaper. He protested, "I never said that." I repeated, word for word, what he had said.

"I wasn't meaning to be racist. I'm sorry if that's how you took it, but can you call the newspaper and retract it?"

I refused.

"You can't do this to me! It will ruin me!"

He had insulted my family; he had crossed the line and I would stand by what I said, come hell or high water.

The paper appeared on the newsstands. On the front page, a profile photo of myself facing off with a profile photo of the Mayor, with the banner headline, *Mayor Forced to Apologise to New Australians.*

Wow. This will set the cat amongst the pigeons. I wasn't sure what the reaction would be until I went into my local Chinese takeaway and suddenly discovered that I was now a celebrity in the local Asian community. There were numerous letters to the paper from sympathetic readers giving me no end of support for speaking out. I felt quite the crusader. There was only one letter that did not support me:

> "Typical whinging Pom, if he can't stand the heat of the kitchen, why doesn't he go back to England!"

I wondered if it was the same chap I had met in the immigration office in Manchester a few years earlier.

The Mayor didn't let it rest and took a complaint about the paper and its editor to the Press Council. He lost.

As any parent would understand, I was fiercely protective of my child. I did my best to save him from the hurt that could befall him whilst he was growing up. I asked Tim, many years later, if he had experienced any issues with racism. His reply gave me some relief.

> "None that I was aware of. Kids growing up often say things to each other, and anyone who's different will from time to time cop some flack. If you are fat, thin, short or tall, brown, yellow, whatever, someone will make an issue of it. It's just kid stuff and part of growing up."

I recalled my own youth. With a large nose, big feet and my Army surplus clothes at school. I suppose I had copped it as well, but I also realised that I may have been dishing it out too. I'm sure many kids do not take it so well, but I was glad that Tim was so pragmatic about it.

So the shadows gradually lifted, and we started to really appreciate all the wonders that Australia had to offer. We drove to and enjoyed the wines of the Mornington Peninsula, and the fairy penguins' nightly walk on Phillip Island. We marvelled at the sights along the spectacular Great Ocean Road and were in awe of the Twelve Apostles - although there were only nine at the time. I believe it's down to eight, but who's counting? The scenery could not get any better.

I think one of my favourite memories was in the Dandenongs. We visited a wonderful township called Sassafras, where we found a cafe. A sign over the door corrected us: 'Miss Marple's Tea Rooms'. Could it get more English than this? As we entered, I realised it could.

Just before leaving England, we had all gone into the Cotswolds to Stow-on-the-Wold, a town visited by thousands of tourists each year on their way to Stratford upon Avon. We had gone to the tea shop, crowded with a coachload of Americans experiencing a real 'English Cream Tea'. A bored-looking waitress had seated us and I enquired as to what tea they served. She seemed puzzled. "Brooke Bond, I think?" I had hoped for Earl Grey but no dice. It was just the standard supermarket brand.

When the tea arrived, I could see the tea bag labels, 'Brooke Bond', dangling out of a battered, stainless steel teapot with a lid that wouldn't close. No doubt it had buckled during several runs in the dishwasher. The waitress returned with mass produced scones, jam and cream and plonked them on the table before us and disappeared just as quickly, before I could ask for the milk which she had forgotten. I managed to retrieve some from the table next door, recently vacated by an American couple. This was our farewell to the fine traditions of the English afternoon tea.

As we entered 'Miss Marple's Tea Room' in the Dandenongs, I noticed that the furniture was pure Victorian. Better yet, waiting at the tables, were immaculately turned out young women in black, with white pinnies and white headbands, looking like 'nippies' transported directly from Lyons Corner House, an institution stood on the Strand in London from 1909 to 1977. The nippies brought back memories of my childhood when my father took me there for tea.

We were seated and the question came from the waitress, as it had in The Cotswolds, but this time with a smile and genuine welcome. "Would you like our cream tea?" I nodded "What tea will you have?"

I was worried that my English accent was a problem so I repeated slowly, "The cream tea, please."

"Yes, but what tea would you like?" I was getting frustrated; she saw this and added, "Earl Grey, English Breakfast, Orange Pekoe, Oolong or maybe Green Tea?"

"Oh yes, of course. Earl Grey would do nicely."

My wife wanted coffee, which I thought would be another challenge. "Coffee, yes of course, no problem." Then she asked "What coffee would you like?"

I was grappling to remember any name of a coffee - Arabica? Or Nescafe? Maxwell House? I was relieved and happily stunned when she offered "Flat White, Long Black, Macchiato, Café Latte, or a Cappuccino?"

Our 'nippy' returned and carefully positioned the fine china tea cups, the silver pot of tea and hot water, a matching jug of milk, and a tea strainer. She offered to pour it for us. A three-tiered plate was presented to the table: the top plate presented a selection of delicately cut sandwiches, the second had our scones, jam and cream on it, and the bottom plate had a selection of little cakes. The afternoon tea served at The Ritz was no better.

I sat in a state of wonder. Here we were - in Australia, up in the hills, in a little country town. How could they serve such an eye-pleasing, mouth-watering array, yet the English girl working in an establishment steeped in the customs and traditions of tea drinking couldn't even find a teapot with a lid that closed? I fear I now understood how Britain had lost its Empire. I have little doubt that at that moment Queen Victoria - and my mother, for that matter - were turning in their graves.

We had grown, in a short time, to love Australia. No more Union Jack bumper stickers. No more 'in England we do it like this'. We had good reason to feel settled. What was there to whinge about?

On the morning of Tuesday 15th October 1991, a very special event took place that cemented our relationship with Australia. My wife, Tim and I, were ecstatic to welcome into the world Charles Langley Griffin. As is the Aussie way, Charles immediately became *Charlie*, and a true-blue Australian, with a certificate to prove it.[29]

Our Aussie family was complete, and life could not have been better. Whatever lay ahead, we looked forward to embracing it. As a family we now could truly call Australia our home.

Chapter 4

#aroundtheworldinthreedays #communityspirit #obsteam

From the *lady* to the *tart*. Before you jump to any conclusions, no, I wasn't misbehaving or straying from the path; nor was I getting stuck into pastries. I had learned from Melbournians that they always considered their city to be more stylish and genteel than other cities. Melbourne was a *lady*, especially when compared to the larger and brasher city of Sydney, nearly nine hundred kilometres to the north, which was simply dismissed as a *tart*.

I loved Melbourne. It was, in many ways, I would agree, more 'stylish'. I had flown to Sydney often on business, and, as the plane descended into Kingsford Smith Airport, I would look down at this massive urban sprawl, wondering how long it took people to get to work each morning. I was not overly impressed.

The Hotel Como became a member of 'Select Hotels', an elite group of individual hotels that banded together to compete with the large chains on marketing. It was the brainchild of Richard Rosebery, a very driven, tenacious and creative marketing strategist, whom I had gotten to know, like and respect over the years. I had been invited to sit on their board, along with Michael Hall who was a legend in the local industry. He helmed the Sebel Townhouse which he'd made *the* hotel in Sydney; all the stars who visited Australia stayed there. I met a number of like-minded directors, including a German guy, Ulrich Renner. He had been GM of Sydney's Renaissance Hotel, and was now working with a Japanese company, The Nara Corporation. Nara was building a luxury hotel in the Blue Mountains in New South Wales, and a luxury 'boutique' hotel on Sydney Harbour. Ulrich mentioned they had engaged Orient-Express Hotels and Trains to manage it, and almost as an aside, commented, "If you are looking to move anytime soon, why not apply for a job with them?"

I was a little taken aback. I had indeed expressed concern to Richard as to what the future might hold for The Como. It had been rumoured that now the hotel was up and running, AGC may divest itself of the property as it was not part of their core business.

With this in mind, I was excited. I had heard much of Jim Sherwood, the entrepreneur and shipping magnate, who owned and ran Orient-Express, and of the hotels that he was buying. A close friend of mine, back in Warwickshire, was Steve Jacobs, a pilot who flew Lear Jets for the Automobile Association (AA) medevac operation, amongst other clients. Steve was meant to have been the best man at my wedding, but had to pull out when Jim Sherwood needed to fly to Moscow. This was not the only occasion that Jim's flight plans interfered with my social life. It was not unusual for Steve to have to cancel at the last minute, or turn up late for a dinner party. Steve would regale us with stories of where Jim was flying and what hotels he was buying. I felt like I knew the man. I had written to the company once before when I lived in England, and was disappointed when I didn't get a reply.

This time I hoped to have more luck. I sent an updated CV and a very nice letter to their head office in London. I did not get a reply. Again. I had almost given up on the idea, when I was contacted by three of the agents with whom I had registered my CV.

As I took the calls, none would disclose the name of the hotel or the company, simply saying it was a luxury boutique hotel on Sydney Harbour. Well, well. I said to all three that I should be pleased if they would express my interest. I pictured that whoever was looking at the applications would see my name on everyone's list. Surely not a bad thing.

It wasn't long before I had a call from Mr Peter Rozee, who had a *very* English accent. He said he would be interested in meeting me and would, with his vice president Colin Bather, be in Australia in the next week. Would I be available?

We met over coffee to chat about me, my work and the plans they had for Sydney, which sounded amazing. The level of investment from Nara and the standards laid down by Orient-Express made it clear that a hotel with this level of luxury would move into uncharted waters for Australia.

Following the meeting, Mr Bather and Mr Rozee retired to their hotel rooms. They asked to see me the following morning. Peter was the hotel expert, but Colin was the formal decision maker on behalf of Jim Sherwood, a sort of majordomo for a number of his interests. Orient-Express owned a portfolio of hotels, along with the famous train, but all were named individually. They didn't brand them as Orient-Express, as other hotel groups did, like the Mandarin, the Shangri La or the Four Seasons.

The company owned some classic properties such as The Copacabana Palace in Rio, The Mount Nelson in Cape Town, and the hotel regarded as the flagship, The Cipriani in Venice. The latter was known as much for its celebrated director, Dr Natale Rusconi, as for the hotel itself. The company at that time owned fourteen hotels, very small by comparison with the major players, but they were all the top hotels in their destinations. This was the intention for the new Observatory Hotel in Sydney.

Colin gave me the news that had me almost cartwheeling around the office. "We would like to offer you the position, if you are interested?"

My response was a poor attempt at appearing calm and measured. "Thank you, when is the appointment due to commence? I would just like to discuss it with the family, although I feel confident they'll agree."

He seemed to be genuinely pleased and there was a very gracious air about him. "I would like you to start as soon as you can get released from your duties here, as there is much to do. We would like you on board during the construction phase, so as to get your input. In the meantime, I will get a contract drawn up on my return to London and fax it to you."

We chatted a little longer and he indicated the salary ballpark, contractual expectations, and other details. I was very happy with all of it; in fact it was much better than I had expected. Later that day as they departed, we shook hands and Peter added with a warm smile, "Best get writing your resignation."

What lay ahead was as exciting as it was challenging. It was strange but I was not at all apprehensive or nervous. I had secured my future away from the tenuous role at The Como. Maybe it was adrenalin. Whatever it was I felt confident and happy enough to walk on water.

Taking Colin's word as his bond, the following day I wrote my resignation letter and placed it into the hand of David to pass on to the powers that be. I walked back to my office feeling very pleased with myself, and thinking how delighted my mother would have been to know that I was now joining the company of the famed Orient-Express: the train of romance and mystery. It would have appealed to her theatrical taste, and she would have had the opportunity to experience for herself the elegant world of Agatha Christie's Hercule Poirot.

I arrived back in my office and the phone rang. The boss would be calling about my letter of resignation no doubt. It wasn't the boss; it was Colin Bather. "Hello Patrick. Look I'm sorry about this but I feel I need to let you know something has come up."

My heart started to sink. God no. So I haven't got the job after all?

"I have been thinking, I didn't tell you when we met but I am leaving the company. As such I feel both politically and for your own benefit, that it might be best if Jim Sherwood should see you and appoint you. Then you would be his choice rather than mine. Could you see him on Monday?"

My mind was racing. I had resigned already. Now I had to meet the God of the company and hope he gives me his blessing? "Er, yes I'm sure I can, I hadn't realised he was in Australia."

"He's not. I want you to come to London. Today is Friday afternoon and he wants you in London on Monday."
"Umm, er, yes of course."
"That's good, let me know what the costs are and we will reimburse you when you get here. Would 11.00am be OK?"
"Yes, I am sure that would work out."

When I was interviewed for The Como, I had to fly back and forth from Perth. Now it's London. How far I had come from those days with De Vere; Coventry to London, at best a trip of one hour. Melbourne to London for the day? Why not?

No sooner was the phone down than I was sprinting back to David's office. He was tidying his desk before heading off for the weekend. "David, have you given him my resignation letter as yet?"

"No, he wanted to get away and rather than ruin his weekend, I thought I would leave it until Monday. Why? Have you changed your mind?"

I explained to him the whole story and how I was now having to go to London for an interview on Monday. "Well, it looks as if you are going to have to 'chuck a sickie'!"

God bless you David. What an Aussie mate you are. With my plan hatched, I got back to the office to call my friendly travel agent. I was just in time, as he was walking out of the office.

I was booked on a flight out of Melbourne on Sunday at 11.55am and would arrive at about 6.00am Monday. I was flying Business Class and there was a lounge where I could take a shower and smarten up before taking a taxi to Sea Containers House, at South Bank, in the city. My flight back was booked with BA leaving Heathrow, Monday night at 9.35pm. The only problem was that this wouldn't get me back until about 8.00am on Wednesday, so not only would I be 'ill' for two days, I would also be late on Wednesday.

I started sniffing and coughing a little, laying on a little drama for the staff, as I was more worried about them finding out about what I was up to than anyone else. I had brought my secretary in on the plan as well, just as a backup in case everything went pear-shaped.

It went like clockwork. The biggest fear I had was a flight delay, but the winds were good and the skies clear. As they swung that lever that opened the plane door, I immediately knew I was back in England: cold wind, grey skies and everyone in several layers of jumpers. I found the lounge, showered and at least felt a little refreshed, albeit jet-lagged. I took a taxi to Sea Containers House and Colin met me.

I sat in his office and waited, nervously going over in my mind what I should say. I watched the clock on his desk; 11 o'clock came and went. It passed 11.45am. I had travelled halfway round the world and managed to get here on time. As I grumpily meditated, I was startled when Colin suddenly appeared. "We're on, let's go."

We headed along a corridor then up a grand staircase, on which was displayed a *very* grand solid-silver trophy, over four feet high. Colin, seeing my interest, explained that it was *The Hales Trophy - Blue Riband*. I had of course heard of it but I had never seen it. It was very famous, given to such ships as the *Queen Mary* and *Queen Elizabeth,* for the fastest crossing of the North Atlantic. It appeared that Jim Sherwood had won it a couple of years earlier with *Sea Cat Great Britain*. It had not been without controversy, having last been won by the *SS United States* in 1952 but the trustees ruled that the *Sea Cat* had in fact met the criteria. The Maritime Museum considered challenging the decision on the grounds that Hales donated the award for ships providing a passenger service, but in the end did not follow up on their objection.

We entered the office on the thirteenth floor of the building with a panoramic window, with a magnificent view across the Thames and the city of London.

Mr James B Sherwood was sitting behind a large desk, that bore a mountain range of files stacked three or four high. He stood up and greeted me. "Come in Patrick, sit down."

He spoke in a strong, yet soft American accent. He was a large man with a warm smile, yet I was struck by the icy blue of his eyes. He was impressive, with an aura of authority about him. He was most certainly a man I would not wish to upset by questioning him on his punctuality for my interview. Judging by the paperwork on his desk, he was without a doubt a very busy man.

He asked me to tell him a little about myself. It took me, at best, ten minutes. He then spoke about the company, its history and his vision. He was certainly a man driven by high standards and a focus on nothing but the best. He completely won me over when he talked of how he saw the role of his managers.

> "Patrick, if you expect to be moved or promoted every two years, like the corporate chains, we are not for you. We like our managers to be the reason that guests return: we want them to say 'I am staying with Patrick at The Observatory Hotel'. I want you to act as if it is your own personal property, and do all the things an owner would do."

No one had ever given me this sort of discretion. If I had written my own perfect management dream, I could not have wished for more. I admired Jim from the beginning, and came to regard him as a visionary and my mentor. If anyone suggested that I had put him on a pedestal, I would have wholeheartedly agreed. For now, I had to return to Colin's office to wait very nervously to hear if in fact I had his blessing. About ten minutes later the phone rang and Colin was summoned. He came back with the contract, waving it as if he were Neville Chamberlain with the 'Peace in Our Time' letter. For me it was even more significant - and my letter was to be honoured, unlike poor Neville's.

I boarded my flight back to Melbourne at 9.45pm on that Monday evening in November 1991. In the mood I was in I could have flown myself! With 52 hours in the air, 15 hours on the ground, and a round trip of 67 hours, I was shattered. The adrenalin I had run on had just about run out as I sat in my seat. I was out for the count. I slept all the way, bar a slight awakening as we refuelled in Bangkok, and was only woken for breakfast shortly before we landed in Melbourne on Wednesday morning. I knew I was home when the door opened and I was hit by a wall of warm air. It was always great to be back in Australia.

I resigned the following day, and started my plans for the migration north to Sydney. We had to sell the house, sort out the school for Tim and to find a new home in Sydney for us all. This time there were four of us with our new addition, Charlie.

The future beckoned seductively. I managed to justify one final business trip to Sydney prior to our actual move from Melbourne, so I could take a look at my future domain whilst *incognito*. I wrapped up my work in the city and taxied to 89 Kent Street.

As we drove down through Millers Point, I looked out on a row of very tired-looking terraced homes, with some kids were playing in the street. I wondered if I had the right address. Hanging on the balcony of one house was a large banner that read, 'Millers Point for the People - HOMES NOT HOTELS.' JBS had described the spot as *an excellent location, within easy walking distance of Reserve Bank Square, the centre of the financial district, yet close to the two great symbols of the Sydney landscape, the Opera House and Sydney Harbour Bridge.* He wasn't exactly wrong but he'd failed to mention that the area was the last bastion of the dockworkers' and housing commission homes, for people on social welfare.

We reached what was obviously the building site, an area cordoned off with corrugated iron and storm fencing. I walked around the block, finding gaps to peer through. The foundations were laid and there was a very large hole that was to be the twenty metre pool in the sub basement. As I returned to the street front I noticed a man drinking a can of beer sitting on the doorstep of his rundown terrace home. He had with him a boy of about eight. My puzzlement soon turned to concern, as the boy picked up one of his father's empty beer cans and tossed it towards a moving car, with the aim of watching it being crushed under a wheel if he got his aim right. He got it spot on, as I could see that his father's beer consumption gave the child plenty of cans with which to practice.

This must be a mistake, surely! How could Mr Sherwood, a shrewd businessman, have considered this a desirable location for what would be the most prestigious five star hotel in Sydney? As if this didn't worry me enough, I heard some screaming and shouting coming from the ill-named 'Splendid Cafe' next door. As I turned to see what the commotion was about, a woman fell backwards out of the door, with another woman standing threateningly over her, holding a handful of hair that had belonged to the first woman, now prone on the pavement. The second one was screaming, "If you come near my husband again I will (*expletive*) kill you!" Rather than get caught up in the dispute, I hailed a cab that was fortunately passing right at that moment, and headed for the safety of the city.

I had hitherto been impressed with Mr Sherwood's vision, but I was starting to feel this was out of whack in biblical proportions. I was to learn over the years, however, that the vision he had was extraordinary. He saw things that I and most others did not see. Hence, he was on the UK's Rich List and I was not. He'd demonstrated this in spades with his shipping containers business; he had seen the potential of it whilst in the United States Navy, when the rest of the world was loading and unloading cargo manually from the ship's hold, a labour intensive and inefficient method.

At the hotel building site in Sydney, it was a struggle, but I kept my confidence that he knew what he was doing, even if I thought it was going to be a far greater challenge than I had imagined.

The date was now set for my departure from The Hotel Como. I was sorry to leave. It had been a very steep learning curve but I had learned about running hotels and life in Australia. I relished the fact that I was actually now an Aussie with two Aussie children. I had left behind any idea of being an Englishman in the colonies. I was as zealous as any convert! The Wallabies were now my team of choice, even at the expense of the Lions when they played against each other. Australians really had no idea of just how lucky they were: their lifestyle had been handed to them on a plate. I often pointed this out when I heard an Aussie whinging, which they usually criticised 'Poms' for. It was a case of the pot calling the kettle black.

We headed for Sydney, having handed over the hotel to a young man, Paul Hussey, who had been my deputy for the past year or so. It was his first general manager's position and was well deserved. Some years later he left The Como and moved to Bali to run a hotel. I was heartbroken to learn that he was among the two hundred and two people killed in the Bali bombing tragedy in 2002. Another friend, Annika Linden, was killed as well. She had gone there with a group of friends just a few days earlier.

On arrival in Sydney we rented a house in Vaucluse, an eastern suburb of Sydney. It was a lovely home that overlooked the harbour and it was not far from Tim's school, Scots College in Bellevue Hill, where Charlie was soon to join him. Sydney was not difficult to settle into and I soon realised that it was 'love at first sight'. Any previous misgivings I had just dissipated in the sun. After all my travels around the world, there is no city that can match Sydney's natural beauty and wonderful climate. Being a coastal city, you're never that far from the beach, and we enjoyed a relaxed lifestyle and lots of outdoor activities. With the harbour, the Opera House, the quaint finger wharves and lush botanical gardens, not to mention the array of restaurants serving myriad cuisines from all parts of the world, we loved our new home. With its diverse multicultural society, the cosmopolitan city of Sydney had certainly grown up in the last fifty years.

I had joined an international, unique and very prestigious company. I'm pretty sure a large dollop of luck was involved but, in achieving this, I had been given the greatest opportunity of my life. I was determined to make it a success.

My first day with Orient-Express was one of discovery. I had no hotel and, yet again, another building site. I guess I should have obtained a better understanding of a few things before accepting the job, but it would not have changed my decision at any rate.

We had temporary offices set up in Harrington Street in the city. Peter Rozee came out from head office in London to help with the initial induction into the workings of Orient-Express, or OEH as the company was always to be called. He introduced me to the owners of The Observatory, the Japanese Nara Corporation, and Mr Saigo who was their representative in Sydney.

Luxury hotels were popping up everywhere at that time. They were mainly Japanese-owned, and Nara also owned Lilianfels in The Blue Mountains, The Observatory's sister hotel, an opulent resort about two hours drive from Sydney. They had also developed Nara Sea World Resort on the Gold Coast in Queensland. It had been the site of a theme park developed by the Australian entrepreneur, Keith Williams, and later became part of Warner Bros Movie World and Wet'n'Wild.

This 'invasion' - driven by investment rather than empire - was mainly due to Japanese banks offering loans at almost zero percent interest rates. It had its critics but I'd often point out we should be thankful for the flow of capital. Owners come and go but the hotels they build will always remain. As things turned out, this is exactly what happened. The void created by the Japanese withdrawal from the Australian market at the end of the '90s was quickly filled by Malaysians, Singaporians and Chinese investors. Economic life goes on.

I had already learned about Japanese culture, as Australia, by and large, wanted to embrace these new investors. In schools, Japanese language classes were replacing French, and courses were being offered by many trainers to enlighten the working population about the complexity of a very different culture. We learned that the Japanese took a long term view on investment, a trait for which I was most grateful. They also expected loyalty, respect and hard work; some of these qualities may have been a challenge to the rather laid back and outspoken Aussies.

We learned that it was customary to bow rather than shake hands. I didn't initially appreciate that this was in itself an art form: the depth of one's bow reflected your status compared to that of the person you were greeting. I noted sometimes that the bowing continued for several minutes, which aggravated my lower back problems. There was also the issue of the business card: always to be presented with two hands and studied closely. *Never* write on it and *never ever* place it in your back pocket. The card represents the company and sitting on is seen as most disrespectful. I was always impressed by the fact that *everyone* had a card. Not to have one could exclude you - how would people understand your position in the pecking order and how were they to know the appropriate level of respect with which to address you? With the Japanese, rather than get it wrong they may, out of politeness, just ignore you.

I will always remember lying beside a swimming pool, when a Japanese man pulled himself out of the water. He produced a business card from somewhere in his swimming trunks, bowed and presented it with two hands to another Japanese man on a lounger near me. Once the formalities were done, they sat together, chatted and enjoyed a beer. It was a minefield even for an Englishman who was accustomed to a formal class system, let alone for Australians with their far more relaxed, egalitarian ways.

Another aspect of Japanese culture was that everything was done in committee. Very rarely was a direct decision made by an individual. This was rather confusing to many westerners as we take pride in being direct and decisive. To this day I admire the culture but there were times when I found Mr Saigo, or Saigo-san, as we addressed him, hard to follow. He was both charming and relaxed, a civil engineer by profession and it was obvious that he came from the upper levels of society in Japan. His family was in publishing and they had the Japanese rights to *Vogue* and *Harpers*. As time went on, I had the feeling that he was a little higher up the social strata than the self-made construction millionaire, Mr Nara, head of the Nara Corporation in Yokohama, where we attended the occasional meeting. [30]

Saigo-san added refinement to the company, but from time to time his guard came down. I arranged a dinner with him and some of our senior head office personnel, one being the very urbane and respectful Peter Parrott, our Vice President of Finance. I chose a very upmarket Japanese restaurant that I knew to be a favourite with Saigo-san, where we all sat on the floor. Thankfully, to accommodate westerners, there was a well into which one's legs could fit under the table, whilst giving the impression of sitting on the floor.

The evening went very well and as the night went on a great many bottles of wine were consumed, and were followed by many toasts with sake. At one point Saigo-san excused himself to answer the call of nature, and he moved away from the table on his hands and knees. He was shortly followed by Peter, who to my surprise crouched down and exited in similar fashion. On Peter's return I was about to ask him if all was well, when I heard him say very politely, "Saigo-san, may I say how much I enjoy the customs of Japan, and how respectful everyone is to one another."

A little unsure as to this comment, Saigo-san asked what he meant?

"I couldn't help but notice that when you rose from the table, rather than disrupt anyone, you remained on your hands and knees as you left the restaurant," said Peter.

Saigo-san thought for a second and burst out laughing. "No, no, that was not a Japanese custom - I have just drunk too much!"

Japanese entertaining captured the very essence of *What happens in Vegas, stays in Vegas*. You work with each other all day, then go out, get absolutely legless in a bar together and make complete fools of yourselves. The following morning, everyone will behave as if nothing had happened and not a word would ever be mentioned about your previous night's indiscretions.

My first task with The Observatory was to understand the issues surrounding the building of the hotel, as it appeared that there was quite a level of politics involved and a rather fractious relationship with the locals. We could see this from the protest hoardings on the balconies of the surrounding houses. Multiplex were the contracted builders, and had established a local residents group in an attempt to handle the objections and general discontent. As a commercial building, the hotel was taking space away from government housing and feelings were running high. I scheduled a meeting with Multiplex and the Local Residents Action Group.[32]

I was more than a little apprehensive of who might be on this committee, as I had visions of the 'ladies' who'd had their disagreement on the steps of the cafe on my previous visit. When I arrived at the Multiplex office, some other ladies (thankfully) were already there. They were first in line for the tea and biscuits the company laid on. I politely said hello and one of the women looked at me. "You must be the young English laddie who's come to run the hotel. Would you like a cup of tea?"

Hardly had my cup of tea been passed to me when the meeting was brought to order. I wasn't sure what to expect, but these people didn't look to me very much like the agitating, militant Trotskyite activists I had been told about. As the meeting continued, I warmed to them; they were simply a group of concerned local residents, whose tight-knit little community, tucked away beneath the real astronomical Observatory perched on the hill above, was about to be taken over, as they saw it, by a large hotel, with an invasion of foreigners and all the noisy activity that this would bring.

Each had their say on building noise, dust, the parking of all the subcontractors' vehicles and concerns about the traffic. I sat and listened, while the construction company discussed their concerns about the building issues. As I had learned before, construction was not something I was allowed to meddle in. Eventually a silence fell. The general gaze turned in my direction.

"Well, Mr Griffin, what do you have to say?"

I hesitated for a moment; whatever I said now would set the scene for our future relationship.

"As far as the points you have raised, I do of course understand and I am sure these will be dealt with by the contractor. As you appreciate this is a building site, and I haven't got a hotel yet. When I have, I assure you we want to be, if you will allow, part of and supportive of your community. You mentioned I was an Englishman; more correctly I *was* an Englishman, I am now a convert and as such a dinky di Aussie."

This brought smiles to their faces, hearing this in my rather Oxbridge English accent.

"But you are right. I am new to Sydney and know little about Millers Point, but I would love to learn. If one of you ladies, or gentleman, have an hour or so I would appreciate being shown around, have a chat and understand more as to how I can help and try to put to rest any concerns you may have."

This had a good effect. They looked at each other and a woman who seemed a little more chatty than the others spoke up.

"I could do that if you would like. But it might start a bit of gossip with me wandering around on the arm of a nice young man."

They all laughed. The ice was broken.

"I'm Fay, Fay Neil, a good Irish name like your own. How about tomorrow afternoon?"

We met the following afternoon and went for a walk. It was evident that most of the residents in Millers Point had been there for many years, mainly due to their husbands being employed on the wharf, which most of the homes overlooked. She had amazing stories to tell.

Millers Point was once 'nobs hill' of Sydney, but during the nineteenth century it developed into a more lively and chaotic collection of wharves, ship builders, repair and maintenance shops, warehouses and bond stores. Millers Point was home to the harbour workers, traders, sailors, wharf owners, waterside workers and their families, as the port developed. The name was derived from Jack Leighton, who in 1814 built a small mill on the hill, creating the nickname of 'Jack the miller'. He came to a nasty end when he climbed one of the mill's sails whilst very intoxicated and fell to his death. The mill was replaced by the astronomical Observatory in 1858. The importance of this building became apparent when I questioned the height of the hotel, and asked why we did not not have more rooms. It had less to do with the residents and more to do with history.

Before radio, the only way to convey accurate time was through a visual signal. Accurate time was especially important to ships setting out on a long voyage as they needed to adjust and calibrate their chronometers for navigation. Initially only a time ball was contemplated to be used, but soon it was realised that a time ball without an observatory and an astronomer was useless. The astronomer needed to observe the sun by day and the stars at night to ensure that the ball was dropped at exactly the right time. It was argued that if the hotel were to be built any higher it would not permit a line of sight to the time ball from the ships moored in the cove below. I didn't like to argue the point that we now had GPS.

As we walked around the streets that made up Millers Point, I was introduced to other residents, including the landlord of the *Lord Nelson*, the oldest pub in Sydney. This was disputed by the next landlord we visited at *The Hero of Waterloo* where they claimed to have a secret passage that led to the wharf and was used by the press gangs to recruit men into the service of Her Majesty's Navy.

Fay pointed out all the places of interest, including the local brothels, old and new. The area certainly had a colourful past. In 1900, Millers Point had experienced Australia's last recorded outbreak of the plague. All the streets were 'tarmacked' as part of the disinfection process, which was a great benefit. There was also the very tenuous belief that the site of where the hotel was to stand had at one time been the home of Mary MacKillop, a nun who was declared a saint and would be beatified in January 1995 by Pope John Paul II.

Fay's tales of the area were boundless. The residents were fiercely proud of their community and woe betide anyone who referred to Millers Point as part of 'The Rocks', a suburb nearby. They were once two clearly defined communities, until the 'Argyle Cut' was built with convict labour in the 1850s to provide direct easy access between Millers Point and The Rocks. It seemed they had very very long memories.

She told me how life had been for the residents and how, on occasion, some of the cargo being unloaded off the ships by their husbands would mysteriously find its way to the residents of Millers Point. They were never short of the odd bottle of whisky, brandy or other goods brought in from faraway places.

Fay and I, together with the other ladies, Doreen Luck, Joyce Sherlock, and the only man in the group, Ron Jennings, became firm friends over the next twenty years. We often shared a cup of tea and they were even there to see me off at my retirement.

The Observatory Hotel's location was indeed an interesting one but how was I to secure it a position on the world map of luxury hotels? This was JBS's goal and the job I'd been given. To meet this challenge I had to find and enthuse a team of the right individuals to help me.

I was pleased with the support I had from London. Peter Rozee was regularly on a flight from England, knocking up frequent flyer points that would take most of us a lifetime to accumulate. He was only topped by another of the Orient-Express team, George Hookham. George was the Director of Technical Services and oversaw the building to the very high standards laid down by JBS.

Although the hotel was owned and being funded by the Japanese, it appeared that Orient-Express, who were to manage the hotel, were given a free hand in its design and specifications. This is where George excelled. I never met another man as capable as George Hookham. When dealing with architects, builders and engineers, his eye for minutiae, and ability to recall in detail the minutes of any meeting were nothing short of amazing. I was often collared by the contractors wanting to know how he did it: did he record his conversations or use a hidden camera? George would refer to a specific conversation or request that had happened six months earlier, with no reference to any notes! [31]

The result: The Observatory was built to a standard that few other hotels could match. The detail mattered, and - as the man who would be left to run the hotel - I was delighted that OEH, the owners, the designers and the construction team actually listened to what I had to say. In my experience, this was a first. I made the most of it. I took my son Tim with me to check out the five star competition in Sydney. We stayed in a very upmarket new hotel that was claimed to have all the bells and whistles. I asked Tim to boil the kettle and make a cup of tea, and as he knelt to plug it into the socket in the skirting board he lamented, "Why do all the sockets have to be on the floor?"

I then went to the bathroom to answer a call of nature, and I was pleased that I could listen to the news on a speaker in the bathroom. The volume control was beside the bathtub: you could lie submerged and enjoy the radio. There was even a telephone beside the loo. I was very impressed with these little touches and made a note. There was however one little problem.

I was going about my 'business' when the phone rang. I was going to pick up the phone beside me in the bathroom however the news was blaring on the speakers. Tim with his own headphones on could not hear me shouting to turn it down and I could not reach the volume control near the bathtub. The caller obviously gave up as the phone went silent. This showed me the dilemma of placing the volume control near the bath and not near the loo. I also duly noted to check this out in our hotel's drawings. As it turned out both problems were mirrored in our own plans. Although it meant a 'variation order', and some cost, the owners agreed for the original bathroom plan to be changed.

On another matter, when we stayed in hotels, my wife was often irritated that I would take a hot shower while she tried to do her hair and makeup in a cloud of steam that was not conducive to cosmetic perfection. Most modern hotel rooms have a desk, so I thought this could be combined to create a dressing table. We had lovely period style desks that were being specifically designed for the hotel, so we asked the designers to make the centre panel lift up like an old school desk, and attach a mirror underneath. Problem solved.

The designers were also going to place mirrors above the men's public urinals. I most certainly felt that one's dignity might be challenged if those beside you could view you as God created. We arranged for a more suitable set of vignettes to hang upon the wall where gentlemen's eyes could rest during this bodily function. [33]

The designers created a visual 'storyboard' of each room so that we could better understand what the finished product would look like. From the drawings of the lounge, I couldn't help but make the comparison to my Uncle's home at Tachbrook, with rich fabrics, deep comfy chairs, drapes and a huge fireplace. During long-ago Christmases, my cousin Tim and I would bounce the glass Christmas balls from the tree to make them touch the high ceiling without shattering; it was not a skill we excelled at. These memories flooded back, so I called the hotel lounge 'The Drawing Room'.

The hotel lighting was a task of monumental proportions. Specialist designers were charged with creating unique effects of 'floating ceilings' in the foyer and corridors to give the impression of height. This was all very new technology for Australia. The marble floor was to be cut from one piece to ensure that the grain matched. The bathrooms had computer-designed shower trays and rain shower heads, with marbled finishes on the walls. One of the public rooms had a magnificent Oriental *trompe l'oeil*, so this restaurant was called the 'Orient Cafe'.

The hotel bar was to take the form of a library. I love books and so was horrified to discover that the team was charged with the purchase of 'forty one metres of books' with no other descriptor, so I gave them one. As the hotel was to be called 'The Observatory', I wanted to theme the library with books on astronomy and astrology - anything to do with the stars. We could only find a limited number of books so we decided to use the Orient-Express theme as well. They happily found forty-one metres worth of antique books on travel, adventure and the stars.

I was having a field day. Never had I ever had so much influence in spending vast sums of money. I was therefore excited to learn that on my next trip to London I was to meet a woman called Sally Lloyd, from a company called Project Art, who was to source hundreds of artworks to be hung in the hotel. We met at the Dorchester Hotel, where I saw many of the same fabrics that featured on our storyboards at The Observatory, as it turned out we shared the same interior designers, Richmond International. The Dorchester's renovation cost many millions of pounds, and was an iconic luxury hotel, so I wasn't complaining.

With Sally being English and Project Art being an English company, I was terrified that the art she might be presenting would be country landscapes in the style of Constable or Turner, or - even worse - cocker spaniels and horses by George Stubbs. I hated the idea of simply replicating a Dorchester or a Ritz in Sydney. As it turned out, The Observatory was later actually referred to by the UK Daily Telegraph as *a Claridge's in miniature, a model of understated elegance.* Claridge's in London's Mayfair was the epitome of timeless elegance, and one of the best five star luxury hotels in the world, so I took this as a compliment and didn't complain.

I explained my ideas to Sally; she was already in full agreement. As part of Britain's colonial empire, many of the artists, whose work depicted the real Australia, were in fact English and had brought their art back to England where much of it had remained. As such, the choice of Australian art was wider in London than back in Australia. Sally put together one of the best collections of Colonial artwork seen outside any gallery or museum in Australia.

When she eventually came to supervise the hanging of the art I was fascinated by some of her choices. I particularly liked the pastels and inks of still life, and sketches of flora and fauna. Sally told me the tale of two of the artists involved. One had lost his coloured inks overboard in the rough crossing of the First Fleet; his fellow artist had refused to share his inks, leaving the first artist no alternative but to use black navigation ink scrounged from the ship's captain. The story intrigued me and was one I was to tell often to visiting journalists. It was not until later when I was telling Sally how well her tale had been taken up by the press that she looked at me, with a smile and a wink and replied, "It is so important to have a good *story* to tell, to gain people's interest!" I realised that there was not one word of truth in what I had been telling everyone. But it was a good story, so I kept on telling it.

We were later to expand our art collection with some serious works, for some of which I take credit. I had never imagined that, under the instruction of JBS, I would be sitting in a Sotheby's auction, my numbered paddle in hand and bidding for a painting with a six figure price tag, an experience I rather enjoyed. JBS and his wife Dr Shirley Sherwood were both keen art collectors. Shirley was credited with reviving a global interest in *contemporary botanical art*. Such was her passion that eventually her collection was to be housed in a dedicated gallery at Kew Gardens named for her. She was also appointed an Officer of the Order of the British Empire (OBE) in the 2012 New Year's Honours for services to botanical art.

We searched for anything that was Australian and antique, which was a challenge as far as European art and artefacts were concerned. We did find a few items: an old fireplace from Elizabeth Bay House, built around 1835, known as 'the finest house in the colony', and this fireplace was placed in the Drawing Room. We also located a rather magnificent station master's desk and this became the *maître d's* spot at the entrance of the fine dining restaurant.

On another trip to London, Sally took me to a little antique shop in Kensington; she had found something of interest. It was a rare 'celestial globe'; there were many 'terrestrial globes' to be found, but one featuring the heavens was unusual. It was very expensive but as it was dated around the time of Captain Cook's travels to Australia we could create quite a story around it. The bar area - or library - with all its books on adventure and travel, the paintings and etchings of native flora and fauna, and now with the celestial globe as centrepiece, gave us the name: The Globe Bar.

We had firmed up the themes around which we were to build the hotel. The astronomical Observatory, in the shadows of which we stood; the luxury travel of the Orient-Express, and some Italian influences - reflecting JBS's love of all things Italian. Finally, but most significantly, an Australian *feel.* This was after all an Australian hotel and JBS put a great store in establishing individuality that reflected the hotel's location.

JBS had started his hotel company with the purchase of The Cipriani in Venice. With this in mind we decided our *ristorante* was to serve upmarket Italian food, which was relatively new to Sydney which had an abundance of casual *osterias* or *trattorias*. 'The Galileo Restaurant' was both Italian and astronomical. It was lavishly furnished, with beautifully carved chairs; the walls were covered in Fortuny fabric, with a silk and gold printed motif. The decor cost a fortune.

We had a large number of suites and to make them a little more interesting we gave them names rather than numbers.

What better than than the Pullman carriages used on the UK train that started the Orient-Express journey. Most had originally been part of *The Brighton Belle*. Their provenance was interesting: we had *Audrey*, built in 1932, damaged in the Blitz, that was to carry The Queen, The Duke of Edinburgh and The Queen Mother to review the fleet in 1953. It was also seen in a TV episode of *Minder* with George Cole and Dennis Waterman. *Perseus* was the carriage built in 1938 used for Winston Churchill's funeral train in 1965. *Phoenix* was built in 1927, a favourite with The Queen Mother and used by General de Gaulle and other visiting heads of state, and had somehow ended up as a stationary restaurant in Lyon, France, in 1973. *Vera* was used on a number of occasions by the Royal Family and for Prince Charles' and Princess Anne's first trip on an electric train in 1954. *Zena* was built in 1928 - my favourite - originally from *The Bournemouth Belle* on which I had travelled as a boy, and was used later in 1976 in the filming of *Agatha*, the story of the famous author herself.

We next had to tackle the twenty-metre swimming pool, with our rather obscure claim that it was 'the largest subterranean swimming pool in the southern hemisphere'. We had commissioned an Aboriginal mural to be painted as a feature wall, but we ran into all sorts of problems. The cost seemed to escalate after every meeting, and the durability of such an expensive work of art was questionable in the humid atmosphere of the swimming pool. Then we discovered that the copyright of the work would create impossible barriers to any photography, meaning we couldn't use it in brochures or even postcards. So the painting was replaced with faux sandstone blocks, although we later createed a *trompe l'oeil* of a beach scene. The mosaics in the pool were computer-designed to give the effect of depth with an undulating bottom as a watering hole, or billabong would have.

The feature that was to make the pool utterly unique was the ceiling: painted to resemble the night sky, with tiny optic fibre lights to represent the stars of the southern hemisphere, with the Southern Cross in all its glory. I was showing off this area, with great pride, to the curator of the Sydney Observatory. As we walked from one end of the pool to the other I said, "It's pretty good isn't it? There are over one thousand optic fibre lights - and they also twinkle with the computerised system we have installed!"

Pride cometh before a fall. He replied, "Very impressive; I can see the Southern Cross, Alpha Centauri and there's Antares; very impressive. Ahhm, not sure how to tell you this, but there is one slight error. It's back to front."

Silence. At first I thought he was winding me up. He was deadly serious. I scurred off to check the drawings used by the electricians. The workers who had set up in the empty pool had laid the drawings on their table and looking up had positioned each light accordingly: which made it a mirror image of the plan. I was forever grateful to the curator, who - to my knowledge - never revealed the flaw in our unique ceiling. I was thankful that there were unlikely to be any passing ships in the night whose safe navigation home would have been reliant on the correct position of the stars above our pool.

We had to figure out how to get a large flotation tank into the health club, located in the sub basement of the hotel. The staircases and doorways - to our horror - were too small. The flotation tank was the latest innovation for health clubs and we were keen to be the first in Sydney to offer this to guests. It was an extraordinary device that had been described to me as a form of sensory deprivation - floating in darkness, naked in a soundproof tank, that looks like a cross between a chest freezer and a coffin. The saving grace being that you were immersed in a solution of warm water and Epsom salts.

I was initially baffled by the idea. Wasn't *sensory deprivation* a form of brainwashing torture? Not a good experience. I then tried it in the USA, feeling jet lagged and tired from a long flight. I was immediately converted. After a single hour-long experience in a tank, having accepted that I wouldn't drown, I slept in such a state of deep relaxation, that I thought I must have been asleep for hours. This was a perfect experience to offer our guests who in many cases would have just flown in from the other side of the world.

Having almost given up the idea of the tank in the hotel due to the impossibility of getting it down the stairs or in the door, Charlie Dodsworth, our chief engineer, came up with a solution. In his Geordie accent he said, "Hey boss, what about through the lift shaft?"

It was this kind of simple but brilliant solution that Charlie was good at. I thought most engineers did everything in the tried and tested way. In the months ahead as we approached completion, we faced many similar dilemmas.

As we got closer to the handover, defects in workmanship or the finish, big and small, were marked by sticking on red dots that started appearing all over the hotel. It looked like the building had caught a nasty case of measles. George Hookham and Charlie had a field day. I saw spots before my eyes everywhere I looked: on the marble floors, on the ceiling coving, in the bedrooms and even in the toilets. I was hard pressed to see what was wrong, but they knew what they were on about. Eventually the dots started to disappear as things were rectified; it was as if a miracle cure had been found for the building measles. I still found the odd red spot about the place fourteen years later.

JBS was committed to quality, style and good taste; so much so that there were occasionally delays due to the fact that some item or other had not personally been signed off by him. He was diligent about any detail that is often overlooked by architects and designers. On one of his visits to the site to inspect the bedrooms, accompanied by George, the contractors and myself, as we left the bathroom, he turned and said, "George, in future builds, please ensure there is a minimum of 18 inches either side of the toilet bowl."

In his book, *Orient-Express A Personal Journey* JBS adds an appendix: 'What Makes A Five Star Hotel Great'. He lists all the attributes of a true five star property. It makes for excellent reading and I only wish I had had such information when first starting out in the industry. His book and especially this appendix, should form part of any young student's syllabus when studying to become a hotelier. I've added some more information about JBS in Appendix A to this book, as he is a most fascinating man.

My executive team was very much involved in developing the detail that would make 'our' five star hotel truly special. Above all, the guest experience of comfort and service at The Observatory was to be both uniquely individual and quintessentially Australian - not following the chain hotel format.

As I have often said previously: no matter how magnificent the hotel may be, or how many technical bells and whistles it may have, in the end the guest will not return if the service is poor. Staff are the key to the success of any hotel.

The first person I needed for my team was a secretary. This role was filled by a lovely young woman, Anne-Marie. The second was a financial controller; this was the only member of staff who required both head office and the owners to sign off.

I interviewed a number of candidates, but only one came up with both the technical background I sought as well as - importantly - personality. He spoke his mind, and could put all the intricate issues of finance in the most simple terms. Having never passed a maths exam, this was the sort of person I needed. Most of all he was Aussie through and through. His name was David Campbell. Peter from head office liked him and he interviewed well with Saigo-san. After their interview, I asked Saigo-san how it went. "Yes - a very good young man, I am sure he has many good attributes - yes."

Wanting to get it all signed and sealed, I took this as a green light, and confirmed David's appointment. I settled back then and turned my thoughts next to the Chief Engineer, who I wanted on board before construction was too far down the track. He would be looking after all the knobs, switches, taps and things that go bang in the night. As things invariably do.

The man I found was he who I have already admired, from Hartlepool to be precise, our Charlie Dodsworth. He had worked on ocean liners, so was used to the intricacies of the hospitality industry and the need to handle guests with care. He had lived in Australia for a number of years and was married to an Australian girl called Margaret. He was a big man with, I soon learned, a big heart. A Pom - yes - but one who was well settled into Aussie culture. I felt he would be ideal. Again I was fortunate. On the very day I found Charlie, George Hookham was in town so I could get them together to discuss the nuts and bolts of the hotel. George liked Charlie and gave his nod of approval in the same way as Saigo-san had liked David. Or so I thought.

I was to have another lesson in Japanese culture. When I had my chat with Saigo-san, I had assumed that he liked David because he had said "yes". David's contract was now signed and sealed. I was therefore rather taken back when the following morning Saigo-san laid a neatly typed note at the threshold of my office. Saigo-san never entered my office, even when the door was open. He would very quietly place any written communication on the floor just inside. I was always baffled as to why he did this, but I became used to it. This morning I read the note and I was horrified to read that he wished to discuss David's appointment; he felt that maybe David was too young for such a position. As David had already accepted the position - from me - I had to think hard and fast as to how I might convince Saigo-san that David was the man for the job. What had changed Saigo-san's mind? After all, he had said "yes"?

I now learned that apparently the Japanese will never say 'no'. I am not even sure there is a word for it in their language. When they say 'yes' they mean 'yes I understand what you have said'. Thankfully I was able to convince Saigo-san that 'we' had made the right choice, and David came on board as planned.

As it turned out, David was an excellent choice and I was forever thankful to him for the way he handled the hotel's finances at a difficult time. Sadly for me, Orient-Express felt he was too good for us in Sydney after a couple of years, and whisked him off to Rio to solve some difficult problems facing the South Americans.

I set about finding the other key team players. As an old school hotelier in the digital age, my belief in surrounding myself with experts in their field came into its own. Having appointed them, I then listened to their advice. I was fortunate to have many young technically astute assistants, but I needed a specialist. I brought back a young man whom I had employed at Hotel Como, Russell Bullen, to The Observatory.

Russell was ideal for putting into action the concepts that Orient-Express wanted. The first issue was the key system. Something simple, you might think, but JBS was keen on maintaining customer interaction, as was I. With the new plastic room keycards being given to guests, the hotel would lose a crucial contact point. We didn't want the old manual key system, so Russell found us something better that had the security we needed. Marlock was an electronic metal key that gave security but could also be hung from a traditional hotel key fob, allowing the guest to leave it with concierge and therefore provide an opportunity for interaction to get to know them. As Russell reminded me some years later:

> "We were the first hotel in Australia to implement the Marlock key system: it was super expensive. Unlike Ving Card, which were standalone units, with Marlock every guest lock/door at OBS had to be hardwired back to a central panel so we could control the lock sequences, lock outs, maid access, and other people's access."

> This allowed us to offer a far greater level of security.

> "We were also the first hotel in Australia to use Landmark with Microsoft Windows 3.1 and 3.112 - unheard of at the time as it only ever ran under DOS."

There were many other innovative technical systems introduced in those early days, but the thing to understand was that they were all done to enable us to offer a more pleasant customer experience, and to give the team access to information that enabled them to make that interaction far more personal. It was never just technology for its own sake, it was all about service - not that I ever really understood the technology.

I then appointed a Director of Sales and Marketing, John Verhelst. He was Australian and also turned out to be a 'Mr Fix It'. His extensive network seemed to stretch globally, which is a great asset in developing a new hotel. Next came Director of PR, Angela Clarke, who was the cornerstone of the hotel's public image. In all my years I don't think I have come across anyone so dedicated to the task in hand. It was Angela's talent that I credit for the recognition and acknowledgement we received in the early years, from not only the Australian press but global media.

I appointed a young Austrian, Gunther Buhosluv as Deputy Manager. (I never could spell his name properly!) Gunther came to me from The Park Hyatt in Sydney, at the time the newest and most stylish of hotels built on the harbour waterfront. His main task was to focus on food and beverage, and he did this with great creativity. In hindsight, I should have kept a closer eye on him, as he commissioned expensive artists to design unique items from glass bowls and platters to banquet stands in wrought iron on which to present the food. In every bedroom we had beautiful bronze stands and hand-crafted amber glass dishes on which we displayed strawberries as a welcoming gift to our guests. They were all amazingly creative and looked magnificent; such was the artistry, the court of The Sun King, Louis XIV of France would have been impressed. Such accoutrements had never before been seen in hotels; neither had such costs. Yet the owners took it in their stride. The budget for hotels of this era reflected the sizable egos and wallets of their owners.

They were indeed heady times. Such extravagance would not be seen again in my time.

The final role to be recruited was the all-important *chef de cuisine*, on whose talents the hotel would be judged - especially in Sydney, home to some of the finest restaurants in the southern hemisphere from classic French, to Japanese, Moroccan, Thai and even Ethiopian.

We looked at many CVs from interesting chefs from Australia, Asia and Europe. We had difficulty finding an executive chef with the depth of knowledge in Italian cuisine that we sought, but struck it lucky with a young chef who we felt would be a massive asset as 'number two'. Francesco Zonta had been working as a chef for The Cipriani, and we were also able to recruit Alberto Tita from The Splendido in Portofino as our *maitre d'*. I was fortunate to have such talent locked in, but was still without an executive chef.

With Peter Rozee's help we found a chef who was working with Anton Mosimann at his Halkin Street 'Private Dining Club', a converted Scottish Presbyterian church in London's swish Belgravia. I had known of Anton Mosimann's reputation from his Dorchester days where his restaurant was one of the few to receive a highly acclaimed two Michelin Star-rating. His cuisine was not Italian but what he called *cuisine naturelle*. Its main characteristic was that it did without such ingredients as butter, cream, and alcohol, with the focus concentrated even more on the flavour of the individual ingredients. It all sounded marvellous. I was very excited about the young chef in question, as in my mind it offered us a wonderful opportunity to differentiate ourselves in the very competitive Sydney restaurant market.

The chef's name was Kit Chan. We had lots of inevitable wordplay on the pronunciation *(kit-chen)*. Kit was Hong Kong-born Chinese - who happened also to be a woman. There were no luxury hotels with a Chinese executive chef nor any five star hotel in Australia with a female executive chef, let alone one with such an exciting pedigree of culinary experience. I flew to London to experience just how well she could cook, but I must confess, not being an indulgent foodie, I was apprehensive about judging. Peter Rozee would be there and he was indeed a foodie, however *my* mind was more focussed on the publicity opportunities. Already having Francesco on board, I was prepared to be flexible. As it turned out no such flexibility was needed; her cooking was superb.

I had my executive team. I was delighted, as I had found a group of experts who were absolute masters in their fields.[34]

As you may have gathered, I have never regarded myself as much of an expert at anything. At best you'd say I was a jack of all trades. What I did pride myself on was the talent to be able to surround myself with true professionals and experts in their craft. My other talent was that - having made my choice - I could then delegate to them the freedom to do what they were good at, applying and developing their own individual strengths. I believe in giving direction, but I have never understood what makes a manager employ a skilled professional, only to then control and micro-manage them and make all the decisions on their behalf. That is never going to be the best use of anyone's time, nor did it offer them the opportunity to grow, to be creative or to achieve the job satisfaction so necessary for the level of success that we sought.

It was now time to find the rest of the staff who would become the face of the hotel. Easier said than done. This was not simply the case of placing an ad and receiving the applications - as was the custom in my younger days. The industry was now using psychometric testing on teamwork, problem-solving, communication, creativity, flexibility and organisational skills. All to avoid putting a round peg in a square hole. An international American-based hotel chain of some repute (that shall remain nameless) had perfected this testing, often conducting as many as four interviews with the aim of minimising staff turnover. They had a rigorous system of training that one senior executive claimed was so good, 'A ham sandwich could run one of our hotels.' It didn't say much for their hotels, to my mind. They believed in total uniformity across their brand - both in design and staff behaviour - down to the words spoken in addressing the guests.

This company's methods made them my nemesis. I was committed to individuality. In my experience, if we employed the right staff then they would, with a bit of guidance, do and say the right thing with sincerity, and particularly when dealing with the cultural diversity of Australia. I did not want parrots as staff, expecting them to repeat the same mantra to every guest. I remembered my conversation with the hotel staffer in the

US with his mindless repetition of "It's a pleasure sir." I wanted people who could be comfortable with what they say, even when doing something as simple as answering the phone. Obviously "G'day mate, how yer doin!" was not going to be sufficient, but neither did I want robotic responses like "Good morning, thank you for calling The Observatory Hotel, John speaking, how may I direct your call?"

My general rule was: be polite, but warm and friendly as if you really do appreciate their call. *(By the way - the unnamed group hotel in Sydney had one of the highest staff turnover rates in town. One staffer even commented in the press that the thorough interviewing techniques made little difference to him as he would move on when he was ready anyway.)*

I am a great believer in the 'first impression'. After all that is the opportunity that a member of staff will have - minutes or even seconds to make a good impression on a guest.

We discussed the best method of recruiting the team and were fortunate to have a very talented Director of HR, Wendy Sawyer, who we had also pinched from the Park Hyatt, our closest rival. We agreed that, initially, we would cast our net as wide as possible and not simply look for staff with hotel experience. I have never believed our business to be rocket science. As I kept repeating to all and sundry, "We can teach the techniques to a person, but we cannot teach them common sense or give them a personality".

Our PR director, Angela, had been busy raising the profile of the as yet unopened hotel, but we were still not sure if our name was out there. We placed a large ad in the paper simply asking for applicants 'with personality who wanted a career in hotels - no experience necessary'. We booked The Adrian Mott Hall, a local community centre near the hotel, in which to conduct the interviews. We set up eight desks, and staffed them with the executive team. We set up tables where prospective applicants could complete a simple form. I wasn't interviewing but would just walk around and chat to people, getting my own first impression of the applicants.

We had no idea as to who, if any, would turn up. Hundreds did, and the queue stretched from the door, along Argyle Street past the Post Office and around the corner into Kent Street to St Bridget's Church! Such was the interest, I was amazed. It was not long before the TV news crews turned up. Some applicants, I was amused to see, hid their faces, obviously concerned that their current employer might see them on the news. Others were more forthcoming. One applicant in particular caught my eye, a very tall young man with great presence and a resonating New Zealand accent. If I was looking for personality and confidence this young man had bags of it. When picked out by the TV reporter and asked why he wished to apply for this job, he made a statement that was to ring through the years and would come back to haunt him. "I'm the face of the new unemployed," he stated in a loud booming voice.

With such presence, and that voice, without hesitation I employed him as a doorman for the hotel. Michael Anderson started in that position but rapidly rose through the ranks to eventually become my Chief Concierge. Along the way he became a member of the greatly respected *Clefs d'Or*, in which he was to play a major role. He was with me to greet and farewell every guest to the hotel over the next twenty years, and gained a reputation as both a source of information and the fixer of every conceivable problem our guests may have faced. One notable guest described him as the best concierge in any hotel in the world.

The recruitment day proved to be a great success. Not only did we have all the staff we needed, we had the *right* staff. I would be hard pressed to recall any round pegs in square holes. As well as Michael, there were many of those who we employed on that day in 1992, such as Elsie and Soshilla in the laundry and Emil Bashay our head housekeeper, who were still working for the hotel until my retirement in 2011, whilst many others were in line for long service leave.

Chapter 5

#supersonictravel #agatherstraintrip #devincibydesign

In April 1992, as part of my induction into Orient-Express, Hotels, Trains and Cruises, I was to experience some of the other company hotels, to give me a better understanding of the standards expected. The timing was to coincide with a group meeting of all the managers and main head office personnel, the first of its kind, with JBS chairing the meeting. This meeting was to be held at the Windsor Court in New Orleans. I loved the city, having visited with my eldest son Steve in 1981. It was one of those American cities that I felt had some real character.

I was able to book my flights through an old friend, and being 'in the trade' and 'in the know' I had the opportunity to book an 'AD75' - a 75% discounted round the world ticket. With such a discount, I could justify travelling in some luxury, hopefully with an upgrade to first class.

My itinerary was set to arrive in New Orleans on Saturday 25th April, with the conference on the following Monday and Tuesday. I would then fly to New York and on to London. I arranged to stay once again at The Ritz, before meeting Peter and boarding the Orient-Express for Venice. We would stay at The Cipriani and then go on to The Villa San Michele in Florence and The Splendido in Portofino. It was a round trip of fourteen days. This trip just couldn't get any better.

Just before I left I had a call. Would I 'mind' if British Airways transferred my flight. I was not happy as my schedule was very tight and I needed to be in London in plenty of time to meet my connection with The Orient-Express Train. They explained a bit more detail. They were transferring my flight to BA2. For a second I was confused, until I realised that this was in fact Concorde. I tried to stay casual, but inside I was screaming *YES PLEASE*. I had only ever dreamt of such a flight. Better than a voyage on the *QE II*.

Door to door my trip to New Orleans took about 24 hours, so when I arrived at The Windsor Court I was jet lagged. I was met by the GM, Philip Wood, an Englishman, who it turned out had originally come from Warwick, my old home ground, so we hit it off immediately. I crashed out immediately. I awoke to a call from Philip with an invitation to join him for dinner. It was still Saturday and as the conference wasn't due to start until Monday, most staff were arriving the following day, including JBS. Philip's charming PR manager met me in the lobby. Philip has been delayed and would I like a little tour of the hotel before dinner?

The Windsor Court was built in 1984, after my visit with son Steve to New Orleans. We wouldn't have been able to stay there as we were on a budget that time. It was the most luxurious and expensive hotel in the state of Louisiana. It was designed on the theme of the House of Windsor, so it was very lavish and decked out with paintings by Gainsborough, Van Dyk and Reynolds. Philip arrived with his wife and we joined him for dinner. The meal definitely set a new standard. He filled me in a little more on my new employer and his wife Dr Shirley Sherwood. The more I heard of them both, the more interesting they seemed to be, although I have to say, I was starting to get a little nervous.

We had all been asked to do a presentation on our hotels. I had cobbled together a presentation of slides and a video which I felt had a real Australian feel to it. On hearing that Jim was rather conservative, and witnessing the formal style of The Windsor Court, I was worried that my presentation was too relaxed and casual. I had even used some humour - maybe this was not a good first impression for my boss?[35]

We finished dinner about 9.30pm but, still being on Australian time and having had a nap earlier, I was wide awake. Philip and his wife bade me good night so I decided to have a nightcap in the bar. The charming PR staffer offered to join me and we sat down and chatted. I have no idea what we chatted about, but even my riveting conversation wasn't interesting enough to keep her awake. She apologetically excused herself, explaining that with JBS's arrival, tomorrow was to be a busy day. I sat alone for a few minutes and, still wide awake, so I moved to a bar stool and ordered another wine.

It was getting on for 11.30pm and I was surprised that, being a Saturday, I was the only customer now left in the bar. I had seen too many movies where the lone man props up the bar, telling a rather bored barman his life story. Surely this wasn't me? Feeling a little guilty about keeping the bar open just for me, I was about to leave when I saw two men standing in the doorway. Their size was such that it was as if someone had closed the doors - the light from the lobby outside simply disappeared. These guys were big. They just stood there surveying the bar until their gaze focussed on me. They said nothing, and I looked back at them and smiled. They disappeared and I sat back on my stool wondering what that was all about.

Suddenly they were back, accompanied by a rather diminutive figure of a man. As he came to the bar he glanced at me casually. Frank Sinatra! He ordered something from the barman, and sat on a stool two seats away from me. I was transfixed. I'd been listening to this man for my entire life, until the Beatles that is. It wasn't just the music - I was a fan of his films too. He had made around forty films; classics like *From Here To Eternity* in 1953, *Oceans 11* in 1960 and - my favourite - *The Manchurian Candidate* with Laurence Harvey in 1962. It was a suspense thriller about a plot to assassinate the US President. A year later President John F. Kennedy was assassinated in Dallas, and rumours were swirling around that his murder might have been part of a Communist conspiracy. Frank Sinatra (whose company produced *The Manchurian Candidate*) hastily withdrew the film from distribution and then suppressed it for twenty-five years.

I sat there, rather in awe. Apart from the two bodyguards and the barman, I was alone with Frank Sinatra. As the barman mixed his drink no one said anything until he turned to me, noticing my almost empty glass, "Would you like a drink?"

I hesitated, "Thank you, very kind of you."

"English?"

I was about to reply "Australian", being rather proud of my newly adopted country, when I remembered that he'd had a stoush with the unions on his visit to Sydney and now he hated the place. He famously said, *A funny thing happened in Australia. I made one mistake. I got off the plane.* So I simply replied "Yes, English."

I was busy running over in my mind what to say next. I had images of us becoming drinking buddies, propping up the bar until the wee small hours of the morning. How did his song go? *While the whole wide world is fast asleep...* This dream rather abruptly vanished as Frank Sinatra downed his drink, turned and left. "Good night."

He and the two large men were gone, leaving me and the barman to review our brief acquaintance with 'Ol' Blue Eyes', 'The Chairman of The Board' - Mr Francis Albert Sinatra.

The next day I was feeling a lot better and in tune with the time zone. There were no formal arrangements until the official dinner that night, so I took the opportunity to revisit some of the areas I had visited with my son Steve ten years earlier. The Americans love to give their cities nicknames: The Big Apple, Sin City, Motown, The Windy City. Then there's New Orleans: The Big Easy. I was curious as to why and was told that, in the 1960s when New Yorkers coined The Big Apple and had the reputation for running around being busy, New Orleans celebrated the laid-back life, The Big Easy.

Nothing much had changed. The French Quarter was still the French Quarter, although not a romantic French accent was to be heard and it was a little seedier than I recalled. Jackson Square was there, with artists sitting around as they do in Montmartre, and where I'd had a cartoon portrait done ten years before, never imagining I would be back under those circumstances. The square, designed after the famous 17th-century Place des Vosges in Paris, had its bronze statue of Andrew Jackson, hero of the Battle of New Orleans and the seventh U.S. President, mounted on a horse rearing up on its hind legs. I had been told on my previous visit, by a passing American tourist, that this statue was the largest or the tallest or the only statue of its kind, of a rider on a horse on its hind legs, or some such superlative claim, as Americans like to do. The city was special and we were to enjoy a little of what the nightlife had to offer during the down time in our conference.

The evening started with a drinks reception. Philip Wood, knowing that I was 'the new boy', kindly stood by my side and introduced me to my future management colleagues. First was Philip Carruthers, of The Copacabana Palace Hotel in Rio. I will always remember him as being an Accrington Stanley football fan, whose name used to ring out when the football pools scores were announced. I never understood what a Brazilian, albeit of English stock, was doing supporting Accrington.

Next there were the Italians. The consummate professional and highly respected Dr Natale Rusconi of The Cipriani, Maurizio Saccani from The Villa San Michele in Florence and Antonio Marson of The Splendido in Portofino. There were the UK managers, from The Turnberry Hotel with its golf course, in Scotland, now owned by Donald Trump, and Brian Miller of The Welcombe Hotel in Stratford on Avon. I knew this hotel from my mother's tales of attending her first formal ball there, prior to it being converted into a hotel by the railways. When British Rail then divested themselves of all their hotels in the 1980s, I had coincidentally gone with my old boss from De Vere Hotels, Reg Constable, to check it out with a view to purchasing it. I remember then it was rather run down and Mr Constable made the comment that if we sold off all the antiques we could probably afford to totally refurbish the place. [36]

There were other managers, a total of fourteen. Amongst these was Nick Seewer, of The Mount Nelson in Cape Town. Nick became a life-long friend and in the years to come we had many adventures together. From head office we had Peter Parrott, vice president of finance, Valerie Le Moyne, VP for sales and Nadia Stancioff, head of public relations. What an intriguing woman she was. Nadia was charming, refined and had an aristocratic bearing. We chatted a lot over the coming months and I discovered just how fascinating and aristocratic she really was. I gathered that her family was very highly placed in the Romanian court, close to the King and the government. When the Nazis invaded she and her brother escaped to Switzerland where, as refugees with little more than what they stood up in, were housed for a time in a mental institution. Eventually, with her family, she arrived in America, where they were able to establish themselves in American society, just managing, somewhat frugally, to survive.

She mentioned going to a ball where she met John F. Kennedy and could not help but notice Jackie was jealous of any young woman who came near him. Nadia later became a friend and confidant of the famous opera prima donna, Maria Callas. She was one of her closest collaborators and a shoulder to lean on during the singer's separation from Aristotle Onassis. Nadia told of how Callas would come and hide in her apartment when Onassis came banging on her door in search of her. Nadia had written a book, published in 1987, about her longtime friend, in which she shared memories of the Maria who gave impromptu concerts of Beatles hits and Mexican ballads. Nadia was so warm and friendly, one of the most gracious women I had worked with, and yet she still had the common touch.

This was evident when she came to visit The Observatory Hotel in her role as VP of public relations. I was doing my best to impress her with the charms that Sydney had to offer, but unfortunately, as we walked along Kent Street, I noticed some graffiti scrawled on the wall in large letters. HOTEL FUK OF. I did my best to redirect Nadia's attention, but the graffiti was hard to miss. She paused for a second and without missing a beat simply said "Ah, another school dropout who I fear can't spell."

The events of the evening in New Orleans were now well underway. Dinner was announced and we filed in. I sat with Philip, who was now more relaxed as Mr Sinatra had checked out early and Mr and Dr Sherwood had been delayed, leaving plenty of time to get his suite cleaned and ready for their arrival.

As we were starting our main course, there was a clatter of cutlery and everyone around me stopped eating and stood up. Mr and Dr Sherwood had entered the room. I was a little surprised at this formality and commented quietly to Philip, "Wow, the last time I did this was when royalty came to dinner."

"You had better believe it; they are Orient-Express royalty."

I was now getting a feel for the company's culture and the respect, mixed with trepidation, everyone felt when dealing with JBS. I felt that my nerves of yesterday were well founded, and that maybe I should seriously be thinking about how I should amend my presentation for the meeting the next morning. I did not have time however.

The next day the meeting started. As this was the first of its kind, we all introduced ourselves and JBS gave a brief update of future plans for the company. It was now time for our presentations. Each hotelier presented a brief account of the financial status of the country, a little about the property and its main market. All rather formal and certainly focussed on the detail. As each progressed I was watching JBS and his reaction. He listened intently and asked the odd question when the GM had finished. I was starting to panic when Natale, of The Cipriani, gave his presentation with the suave sophistication that Italians exude, accompanied by a video of the beauties of Venice, the style, the history and the architecture, all accompanied by Vivaldi's *Four Seasons*.

Only one thought ran through my mind, as Natale sat down and JBS nodded in deference to him: *Oh shit, I'm screwed.*

How could I follow that? I nervously got to my feet and stood before all these GM's with their École hôtelière de Lausanne training and years of experience in some of Europe's most classic hotels. In front of JBS, I was fearing my OEH career was about to come to an abrupt end, before it had begun.

As JBS looked on, I thought of the words of another American, Franklin D. Roosevelt: *The only thing we have to fear is fear itself.*

I took a deep breath and put up my first visual: a picture of a map of the world that I had found in a souvenir shop, called *McArthur's Universal Corrective Map of the World*. It was a map of the world depicted upside down, with Australia at the top. I started with the true Aussie greeting.

> "G'Day! Now for those of you who are unsure of our location, first we are Australia and NOT Austria, and this is how we see ourselves in relation to the rest of you in the world. Please note that WE are on top."

There was a stunned silence. JBS gave a little smile, at which point everyone laughed. I gave a sigh of relief. I followed this with a video borrowed from the NSW tourist board, which had a backing track from the band AC/DC - about as far removed from Vivaldi as one could get. The drum beat and the guitars perfectly synchronized with the video of the surf boats crashing into the waves of Bondi. It showed the youth, the excitement and vibrancy of Australia at its best. At that moment I was very proud to be an Australian, and almost wished I was back there. The presentation was a resounding success and even got a genteel round of applause, along with a nod of approval, from JBS.

By the end of the two days we all agreed that the meetings had gone very well. I had made my mark and made a number of good friends. Some were still a little confused, however, and not sure what to make of this cultured Englishman speaking 'Strine'.

I was not to return to New Orleans until 2007, almost destroyed by Hurricane Katrina. I was appalled to see how little reconstruction had been done. Everyone blamed the lack of federal support and corruption in the city; to this day I'm not sure it has recovered. We still managed to have a good conference and were entertained at The Mercedes-Benz Superdome. Even though it was a chilly day there was plenty to keep us warm.[37]

On my way out of the US on that first OEH visit, I stayed at The Mark Hotel on Madison Avenue at 77th Street, New York. I loved this hotel with its black and white Art Deco style, run by the charming Raymond Bickson. [38]

I was up and out early to JFK airport as I didn't want to miss my Concorde flight to London. British Airways had a completely separate check-in desk for BA2, and our own lounge with a panoramic view of the tarmac on which sat the majestic aircraft just metres away. Although early we sipped our vintage champagne; at nearly £5,000 a ticket, it was only to be expected.

When we boarded, the first thing that struck me was how small it seemed. There were two seats, all one class, either side of the aisle, in two compartments, and not a great deal of headroom. My seat was in the front of the second section, with a screen that displayed the speed at which we were travelling. I made myself comfortable in the leather seat; it reminded me of a large bucket seat of an expensive sports car, with just about enough legroom for my six-foot-four frame.

I could now appreciate why the Concorde would never be a commercial option on the longer Sydney/ London route. Apart from the noise and pollution, there were problems with supersonic travel over land, and even though it was comfortable, you couldn't sit in this confined seat for the 17 hours, 3 minutes, 45 seconds it took. It also needed to refuel in Singapore, at which point most passengers alighted and continued in greater comfort aboard a Jumbo.

For now, I was more than happy to sit on board this exquisite piece of European engineering ready to wing its way to London. The Captain announced "Good morning ladies and gentlemen, we will take off shortly on BA2 flight bound for London Heathrow, with an estimated flight time today of 3 hours and 4 minutes."

Did I hear that correctly? The last time I flew New York to London it took nearly 10 hours! He went on to explain what to expect, and that he would let us know when we hit supersonic speed. When we took off, it felt as if we were rising vertically. We weren't of course, but we were climbing very steeply. As we flew over the Atlantic, the pilot really started to speed up, as I could see on the screen in front of me. Apparently the Americans had all sorts of restrictions on speed in their airspace. The British of course believed it was out of envy; they just didn't want Concorde showing up their planes!

I sat mesmerised by the digital indicator. The acceleration felt disappointingly slow. I had rather hoped it would be a 'Star Trek' experience but there was no "Warp factor five, Mr Sulu". As the airspeed did increase closer to the Mach 1 mark, I looked out of the small window. It was very dark outside - as if we were going into orbit. The Captain's voice again: "Ladies and gentlemen, we are now going supersonic."

Great - now was my 'Star Trek' moment! I watched the numbers click over to Mach 1 and there was a tiny wobble. I wasn't sure if it was the pilot wobbling the plane for effect or if it really did wobble as it broke the sound barrier. There was no audible 'boom'.

Just as I thought 'that was it, I have now flown faster than the speed of sound', I noticed the number on the screen kept climbing. We eventually passed Mach 2. This was amazing. I was now flying faster than the F-111A fighter plane that I had watched with excited wonder in the '60s at an airshow in the UK. I looked out of the window, wondering just how high or how fast we could go. I happened to touch the window and it was very hot, so hot that I drew my hand away sharply. Was this a problem? I buzzed the flight attendant. She smiled as if she were comforting a young child. "No need to worry sir, it does get very warm due to the friction at the speed we are travelling. In fact at the nose it can reach a temperature of 153°C *(307°F)*. Quite impressive when you consider that the outside air temperature at this altitude of 17,000 metres *(56,000 ft)* is only -57°C *(-70°F)*."

She had said it a thousand times. And as if this hadn't made me nervous enough, she added "And the plane itself can also stretch by 12 to 30 centimetres *(5 to 12 inches)*, but no need to worry. It's only the temperature that stops us from going even faster."

I looked around to see if any of the other passengers showed any concern. I realised just how few people there were on board. No celebrities as I had thought there might be. A handful of rather plump business executives, whose companies were no doubt paying for the ticket, nearly 30 times the cost of the cheapest option to fly this route.

As I had actually shown some interest, the flight attendant returned and asked if I would like to visit the cockpit. There was no need for an answer as I was already out of my seat. "Come in, not much room I'm afraid." The captain was right, but I was in awe, thinking that this was about as close I was ever going to get to going into space. [39]

I returned to my seat, sat back, accepted a glass of Dom Perignon champagne and chose from a menu of Angus beef, Scottish smoked salmon, caviar, lobster, guinea fowl, truffles, and foie gras. As I ate my caviar, I gazed out of my window at the darkness of the stratosphere, speeding along at more than 1,300 mph, faster than a bullet, and over 10 miles above the earth.

We landed on time, and I headed for London's Ritz Hotel. As I sat in the cab travelling at a much gentler pace, I marveled at what I had just experienced. If I had flown in the other direction, London to New York, I would have arrived before I had taken off. Now that's what I call travelling.

I did enjoy staying at The Ritz. Who wouldn't? In addition to the luxury and my friendship with Terry Holmes, it was just so convenient. And, I learned, traditional. At fifty years of age, I had bought my first pair of jeans in over thirty years. Proudly sporting my new groovy jeans in the lobby, I was diplomatically and charmingly directed to a secret lift by Michael, the concierge, so as not to offend the guests sipping expensive tea in the Palm Court. Their loss.

With the flight change I found that I was to be in London for two nights rather than one. It was early evening so I decided to wander out and stretch my legs. I had wanted to go to Langan's, a well known restaurant that was out of my league anyway, but I didn't feel like a full dinner. I remembered The Stafford Hotel, a lovely little hotel tucked away in a mews full of character and geranium-filled hanging baskets on white walls, just a short walk from The Ritz.

The American Bar at The Stafford was one of the longest surviving American bars in London, with an elegant yet delightfully relaxed decor. Every available wall space and surface is crammed with artefacts, knick-knacks and signed celebrity photographs donated by patrons and guests over the years. I ordered a glass of wine and a Shepherd's Pie from the bar menu, happy to enjoy a little comfort food. It arrived a few minutes later on a tray, the bottom of which was padded with a 'bean bag' so as to sit comfortably on my knees. I had never before had to eat off my lap in a pub, but it worked and the pie was delicious. In time, I became a regular at a number of fine restaurants in town, a welcome augmentation to my hedonistic lifestyle. Thankfully, and certainly fortunately, I got to know Richard Shepherd CBE (one up from an OBE), who, in partnership with Sir Michael Caine, owned Langan's. This led to my association with the wonderfully flamboyant Roy Ackerman CBE, who owned The Gay Hussar and

L'Etoile restaurants, favourites of Roger Moore. There's nothing quite like a night out in an exceptional restaurant - especially when you know the boss! [40]

At the Ritz, Terry had kindly put me in a suite. This was a regular occurrence when staying in a colleague's hotel, and although the gesture was appreciated, I would have rather preferred a standard room. Being on my own, I seemed to rattle around a big suite. Nevertheless, I slept like a log.

The following morning I went to Sea Containers House, OEH head office, to catch up with Peter and bring him up to date on the meeting in New Orleans and the status of The Observatory. I didn't mention my adventure on Concorde; I was a little worried as to how such an extravagance may be viewed, even though it was at no additional cost to the company.

Peter took me around to meet a number of the team based at head office. All were very friendly, and I felt welcome. We ran into Peter Parrott, who I had briefly met in New Orleans. Vice President and Treasurer of the company, he was a tall, dignified man, who looked as if he belonged in the Guards. Anyone who was high up in finance made me nervous, as I was not confident in matters financial. Paul White, the finance manager I had been working with on budgets in Sydney, was much more approachable, relaxed and easy going and had the ability to put the intricacies of accounting into layman's terms. He was a sports-mad chap, obsessed with Ipswich City FC and cricket. I was not at all keen on football but less averse to cricket. On the weekends when Paul was in Sydney he would join me to watch my son Tim play at school, in the grounds of Scots College with magnificent views across the harbour with yachts' sails reflecting the bright sun.

As Peter Rozee and I sat chatting, Peter Parrott popped his head around the door, with "Are you doing anything this evening?"

Not waiting for an answer, "How about dinner and afterwards *Carmen*?" I was taken by surprise at such an offer from one of the senior VPs of the company. I nodded. "Jolly good. You're staying at the Ritz?" Not a bit impressed by my residence. "I'll pick you up at 6.00."

His head disappeared and I sat there with nerves on high alert. Was this another test? Would he delve into my knowledge of finance? Why *Carmen*? The closest I had come to opera was Gilbert and Sullivan. Sensing my concern, Peter Rozee reassured me that Peter Parrott was a very nice guy and just wanted me to feel welcome. "Obviously he thinks that this is your style and taste in music!"

My, how wrong he was! Even Gilbert and Sullivan didn't excite me. Give me Phil Collins or Fleetwood Mac any day. Wishing not to make a complete idiot of myself, on my way back to The Ritz I stopped off in one of my favourite stores in London, Hatchards, right next to my second favourite store, Fortnum and Mason. Hatchards had been around since 1797. Behind its Dickensian shop front it was stocked - from floor to ceiling over five floors - with many thousands of books.

With some help from an assistant I started to search. Having seen *Porgy and Bess,* a rather more modern version of the *Carmen* story, it was starting to sound familiar. I found the book I needed and moved into a quiet corner to get up to speed.

An opera in four acts, by French composer Georges Bizet. *The libretto was written by Henri Meilhac and Ludovic Halévy, based on a novella of the same title by Prosper Mérimée. Carmen was first performed by the Opéra-Comique in Paris on 3 March 1875. Bizet died suddenly after the 33rd performance, unaware that the work would achieve international acclaim in the following ten years. The "Habanera" from Act 1 and the "Toreador Song" from Act 2 are among the best known of all operatic arias.* Of course!

The Toreador Song! I had heard it dozens of times. I now felt confidently equipped with sufficient knowledge to manage an evening at the opera.

Peter Parrott picked me up on time and, true to the other Peter's assurances, it was a delightful evening, relaxed and easy going. Peter was a charming man. I was really starting to enjoy this company; everyone seemed so *gentlemanly* and welcomed me so warmly into their club. It was the start of what was to be a wonderful experience with genuinely nice people, who I grew to admire and respect.

I arrived the next day in plenty of time to meet Peter Rozee on Platform 2 of Victoria Station, where we were to board the Orient-Express. To be more precise we would board the Pullman, which would take us to Folkestone from where we would cross the English Channel to Boulogne. It was there that we would board the actual Venice Simplon-Orient-Express. Peter was my travelling companion to The Cipriani, then to Florence and The Villa San Michele, then to Portofino and The Splendido, whence I would learn of the quality and service standards JBS expected in his hotels.

I checked in at the small Orient-Express lounge; Peter was already there. There were a number of stewards on hand to take care of our luggage and ensure we were settled. They looked very smart in their blue and gold braided uniforms with their matching French képis. I was now starting to feel imbued with the spirit of Agatha Christie, without whose famous novel neither I nor the other passengers would likely be standing on this drafty platform with such eager enthusiasm.

I wasn't sure what to expect. The other passengers consisted of some retirees, one or two unmistakable honeymooners, but in the main American tourists. All were couples intent on a romantic journey to Venice. Their style of dress was varied; some were dressing for the event, others were in holiday attire. I was in my blazer and slacks and did not feel out of place. Peter and I took our places in the dining car, which was named *Zena*. Peter told me it was used in a film about Agatha Christie in 1976 and was originally part of *The Bournemouth Belle*. I convinced myself that I was travelling in the same carriage as I had as a boy with my father when returning from one of our trips to London via Bournemouth West before boarding our less salubrious train on a branch line to our home in Swanage.

We sat back and watched the grubby backyards of the terraced houses of Brixton go by as we travelled through the suburbs, heading south. I wondered how train travel had developed a feeling of style and romance, as railroads tended to pass through the less attractive areas of any city, churning out smoke as they steamed through, leaving indelible black soot over every building within a half mile of the railway line, creating the least romantic views to look out upon. [41]

Leaving London behind, we chuffed through the English countryside, 'a green and pleasant land'. We were served a splendid early lunch, accompanied by a very nice wine. Before I knew it, we pulled into Folkestone Harbour where we were to board a Sea Cat for the Channel crossing to Boulogne. Thankfully the sea looked calm. I still had bad memories of boats after my trip back from Holland twenty years ago.

We had a smooth crossing and were escorted to the train. It was as magnificent as I had imagined it would be and certainly lived up to the glossy brochure presentation of its blue and gold livery and shining white roof. JBS insisted on this, to ensure that as it travelled through the countryside it was unmistakable. The maintenance staff were not quite as enamoured with the white roof, as they had to scrub it after each journey to maintain its pristine appearance. Our cabins were small but very comfortable, with a footstool and small table, and a banquette sofa that would be converted into a bed. There was my bathrobe and a pair of slippers. In one corner, a decorative Art Deco bow-fronted armoire opened to reveal a wash basin that looked original, with hot and cold water, and towels and toiletries all provided. I had not thought to ask but realised on boarding that the carriages had no showers whatsoever and the closest lavatory was at the end of the corridor. I had some concern as to how the wash basin might be utilised by some of the more elderly travelling men who found the need to answer the call of nature during the night, but I put the thought to the back of my mind. The cabin was beautifully decorated in various woods and magnificent marquetry; the furniture was upholstered in rich fabrics, the style of which evoked a more elegant age.[42] [43] [44]

Once settled, Peter and I headed to the bar for a drink before dinner. We were to eat at the first sitting. The view was rather unexciting as we passed through the French countryside towards Paris, but the atmosphere and experience inside was wonderful. We walked through the dining cars to reach the bar: elegant in the extreme, in the *art deco* style, with beautiful marquetry and wonderful Lalique crystal decorative panels. The bar was busy. I looked around at the couples engaged in intimate conversation, or just listening to the pianist, sipping their champagne. I realised that Peter and I were the only two males travelling together, and eyes fell on us with some curiosity. I was even more conscious of this when Peter leaned over very closely to chat. "Sorry, but I am rather deaf in one ear and with the piano it is difficult to hear." I raised my voice somewhat with which he sat back a little, and I regained some comfort in my personal space, and fewer prurient stares from the other guests!

Dinner was served in *L'Oriental* dining car; the others were called *Lalique* and *Etoile du Nord*, each with their own design. We dined on baked lobster in brandy sauce with spring vegetables, followed by roast duck supreme, with white truffled *foie gras*. This was one of the most memorable dinners I was to enjoy: beautifully prepared and served, in a marvellous atmosphere. The table was laden with crisp white linen, VSOE-crested fine china and glass, an art deco table lamp and a small silver vase with a single rose.

During the meal we were visited by the Executive Chef, Christian Bodiguel, who had - in the strict confines of the train's galley - produced this gourmet delight. I was very flattered to hear, "Mr Griffin, I am so happy to have you aboard our train." [129]

I was so surprised and pleased at the warmth of his greeting, and the fact he knew my name. Everything about this trip was enforcing just how unique this company was; not simply the products, which were indeed very special in their uniqueness and individuality, but the professionalism, the respect, the warmth one received from all the staff.

We enjoyed our wine and finished the meal with a cognac as we were pulling into Paris Gare de l'Est. We retired to the bar to listen to the pianist playing a selection of George Gershwin tunes, as we watched new passengers board the train. I was a little disappointed that there was not a Hercule Poirot in sight, but we certainly had the odd countess or two by the look of them. The French and Italians are so stylish. We left Paris a little after 10.00pm for the overnight journey to Innsbruck, and we retired shortly after to our cabins. My day compartment was now transformed into an elegant bedroom: monogrammed linen sheets turned down, bathrobe laid out, slippers positioned at the foot of the bed, a little 'turn down' treat on the pillow. The lights were set for 'bed'. I shuffled down the corridor to the loo, rather expecting to join a queue but was pleased that the corridor was deserted. A steward was stoking a small, antique-looking boiler that heated the hot water. He slept beside it on a drop-down seat that looked incredibly uncomfortable. As I returned to my cabin I noticed all the other cabins had their blinds pulled down already. I was the last crazy kid to retire.

Whether it was the brandy or the gentle rocking of the train I do not know, but the bed felt surprisingly comfortable and even fitted my six-foot-four frame. As I drifted off, I thought of Hercule Poirot and of all the many ghosts who must haunt these carriages from all over Europe. I wondered if I was in the carriage that had been found in Limoges which had been used as a brothel during the war? Ah, if only walls could speak. I slept well; there was no shot fired, not a scream heard, and nothing went bump in the night. I awoke as the dawn broke over the mountains. A lake came into view with early morning mist floating above the water.

I washed and dressed and there was a tap on the door. I opened it to find the same liveried steward from the night before, still looking immaculate, with a cheerful, "Good morning Monsieur Griffin, I hope you slept well, I have brought your breakfast." He placed it on the small table, positioned to be easily accessible. "We are well on time to arrive in Innsbruck after 11.00am. Just ring when you would like me to put away the bed so you may be more comfortable for the journey down to Venice." With which he retired, and I sat down to enjoy my continental breakfast.

At about 10.00am there was another tap on the door and Peter poked his head in. "How did you sleep? I thought we could have a coffee in the bar car before it gets busy, and I can fill you in on the rest of the trip?" I was suddenly reminded that

I was not a tycoon, however much I might have imagined myself to be, but that I was actually here for work. But what a wonderful work environment to be in.

As we had travelled through the various countries it was interesting to see not simply the change of scenery but the people, especially the staff at each of the railway stations. The French, casually doing their job as if a little bored. The Austrians, serious, methodical and industrious, and then the Italians - a new level of indifference. Yet the trains still run on time, although Mussolini was a high price to pay for punctuality.

We travelled across the Alps, through magnificent scenery, lush green pastures against a backdrop of snow-capped mountains. The views took our breath away as we sat in luxurious comfort sipping another glass of champagne. What a wonderful life the wealthy live. I was reminded of my mother's flippant comment once: "My dear, if you are to enter marriage, always pick from the same drawer or the one above, preferably with money. Don't get clouded by emotion - if it is not happy marriage, being miserable with wealth is much better than being miserable in poverty." Although I never followed her lighthearted advice, I could certainly have done so now, sitting on the Orient-Express, champagne in hand.

Having crossed the Italian border and enjoyed a wonderful lunch prepared by Chef Bodiguel of *foie gras* followed by pan fried John Dory, with butter beans and the best mashed potatoes I have ever tasted, we pulled into Verona. My thoughts immediately ran to William Shakespeare and school-boy memories of *The Two Gentlemen of Verona*. I wonder what my English Lit teacher would say now if he were to see me and Peter, a modern day Valentine and his chum Proteus. Thankfully though, we did not get into the same troubles with broken vows to lovers and outlaws and angry fathers of lovely daughters that the originals did, although avid readers will know that I had already been there in my younger years.

After a short stop we headed on for our final destination: Venice. It was early evening and the warm breeze had a taste of the sea mixed with the usual smells of a railway station. It took a couple of minutes to adjust to the fact that the ground beneath my feet was no longer rocking with the motion of the train. We tottered off to our cases that had been neatly lined up on the platform. I had purchased, in Bangkok, what I thought to be an exceptional copy of a Louis Vuitton suitcase, which I felt would be ideal for a stylish young man to carry on the Orient-Express. As I approached to collect my "LV" suitcase, I saw that it sat between a number of cases that were undoubtedly the genuine article. Mine now looked very dowdy and different from the case I had been so impressed with in the markets in Bangkok. I held back and watched the cases get picked up by their affluent owners. A Japanese couple even pointed and joked with each other over the rather obvious 'knock-off' in the midst of their $5,000 originals. I was in two minds about whether to abandon it there and then; but had I enough clothes to wear? Upon arriving at the hotel I discarded it as discreetly as possible. I often wondered if Natale Rusconi was ever aware of the shameful piece of luggage that would have been found in my room. Ever the discreet professional, he never mentioned it.

Peter directed me to the jetty where the launch was waiting. To confirm we were in Venice, the equivalent of the black London cab was waiting for us: the water taxis or *motoscafo rivas*. Our launch however was a little more special, sent by The Cipriani. It was a magnificent timber-decked launch with pristine white cushions and a uniformed Venetian boatman. The launch was named *Shirley*, after JBS's wife, a charming gesture. Peter and I set off to the hotel, set on Giudecca Island, a twenty-minute cruise from Venezia Santa Lucia Train Station. As we passed along the canals Peter pointed out various landmarks, and we entered the Lagoon and passed the Basilica di Santa Maria della Salute. As I nestled in the deep cushions, I thought of Dirk Bogarde in *Death in Venice*, the haunting adaptation of Thomas Mann's classic novel set in the pre WWI period, with the dramatic Mahler soundtrack. It was about an outbreak of cholera, which I hoped would not be a problem during my visit.

The launch pulled up to the landing steps of The Cipriani where we were met by a smiling porter who took our bags. As we entered the hotel, Natale appeared and greeted us warmly. What a lovely man he was, such a stylish bearing. He was the epitome of the sophisticated international hotelier. We were shown to our rooms, in the annex, as the hotel was busy. It had been a private home adjoining the hotel, the 15th-century Palazzo Vendramin, with mesmerising lagoon vistas. It was breathtaking. It would to be occupied by Princess Diana on her 1995 trip to Venice.

We had a delicious dinner with Natale who was very agreeable company and went out of his way to make me feel welcome to the Orient-Express family. Peter ever-so-subtly kept me on track when it came to my minor indiscretions, such as pronouncing Cipriani with 'ch' sound and not an 's'. He was so tactful, he didn't tell me in a pointed way, it was as if he were just making an interesting observation about Italian pronunciation. Another little tip was dropped in conversation, "It is interesting that the Italians never use a spoon to eat pasta, just a fork."

Thank God he made that clear! Even after years in hotels I, with many other Englishmen, use a spoon to help twirl spaghetti around the fork. I could see that this was going to be like learning to eat food with chopsticks, so that evening I played it safe and ate risotto. Peter's advice always came in the form of a little story, a question or he would simply say "did you know" or "as I am sure you know", when I usually didn't. I never felt any put downs or had the feeling that I should have known that. He was a great travel companion and it was the start of another lifelong friendship.

The following day we rented a very comfortable BMW and headed at speed for the next hotel on the itinerary. The trip was hairy to say the least as there appeared to be no speed limits or, if there were, they were totally ignored. Peter was quite happy to roar along. At one point we were overtaken in our BMW by a little Italian Fiat 500. I had no idea that car was capable of such speeds, but his driving was similar to that of Mario Andretti, the famous F1 driver.

We eventually arrived safely at The Villa san Michele. JBS had bought it from a Frenchman who had made his money as an arms dealer in the Vietnam War. According to the brochure: *a 15th-century national monument set in terraced gardens on the slopes of the Chianti Hills overlooking Florence.* We were greeted by Maurizio Saccani's wife as he had not yet returned from the USA. She was a lovely woman and enhanced the family feel of the company. Peter had some work to catch up on so he suggested I take advantage of the afternoon off and investigate Florence.

I understood why it was known as the "cradle of the Renaissance", with its monuments, churches, and buildings, and its domed cathedral, Santa Maria del Fiore, The Duomo. Of course there was also Accademia Gallery, home to the world's most famous sculpture of the Renaissance, Michelangelo's *David*.

I was in awe, because it was so much more wonderful than the copies set in the most unlikely of places. I thought of a replica I had seen recently displayed in the Raptis Plaza, a shopping centre in Surfers Paradise on Australia's Gold Coast. Regrettably it did little to add culture to the brash holiday town.

It was a special afternoon, made even better by a walk across the Ponte Vecchio, which along with London's Tower Bridge is probably the most photographed bridge in the world. It is best known for the wooden-shuttered goldsmiths' shops that line both sides of it, and for the Vasari Corridor that runs over it. Peter's knowledge of Italy came to the fore again as I learned this was a private aerial walkway built in 1561 so the Medici family could move between the Palazzo Pitti and the Palazzo Vecchio, safe from the risk of assassination in the streets below. Thankfully this was not a risk for me during my walk.

In a small sidestreet I made a surprising find: a little shop that sold every conceivable shaving accessory. It seemed so out of place in its medieval surroundings. I had been searching all over the place for a particular shaving mirror for our bathrooms, as none so far seemed to work, and here in the most unlikely of places, I found exactly what I wanted. After some discussion I bought one and the kind shopkeeper, with some amusement at my excitement, also gave me the name of the company from whom I could purchase the quantity I would require. With the most unusual souvenir of Florence under my arm, I returned to the hotel and prepared for dinner.

I met Peter and a young man who had been given the task of showing us around the hotel. It had been a monastery, and it was the first time I had checked into a hotel where the reception desk was a carved stone tomb. It gave a touch of unique quirkiness. The architecture was very grand in a monastic way. I was admiring the external structure when the young man engaged me in conversation about my hotel in Australia.

It seemed that everyone I met wanted to go there, which I found pleasing, and I started to appreciate how lucky I was.

I suppose when you live in highly populated cities, amongst buildings with hundreds of years of history, there was some appeal in visiting a new country with wide open spaces. I spoke enthusiastically about The Observatory; I explained that we had started with one of Australia's leading architects, Philip Cox, who had recently designed the Rod Laver Tennis Arena in Melbourne and The National Maritime Museum in Sydney, and who had been asked to design The Observatory to sympathetically fit in with the local surrounds. He looked very interested but I was about to have a lesson in humility. "Yes, I agree it is important to have an architect with this belief of designing a building that blends well. Here at Villa san Michele we were very fortunate to have Michelangelo." That's all he said, so, realising that maybe it would be best not to try a game of one-upmanship, I quietly listened as he took us around.

We had dinner on the vine-covered terrace of La Loggia, with spectacular views over Florence. The meal was typically Tuscan, characterised by simple food, not covered in heavy sauces, and cooked with olive oil, not butter. This was very different again to my Venetian meal, which was itself simple and tasty but had been a unique combination of soup and thick risotto made of fresh peas and rice, with pancetta. A dish that is one of my favourites to this day.

Following dinner we retired to the bar where a pianist played. He was not what I would call the usual background pianist, but was a jolly little fellow who bounced around on his stool and had a small puppet that sat on the piano and was serenaded. His style reminded me of another famous Italian singer and pianist, Paolo Conte, notable for his resonant voice and his colourful and wistful compositions with melancholic lyrics. This pianist was quite unique and was fun and not the formal performer one might have expected in such a setting. A few years later I was in the bar at the Mayfair Hotel in London and there he was again. As the Italian hotel closed for the winter months, as did most, he would pack his puppet and perform in London's equally prestigious establishments, to the joy of the patrons.

The next day we were on the road again. Peter wanted to leave early as the road leading along the coast to Portofino became congested with tourists as the day wore on. We arrived at The Splendido in the late morning and were welcomed by the general manager, Antonio Marson. This hotel also used to be a monastery and I pondered the irony of ascetic medieval monasteries being converted to luxury hotels.

The Splendido was perched on the cliffs overlooking the bay of Portofino. It had long been one of Italy's most glamorous places to stay, proven by the display of photos of the rich and famous above the concierge desk. Elizabeth Taylor, Richard Burton, Lauren Bacall and Humphrey Bogart, David Niven, Rex Harrison and many other stars of the golden days of Hollywood had their photos on the wall. One photo that was definitely not displayed was that of Eva Braun, Hitler's mistress, who was seen there in her home movies taken when holidaying at the hotel with family and friends in 1940.

Before lunch we had a tour behind the scenes and two memories stayed with me. The size of the kitchen for a hotel of this size made ours back in Sydney look palatial in comparison. It was located in the basement of the hotel with no natural light, and a flight of stairs for the waiters to climb with each dish for the restaurant. I can only assume the waiters were extremely fit.

The second memory was in the staff dining area where the steward was setting up for lunch. I watched in surprise as he placed bottles of wine on each table. Peter said, "Patrick, this is Italy, people don't drink water." I was now even more impressed with the resilience of the waiters; not only were they fit enough to climb all those stairs all day long, but they could do it after a few glasses of wine. Obviously Italy had less demanding health and safety regulations.

We sat on the terrace for lunch. The seafood was so fresh that the chef must have been out in his boat before dawn that morning. I had now had meals in three hotels that were all a delight, yet all so different. I realised how simplistic we were in Australia when it came to giving the label 'Italian' to food. That one word I realised was utterly inadequate.

The restaurant, which overlooked terraced gardens and rose arbors, had a wonderful view of the super yachts moored in the harbour below. I was admiring the scene and commented to Peter, "What beautiful yachts, they must be worth millions! You can have the large one and I will be quite content with the little one next to it."

The waiter serving our meal overheard my remark. "That one sir, is owned by the King of Spain. Maybe you would like to make him an offer, he is seated at the table over there." Sure enough, there he was, but knowing that my credit card was probably maxed out, I chose to forgo the purchase.

We went down to the harbour after lunch for a walk. It was like a little fishing village in Cornwall, but more colourful and vibrant, what with the restaurants, cafes and the superyachts. Hmm, on reflection, maybe not so much like a Cornish fishing village...

One disadvantage with the hotel's location was the climb back up the cliffside - the price to pay for the finest views in Italy. The walk had taken its toll on me and was the final straw of exertion after nearly three weeks of travelling the world, even in such luxury. I was quite exhausted, and Peter, seeing this, suggested I retire for the day, have a bite in my room and an early night. This was not the way I wanted to finish my adventure but I took his advice.

The following morning I was feeling better, and after a wonderful breakfast on the terrace, we bade farewell to Antonio and set off for Genoa, and from there the long journey back to Sydney. Door to door, I estimated it was unlikely to be less than thirty hours, so I put it to the back of my mind and just sat back and enjoyed the last views of the magnificent Italian Riviera.

Back in London, I said farewell to Peter, my travel companion and now close friend, and headed for the international terminal. As I joined the line to board the evening BA flight to Sydney, my boarding pass was taken and popped into the machine only to be spat out. I thought grumpily 'oh no, they are changing my seat' - it was one I had particularly asked for. "Mr Griffin, I hope you don't mind but we need to change your seat." I was tired, and had already started to wind down, and this was the last thing I wanted.

> "Oh come on. I booked this seat weeks ago. Surely you are not going to move me now?"

The attendant gave me a look which was hard to read, and then rather disarmingly said, "Oh that's OK, if you prefer *not* to be moved to first class, then I am sure that will be alright." I coughed and sputtered a little, before I was able to reply. I almost took her arm off in my rush to grasp my new boarding pass. "No, no that's fine, thank you, thank you very much."

I don't even recall the flight back, as I slept all the way, with the exception of the little bump I felt as we landed to refuel in Bangkok. I was thankful that we were not all kicked off during the refueling process, as they do now, and once in the air again I didn't wake until I was gently shaken by a flight attendant for breakfast. Even in first class, it was something of a letdown compared to the last breakfast I had enjoyed, overlooking the harbour in Portofino.

Once back home I reflected on my journey. Had it all been a delightful dream? To this day it lives bright and clear in my memory. Unless I win lotto or come into a fortune it is unlikely to ever be repeated. But I had done it, and was a far better hotelier for it. I could only wonder at just how incredibly fortunate I had been, to do what only the rich are able to do. And it had not cost me a penny.

My knowledge and appreciation of Orient-Express Hotels, Trains and Cruises was now very clear. I realised just how far the bar had been raised from anything I had done before.

Chapter 6

#princesn'presidents #tigerloo #filmsn'phantoms

During this period, Australia saw a number of hotels launch with much fanfare and extravagance; film stars and celebrities were flown in, each company trying to outdo the previous opening night party. There was Sir Peter Abeles' Hayman Island in 1987, a $300 million development for which he had bought a marble mine at Chillagoe to ensure that there would be no shortage of the prestigious rock, and pink marble was imported from Italy for the hotel's main foyer. The grand opening was spectacular. Sir Peter was not without controversy but, upon his death, the late former PM Bob Hawke said "Of the 5.5 million immigrants and more than half a million refugees who have made Australia their home since World War II, none can match the breadth and magnitude of Sir Peter Abeles' business achievements".

Then there was Observation City, in Perth, opened by Alan Bond, another immigrant, which cost close to $100 million to build. The grand opening there in 1987 cost $2 million and featured 20 bands and soloists in five separate areas of the hotel, a full buffet and bar and fireworks that were the talk of Western Australia.

A year later in 1988, Christopher Skase opened The Grand Mirage on Queensland's Gold Coast. Skase was known for his ostentation, with a lavish fortieth birthday party that year, and a company Christmas party that cost $450,000. In one particular incident, he had his private jet fly from Port Douglas to Melbourne to pick up a dress for his wife, Pixie.

The ego and the extravagance driving hotel development around this period were astonishing, but really just bordered on kitsch. The dodgy acquisition of the money squandered by Bond and Skase was soon to become evident. In 1992, Bond was declared bankrupt with personal debts totalling A$1.8 billion. He was subsequently convicted of fraud and imprisoned for four years, dying in 2015. Skase became one of the country's most wanted fugitives after his business empire crashed spectacularly and he fled to Majorca, Spain, where he died in 2001.

I concluded that there had to be a classier way to open our hotel, that would generate publicity whilst generating goodwill. The one thing I had learned of Orient-Express was that we offered a tasteful, understated and above all *discreet* form of luxury. There was also a very subtle diplomatic issue to be handled. If we wished to have a lavish grand opening both JBS and Mr Nara would attend - and we only had one 'Presidential Suite'. Then there was the question of culture. Mr Nara would no doubt wish things to be done with due ceremony in the Japanese manner; JBS would wish things to be done in a more western style, reflecting the qualities of Orient-Express.

The solution we found was helped by the busy calendars of both bosses: we'd hold two 'official openings' and one soft opening to which we would invite the press.

The soft opening of The Observatory was in late January 1992. [45]

We broke the conventions by inviting residents in the surrounding neighbourhood and those associated with the building of the hotel. Many people counselled against this, somewhat unkindly, expressing concern as to the integrity of some locals. I however had got to know many of them and although they were not exactly our target market, they were down to earth solid citizens who had put up with much inconvenience during the construction. What better way to show our thanks, and to build on our relationship by allowing them a feeling of some ownership of this new 'posh' hotel in their community? I was convinced it was a good move, and was proved right. On the day the locals all turned up in their 'Sunday best', delighted to have been invited and fascinated to see the hotel.

Following the event we got excellent press, with recognition that we had been such thoughtful and considerate neighbours. The press were by now tired of the extravagance of the glittering events that were hardly newsworthy now. Better still the cost was minimal against the cost of a lavish party and we gained more interest and column inches than the others ever did.

This event was followed by two more formal events. Mr Nara, the owner, hosted the first one in the Cornwallis Suite, the largest banqueting room we had, and it followed a distinct Japanese theme. A majority of the guests were Japanese, as one might expect, and this made the evening very stressful. We worried about the Japanese cultural protocols we were expected to follow. We knew little about it, and it was fraught with danger. The women appeared in magnificent kimonos; it took two people to assist Mrs Nara to dress. The men were dressed rather disappointingly in standard dinner jackets, with not a shogun in sight.

It was here that the cultural differences became apparent. Men in the west traditionally give way to the ladies, however this was not the case this evening. The ladies elegantly, and one might say obediently, followed their husbands, standing behind the men at all times and not entering the conversation. They simply bowed to Mr Nara and his guests, and ensured that their needs were met. I am sure that some of the Australian men present would have loved to adopt these customs, however it was evident from their bemused wives that this was one wish that was never going to come to fruition. Speeches were made, in Japanese, again with the wives standing demurely behind their husbands as they spoke. Thankfully the evening went off without any hitches.

I dutifully bowed a lot, at any and every opportunity and to any Japanese guest who noticed me. Quite abruptly, at ten-thirty, as if by a secret signal of which I was unaware, everyone got up and departed. It was not exactly a party but all seemed happy and formalities had been met.

The second official launch party was under the banner of Orient-Express Hotels, Trains and Cruises, hosted by Jim Sherwood and his wife Dr Shirley Sherwood, who had flown out from London to attend.

This nearly proved a disaster. We had planned to hold the dinner in the Cornwallis Suite as we had for Mr Nara's event. It was to be a very stylish event, with as many guests as we could squeeze in, the list having been vetted and added to by JBS. There was a number of Australia's 'nobility', mainly from days when Imperial Honours were bestowed on those deemed worthy, such as Lady Sonia McMahon, the socialite and widow of Sir William McMahon, a past Prime Minister who had died ten years earlier. I had met Lady McMahon in Melbourne and was to become well acquainted with her in the years that followed. She took a liking to the traditional style of The Observatory and became a regular at all our social events.

Another was Lady Mary Fairfax, the Polish-born Australian businesswoman and philanthropist, third wife and widow of wealthy media tycoon, Sir Warwick Fairfax. Lady Heather Rossiter was a personal friend of JBS, an interesting woman who had been a research scientist for the UK Atomic Energy Authority and the US Atomic Energy Commission, as well as a teacher, author and vine-grower in Australia. There were several high-profile businessmen and women, together with a number of highly placed politicians and, of course, the odd celebrity.

Jim Sherwood arrived from London on the afternoon of the event. We had of course pulled out all the stops, with a superb menu accompanied by the finest wines, the room decked in flowers carefully chosen to compliment the rich colours of the drapes. The team had done a magnificent job. JBS called me to run through what had been planned for the evening, and the guests who were to attend. We entered the Cornwallis Suite, and - far from the happy reaction I had been anticipating - there was silence. The tension was palpable. "Why are we in here?" he said. Not waiting for a reply he continued, "Tonight is meant to showcase the best The Observatory has to offer to society and business leaders, so why tuck us away in a banqueting room?" Again not waiting for an answer, "The Galileo Restaurant is the best place for the event. See you at seven." [46]

There was to be no discussion; the decision was made and he retired to his suite. The staff handled the last-minute changes calmly and professionally, with hardly a murmur, which was to become the hallmark of the wonderful team that I had been so fortunate to build around me. The evening was a great success and JBS seemed happy with, the guests and, thankfully, the cuisine and wine we had selected for the evening.

And so it was that The Observatory Hotel was now officially launched onto the Sydney stage, and more ambitiously the world stage, to take its place beside the other grand-dames of The Orient-Express Collection. Well - in time it would.

I had grown to like and respect JBS but was always rather nervous when attending meetings with him. He was not a man for small talk or humour in a business setting and you had to have all the facts at your fingertips. In London once, on being invited to lunch with a few other general managers, I joined my colleagues as we assembled. They all had bundles of documents, and I had none. I asked them why they carried all these papers around... weren't we just having lunch? The answer terrified me. "JBS never 'just' has lunch".

Over lunch he went around the table. I was lucky as I had been placed on his right, and he started from the left which gave me time to think of some answers. I just scraped by in not sounding too much of an idiot, and still had my job at the end of lunch. At the next meeting I wasn't sure if I would be so lucky.

In 1993 our meeting in London was one of the last to be chaired by JBS, before his stepson Simon Sherwood took over the reins in 1994. It was not a nepotistic move on behalf of JBS; Simon was actually the best man for the job, with a Cambridge and Harvard background and a better knowledge of the company and its aims than anyone. JBS would still be overseeing the hotels at arm's length.

This managers' meeting was significant. A VP of sales had been appointed and understandably wanted to increase the number of staff in his department, however, amongst the general managers it was generally felt that with only fourteen hotels to share the cost, it was an extravagance that we could not afford. OEH was a unique company. There was no common Orient-Express Hotel branding. All properties were individual and were marketed by the properties themselves. We were not like Ritz Carlton or Hyatt. Our objection to the extra cost, however, was like Canute trying to turn back the waves. There were a lot of grumpy murmurs during the meeting. Nick Seewer, from The Mount Nelson, and I chatted later over coffee. We both felt strongly about this issue but no one seemed prepared to speak out. Nick and I made a pact; he would make the first comment having been with the company longer and I would then follow up in support. In the meeting, we happily found we were supported by all the other GMs.

To our surprise, JBS agreed that if we felt strongly about it, then it would not go ahead. We had won our case, after which Nick and I became inseparable. I was however a little nervous when Peter Parrott, the CFO, commented to me in passing, "That was very courageous of you Patrick, very courageous."

Having been a fan of *Yes Minister* I knew that when Sir Humphrey Appleby said that to the Prime Minister, it did not bode well. The head office sales department shrank and eventually disappeared until it was revived some years later when the company had grown and it was financially viable. I was also pleased that the two people who took on those future roles of VP Sales were two of my own team.

I survived and became very settled at The Observatory. I even gained a new title of *Regional Director - Orient-Express Hotels (Asia Pacific)* courtesy of the Japanese culture. With such a title, one could gain better access to highly placed directors in the Japanese companies whose business we sought.

I think I was accepted by my colleagues at Orient-Express. This had often played on my mind, as most of them had had elite training at Swiss hotel schools followed by experience in hotels that were somewhat more prestigious than where I had worked. Whether it was confidence, bluff or the ability to treat life as a game, somehow I made a success of the opportunity I had been given.

It was almost thirty years to the day since I had donned an apron and stood at the sink at the Manor House Hotel with a pile of dirty pots before me. Every day had been an exciting new adventure and I can truthfully say that at no time had I woken with dread at the thought of going to work.

My father had always pointed out the home of J.B Priestley, a notable British novelist, who lived in Alveston, near Stratford-upon-Avon, not far from our home. Priestley rather summed up my own take on my chosen career: 'I have always been delighted at the prospect of a new day, a fresh try, one more start, with perhaps a bit of magic waiting somewhere behind the morning.' So it had been and so it was to be for each day of the next eighteen years.

The Observatory Hotel was, on per room basis, one of the most costly hotels to build in Australia but as I have said many times, no matter how much money is spent on the bricks and mortar or how magnificent are the gadgets on offer, no guest will return to the hotel if they are not treated well by staff and offered the service they might expect when paying the rates we charged.

We were fortunate to have found the right team. Not only were they masters of their crafts, but they had individual personalities and a passion to provide for the needs of each individual guest. It seems to me that hotels train their staff to enable them to conform to a company's detailed rule book: what to do, how to do it and how to say it, but with no ability for the employee to have input. We are not robots, we are individuals, and my strategy was to nurture the strengths and improve the weaknesses. Don't take the easy way out and dumb them down to a common denominator. Promote individualism, and in so doing make the hotel experience unique and special. Our team did so. [47]

Recognising the individuality of the staff of The Observatory helped us recognise the individuality of our guests. Over the next few years we were to welcome many intriguing people, some great, some good, some less so and some just simply bloody awful; but all were to leave their mark on The Observatory Hotel, and on me.

It is hard to know where to begin, so I'll start at the beginning.

Within days of opening I had a call from my old friend from Melbourne, Barry Everingham who had handled public relations for me at The Hotel Como. He hated being called the ' royal watcher' however in the first breath of our conversation there was a reference to royalty. "I have an HRH I have to entertain for lunch when we are up in Sydney next week, I don't suppose you could host him?"

By 'host' Barry of course meant 'can I lay on an impressive lunch that he would not have to pay for'. It was unclear at this stage who the HRH was, apart from being a man. Was it one of 'the boys', maybe Edward or Andrew? In any event it sounded like a good start; royalty visiting in the first month. "OK, I think we could do that, are you able to tell me who it is?"

"I would rather not until I have cleared it, if that's OK with you. I should be able to get back to you tomorrow."

I awaited his call back the following day. "It's all on for the sixth of March, it will be just the three of us."

I could hardly contain my excitement. An intimate lunch with His Royal Highness. "That's great, can you now tell me who it is?"

"Oh yes of course, sorry I thought I had told you. It's HRH Prince Tomislav of Yugoslavia."

"Who?"

Barry picked up on my disappointment, and tried to explain. It sounded like a script. "Prince Tomislav of Yugoslavia is a member of the House of Karađorđević; the second son of King Alexander I and Maria of Yugoslavia. He is a younger brother of King Peter

II of Yugoslavia, and is the nephew-in-law to Queen Elizabeth II and Prince Philip, Duke of Edinburgh."

With that rather tenuous connection, I agreed to provide lunch. He was a charming man and we were soon chatting comfortably. In 1934 when he was only six, his father was assassinated and his elder brother Peter succeeded to the throne as King Peter II of Yugoslavia. It was here that a little light lit up in my memory. I remembered one of my favourite films of the 60s, *The Yellow Rolls Royce*. Ingrid Bergman and Omar Sharif discuss Prince Peter who was part of the plot, as Germany invaded Yugoslavia. It is amazing how much education you can pick up from the movies.

I was intrigued to hear about his experiences. He had been educated in England and had attended Oundle School (a public school I might add to which I had failed to be admitted). He later worked in the summer holidays as a field hand on a farm, and eventually bought an orchard at Kirdford, near Petworth, in West Sussex growing apples. He was in Australia on a diplomatic mission relating to the conflict between Serbia and Croatia, that was to become one of the most horrific conflicts since World War II. [48]

Not long after that we had another royal visit - well, Australian royalty anyway. John Farnham, one of the country's best-known and most popular performers. The fact that he was actually born in Dagenham, Essex, didn't really matter. Australia has a lucrative strategy of claiming people as its own once they become famous as they did with Olivia Newton-John who was from Cambridge, England, and Sam Neill, from New Zealand. They too become regulars at The Observatory. [49]

Farnsie was quickly followed by Bruce Samazan, who set some young hearts fluttering amongst the receptionists. He was an Australian actor born in Madagascar who appeared in several soap operas and drama series on Australian television.

He was the only actor to have played regular roles in Australia's 'Big Three' soap operas of the 1990s: *E Street, Neighbours* and *Home and Away*.

Other true-blue Aussie guests in our early days were John Wood and Ernie Dingo, delightful men, as was Ray Martin, the iconic television journalist and entertainment personality. Metallica graced us, and Lars Ulrich, a keen tennis player, played a game with my son Tim. As Tim's father I claim the bragging rights that Tim beat him, going by the smile on his face. [50, 51, 52, 53]

Things became more serious in May when I had a visit from two rather mysterious men and a woman wishing to view the hotel, insisting that they would only speak with me. They wanted to see the hotel from top to bottom and asked a lot about the back of house staff areas and access. On checking the presidential suite, I heard one murmur something about Observatory Hill and line of sight. I was fast coming to the conclusion that these were not normal conference organisers.

After an extensive tour and numerous questions, all of which could have been handled by the conference department, they asked to go somewhere private where we might have a discussion. Turns out I was chatting with ASIO and the AFP. The Prime Minister of Vietnam was to visit Australia, the first such visit by their leader since the end of Australia's involvement in the Vietnam war. Hence the need for high security.

I felt more than qualified to understand such things. After all, I had had dealings with Prime Ministers, Royalty, even Mrs Golda Meir of Israel, so no problems. Little did I realise just how times had changed since the 1970s and the level of security they had in mind. Days before the arrival, the dog squad came in for an initial sweep, then the AFP came around and - much to my annoyance and that of our chief engineer, Charlie Dodsworth - started checking every duct, cupboard, and everything that opened. Having done so they proceeded to stick tape across the doors, much like those pricing tags that fall apart when you try to remove them. This took months to remove from the lovely new paintwork after the visit and Charlie was not a happy man.

After further dog checks and police checks that included all the staff, a number of supposedly inconspicuous plain clothes officers positioned themselves around the building. I was hovering in the foyer before the expected arrival, when a couple of young men in blue overalls came in. Over their shoulders were bags roughly disguised but quite obviously holding rifles. They were the snipers who were to position themselves on the roof. I was advised to keep a watch for any demonstrators. As it turned out there were none. It appeared that the word had got out, by accident or design, that he was staying at another hotel in the city. With no small irritation, the manager of the hotel overlooking Hyde Park was faced with a throng of rather noisy demonstrators, with no idea as to why they were there.

The Prime Minister arrived with his wife and entourage with little fanfare. He was all smiles and with little bows from all around we escorted him to his suite.

Prime Minister Vo Van Kiet was a humble man. He had been born into a sharecropper's family in the Mekong Delta in the 1920s, and joined the anti-French revolution at 18 when he fled into the jungle after an abortive local uprising. He later emerged as an important member of the Việt Cộng insurgency in South Vietnam. His first wife and children were killed by American bombs, and their remains were never found. Mr. Kiet's second wife, Phan Luong Cam, was a scientist.

He struck me as a noble and sincere man, hardly the man who in the '60s we were taught to hate. It brought home to me the futility of war - less than twenty years before we were killing each other, and now we were shaking hands and welcoming him as a

VIP, into a hotel, which happened to be owned by the Japanese, with a German deputy manager. I won't even mention our friends, the French with whom as an Englishman my ancestors were at war for over 500 years. Propaganda and politics have a lot to answer for.

His stay was uneventful other than the odd cultural anomaly. The first arose from the decorative Chinese bowls which were around the hotel, filled with a pot pourri mix intended to add a gentle scent to the air. With a little surprise we saw some of the Vietnam delegation tucking into them with gusto, regarding them as a complimentary snack.

The second 'incident' was at the formal State Banquet in honour of his visit. I was seated at one of the VIP tables with the NSW Premier's protocol team. The Australian Defence Force Band were playing the music, decked out in full mess kit. I was thoroughly enjoying my meal when I noticed the band was playing the score to one of my favourite musicals. Even though it had a Vietnamese setting, I wasn't sure that *Miss Saigon* was the most appropriate choice. I casually mentioned this to the Premier's protocol man who shot out of his seat. "Oh shit!"

A word in the ear of the conductor and the music cleverly segued into another tune without missing a beat. On his return to the table, the protocol guy mouthed a thank you and then whispered "I don't think they noticed, doubt that particular musical has reached Hanoi yet!"

The following Sunday they were to depart. I was at the entrance to say my formal farewell. As he approached one of our more elderly local residents, Joyce Sherlock, had arrived at my side, in her hat and Sunday best on her way to church, curious to see what was happening. Before I had time to usher her away, the Prime Minister was in front of me, hand outstretched with a cheery smile. "Thank you Mr Griffin, for a very nice stay." And then seeing Joyce, gloved hand outstretched, took her hand, "Mrs Griffin so nice to meet you."

With which he was escorted to his car and whisked away with police outriders and his entourage in hot pursuit. I stood dumbstruck, whilst the doorman beside me couldn't contain a laugh. Joyce looked up and smiled, "What a nice man. Who was he?" and headed off to church.[54]

That first year we also had the pleasure of welcoming Reg Grundy and his wife, Joy Chambers. Readers will recall I looked after them at The Como, even deconstructing the sealed windows to accommodate his liking for fresh air. Fortunately The Observatory's presidential suite already had windows that opened. Their assistant Di Ayres was still with them. They were to visit regularly and were on my 'favourite' list. Our friendship was as warm and friendly as ever and lasted until I retired from The Observatory in 2011. Reg passed away in 2016. In 2019, Joy visited the hotel again, where it was serendipitous that she was greeted by my son Charlie, who had followed me into the hotel industry and was then a duty manager. True to form, she discovered the connection and talked of the times she had known me and asked that she be remembered to me.

In October of 1993, we had a visit from Michael Crawford, who I could only think of as Frank Spencer in *Some Mothers Do Have 'Em*. I had never been a fan of his musical abilities, having first seen him in the early '80s on stage in *Barnum*. A few years after that he really made a splash in *Phantom of the Opera*. I had seen him as the Phantom but I preferred the Australian cast with Anthony Warlow and Marina Prior.

Whilst with us he was interviewed by a young Richard Wilkins, who presented him with an award for record sales. The room had been set up and the timings agreed. Guests were invited and all were enjoying a drink as he circulated amongst his fans. An announcement was made of a 'surprise' award to Michael, and the reaction was about as theatrical as it could get. His gasp of amazement, the show of disbelief, the humility and then - after persuasion - his acceptance of the 'platinum disk' was a performance all of its own. He is talented, no question about it, as attested to by the millions of fans who adore him and the joy he brings to so many, but I was still left feeling that you could never take Frank Spencer out of Michael Crawford. Andrew Lloyd Webber was our guest the following year. [55]

Daryl Somers was another Aussie TV icon. He'd hosted an enormously popular TV variety television program *Hey, Hey It's Saturday* which ran for 27 years until 1999. He was to stay with us regularly from the first year we opened and long after my retirement in 2011. He was a lovely man, warm, friendly and popular with all the staff.

We brought our first year to a close with the arrival of a guest I had heard a lot about from my film producing brother Chris, who had worked with him on a number of productions. David Puttnam, or Baron Puttnam as he became, was a film producer whose works included *Chariots of Fire,* which won an Academy Award for Best Picture, and later *The Killing Fields*. He and his wife stayed with us in December and he asked me to convey to my brother the fact that he owed him one, as the series Chris had produced for him was due for a rerun, and they'd get the royalties. I fear the message was not so well received, as Chris believed he should have had a greater reward for the series that Chris had worked so hard on, whilst David was in Thailand filming *The Killing Fields*. David and his wife liked the hotel but he was a chronic allergy sufferer, and asked why hotels could not have rooms without carpets, and with hypoallergenic bedding? We ran out and purchased hypoallergenic pillows and sheets for any future guest who might suffer from the same ailment, although our new carpets did remain [56]

We also hosted the French film producer, Jean-Jacques Annaud who made *The Lover*, an erotic movie of the type that the French seem to do so well, *Seven Years in Tibet*, with Brad Pitt and *Enemy at the Gates*, based on the battle for Stalingrad, starring Joseph Fiennes, Jude Law, Bob Hoskins and Ed Harris.

Robyn Dalton stayed often and was an absolutely fascinating woman who I got to know well. She was an author and I still have her book, *Aunts Up the Cross,* her memoir of growing up in the bohemian Kings Cross area of Sydney with her doctor father. Her film-producing included *Oscar and Lucinda* and *Madame Sousatzka*, among others. Most of all I was intrigued to hear her tales of when she worked in intelligence in the '50s. This came about through knowing Prince Chula of Thailand and the work appeared to consist largely of putting the Thai government in a good light. As a press attache in London, she wrote earnest letters to *The Times* and *The Guardian* and managed the press for the first Southeast Asia Treaty Organisation conference in 1955. She had certainly lived life to the full and was quite an inspiration.

Another regular visitor was Scott Hicks, best known as the screenwriter and director of *Shine,* his Oscar-winning biopic of pianist David Helfgott. For me his best movie was *Snow Falling on Cedars*, a beautiful-looking film, with the most memorable snow scenes I have seen since *Doctor Zhivago*. Scott was a lovely man; very self-effacing, with the groovy look and style of a 60s hippy.

1994 arrived and the year was notable for the various Royals who came to Sydney and whom I met. I was still very much the monarchist at that time, although by 1999, when the referendum was held, I actually voted in favour of becoming a republic.

Seeing how well William has turned out, and the fear of ending up with a President like Donald Trump, I do not think I would vote that way again.

In January 1994 Prince Charles came to Sydney promoting his passion on matters of ecological concern. To everyone's horror, a young man, David Kang, decided to take a shot at him. Thankfully it was only a starting pistol. He was protesting the treatment of several hundred Cambodian asylum seekers held in detention camps. How little has changed, sadly. He could have faced twenty years in prison but ended up with 500 hours of community service. Kang now practises as a barrister, specialising in criminal law.

It was the day after this event that we were invited to a garden party at Parliament House, when I was to meet the Prince again, the first time being in Kenilworth in the 1970s when he was still single. He was giving a presentation in the chamber and I realised just how difficult it must be to be constantly in the spotlight. The chamber was not large and we all sat in the main area, while the press were seated in the gallery above, only a few metres from the stage where the Prince sat. As he started to speak the long telephoto lenses came out, with flashes going off left, right and centre. As he spoke, the first flashes settled down but then I noticed whenever the Prince coughed, swallowed, or touched his ear, nose or hair, it started up a barrage of flashes. No doubt they were desperate to get a photo of him with a finger in an ear or up his nose. I really felt quite sorry for the scrutiny he underwent constantly in front of the *paparazzi*.

After the speeches we all headed onto the roof garden for cocktails. I was with my group of hoteliers and Australian Hotels Association colleagues. At one point the official photographer came over to take a photo of the hotel group. The chairman of the Association, John Thorpe, a no-nonsense pub owner, stopped the photographer. "Hang on - we want Charlie in this shot with us."

With which he hurried over to the Prince, who was in conversation with another group of dignitaries, took him by the elbow, said something and frogmarched him over to our group, holding his elbow should he try to escape. I was horrified, having seen all the formalities of royal etiquette in England - this was indeed a breach. I was convinced that when next visiting the UK I would be unceremoniously tossed into the Tower. To my surprise, Charles was mildly amused by the whole thing, and took his place amongst us with the joking comment, "I do hope I don't manage to break your camera." [57]

Photo taken, he smiled and nodded at us and was rescued by his equerry. How different he was here than in England; so much more relaxed, he even appeared to enjoy the somewhat irreverent Australians.

The next royal encounter came via an invitation from Lady Fairfax, who had been a guest at my table for JBS's hotel opening function. She held a fundraiser at her home on Sydney Harbour, *'in the presence of His Royal Highness Prince Edward CVO.'* He the Queen's child whom I had not met, and I rather liked the idea of continuing to build up my set.

I arrived at *Fairwater* in Double Bay, a sprawling mansion on the largest privately-owned harbour side landholding in Sydney. I had driven past it many times yet had not appreciated how large it was. (After her death in 2017, it was reported that all the live-in servants were allowed to keep living there. It then sold for $100 million, Australia's most expensive house to date, to who else but a tech billionaire - Mike Cannon-Brookes.) On arrival, I was ushered onto the terrace overlooking a beautiful lawn leading down to the harbour foreshore. I was greeted by Lady Fairfax.

I wasn't sure if she remembered me or had any idea who I was, but she was charming. A waiter offered me some 'frivolities' as they were referred to on the menu, with a glass of Veuve Clicquot Ponsardin 1985, a most suitable choice: it was known as 'The Widow' as Madame Clicquot had taken over her late husband's business, becoming one of the first women in the early 1800s to run an international business. Lady Fairfax was well acquainted with such a situation.

Prince Edward eventually arrived and the twenty or so guests were formally presented, and we were led into the house for dinner. It was a large oval table and I found myself three seats to his right, with a young woman and two men between us. The menu of seafood, roast venison and a dessert of summer fruits were served with vintage wines. [95]

All I could see of Prince Edward were his hands which struck me as being rather small and pudgy; he had a large signet ring on his left hand. There was little humour and the conversation was very stilted. It was one of the more boring VIP dinners I have attended. Prince Edward was dull, lacking the spirit of his elder brothers. We made attempts at conversation but it was all very dry. After coffee, Prince Edward retired and we were left to our port and brandy. I excused myself and headed off to find the lavatory. Eventually, a butler pointed me in the right direction. On entering, I was taken aback. The entire room was done up in a jungle theme with tiger skin wallpaper; very *trompe l'oeil*. It was extraordinary. I could not imagine how this kitsch could be found in such a grand mansion. I was still chuckling to myself when I took my place back at the table. I wanted to tell my dinner companion to go and take a look at the ridiculous decor. I turned to the man, "Have you seen the loo?".

Before I could comment any further, he replied, "I certainly have, I designed it."

I rapidly changed my laughing tone to one of interest, thanking my lucky stars he had interrupted me. It turned out that he was an interior designer who did a lot of work for Lady Mary Fairfax. In 1988, one of New York's great hotels, The St Pierre sold the 41st and 42nd floors to her. She immediately set about trying to make a splash in New York society by transforming the Pierre Roof into a palatial private residence. One of the guest bedrooms, called the Scottish Room, was decorated with a green tartan plaid and a set of bagpipes. The other, the Arabian Nights Room, was decked out with Middle Eastern murals. The Grand Salon had been outfitted with an 18-foot-high limestone fireplace and mantle, originally from a French chateau, that Lady Fairfax had found in an architectural salvage shop near Paris. A huge tiered crystal chandelier was hung at the centre of the double-height room. She did have some eccentric tastes, so her bathroom may well be regarded in hindsight as being rather understated by her standards.

Later that year, something occurred that truly made me appreciate the egalitarian values of the Australian culture. Kate, my secretary at the time, said a member of the staff was on the phone and wanted to speak with me on a personal matter. Justine Mainwaring was at the time a young waitress we had employed in the Orient Cafe. I was racking my brains to put a face to the name, when Kate put her through. "Good morning Mr Griffin, I am sorry to bother you but my father has a friend who would very much like to see the hotel and asked if I could show him around."

I of course agreed as I was delighted when the family took an interest in where their children worked.

"He is also a friend of Mr Sherwood." This made me sit up and take a little more notice.

"Of course that's fine, and if I may I should also like to meet him and join you on the tour. What is the man's name and when does he want to come and see us?"

There was a moment's pause as she relayed the request to someone with her. "Would later this morning be OK? It's Prince Michael of Kent."

I was stumped for words. I suggested under the circumstances I felt it would be better if she wore her normal clothes rather than the Orient Cafe uniform.

This raised so many questions in my mind. Who was Justine? Who were her parents? My mother's favourite questions. I asked Kate and it turned out that the father was a judge and Justine came from a very good family. The old English class system popped into my mind. In England I had often received a call from some well-placed father asking if I would consider their son or daughter for a position. It was par for the course for a parent of note to pull rank for their child to enter employment, and most certainly a judge in England would have done so. It was therefore refreshing that Justine had simply applied on her own merits and reinforced my appreciation of the egalitarian culture of Australia.

Justine arrived early and we awaited Prince Michael's arrival. When he arrived I greeted him formally, and we headed off on a tour. He explained that he was a good friend of Jim's and had visited a number of his hotels. Most of his chat took place with Justine, and I just opened doors, but he was relaxed and pleasant enough. He left after about an hour and promised to return. [58]

He did in June 1999, and stayed for a few days, as a guest of JBS. He was friendly and surprisingly chatty. I mentioned how our paths had crossed before, or more accurately 'passed'. He was with Lord Montagu of Beaulieu in a car on the London to

Brighton Run, and they had flashed by me as I rode in the 1898 Daimler Benz. On check out, I explained that his account had been taken care of by JBS, of which he was most appreciative, and made a remark I have since always found amusing. "That is so kind of him as nowadays I am but an impoverished peer." He was reportedly £2.3 million in debt. These days he has recovered, and is worth around $40 million.

Prince Michael left me a very nice crested silver letter opener, which now joins many others as an out-of-date relic, much like myself, in this digital age. He also left me with the quote that I often use nowadays in referring to my own situation, with a slight adaptation, that of being an 'impoverished pensioner'.[59]

Sarah Ferguson, The Duchess of York, known simply as Fergie, visited in 2002. Things fell apart after her divorce from Prince Andrew in 1996, when scandalous photos appeared in the popular press of her sunbathing topless, having her toes nibbled by an American financial manager, for which she was ridiculed. By the time she came to stay with us at The Observatory she was gradually regaining some respect as a writer, charity patron, film producer, and television personality. I knew her sister Jane Luedecke quite well as she lived in Sydney and it was Jane who recommended that she stay at The Observatory.

Fergie was with us when she was promoting Wedgewood china and porcelain, and - as with all events that include someone with royal connections - we got a good turnout. We had closed the Galileo Restaurant to host the event, which we had planned to open again later in the evening, but unfortunately due to the long wait for her entrance the event took up the whole evening, to the irritation of those who had booked for dinner. After this shaky start she got a bit better. Fergie was very approachable although a little too much of a jolly hockey sticks type for my taste. [61]

It so happened that at the same time we had Gabriel Byrne staying with us. He is a wonderful Irish actor with the soft voice that was a characteristic of so many of his countrymen. He popped up in so many films, but for me it was his D'Artagnan alongside Leonardo Di Caprio in *The Man In the Iron Mask* who I loved the best. Fergie approached me and said, much to my surprise, "Did I see Gabriel Byrne in the restaurant?" She was as excited as any adoring fan.

"Yes, he's staying with us."

"Please could you do me a favour, I think he is amazing and he must be my favourite actor, do you think there is any chance you could arrange for me to meet him?"

As a monarchist I found this a strange position to be in. Here was a woman who had been married to an English prince pleading for me to arrange a meeting with a famous actor. Prior to this it had always been the actors lining up to be presented to the royal personage. This was no different to the girls standing outside the Hotel Como begging to meet Bono. Gabriel Byrne was just finishing his breakfast when I approached him to explain the situation. He could not have been more charming. "Of course I should be pleased to, where is she?"

I arranged for a quiet corner table in the Globe Bar that was empty at that time of day. When they met they hit it off from the start and chatted and laughed for over an hour. I couldn't help but wonder, rather scandalously, if Gabriel Byrne's situation of being between marriages may have been any help.[62]

The favour was rewarded with a gift of a fine Wedgewood china clock suitably signed, together with a rather glamorous photo of Fergie with the message,

Dear Patrick, Best wishes and thank you for all your help - I am so looking forward to coming back. Sarah, Duchess of York.

She never did come back.

In 2009 I was unfortunately diagnosed with prostate cancer, which I am delighted to say I saw off, but as a result missed the visit of Princess Anne or - as she is now known - The Princess Royal, a title customarily awarded to a British monarch's eldest daughter. From all accounts she was warm, friendly and even signed the 'Golden Book' alongside other celebrity signatures. How she had mellowed. It seems she was very different from the Princess who had put me in my place for having the cheek to speak to her when she was attending the Royal Agricultural Show over thirty years earlier.

Another guest brought back memories of a story my mother had told me about the Coronation of Queen Elizabeth in 1953. A smiling and waving Queen Salote of Tonga, wearing traditional dress, won the hearts of the crowd as she remained undaunted by the rain throughout the long procession and refused to raise the roof of her carriage for protection. Her son King Tupou IV became a regular at the hotel; he would book through the reservations department and check in as any other guest might do. He gained the respect of all the team for his unassuming manner and made no demands on anyone, possibly because of his upbringing in Australia. He was educated at Newington College and studied law at Sydney University while resident at Wesley College. We all loved the man and when he was in the hotel we were hardly aware of it.

Upon his death in 2006 things were to be a little different with his son King Tupou V. He had attended King's College in Auckland, New Zealand. This was followed by periods in England at The Leys School in Cambridge, and another school in Switzerland. He then went on to study at Oxford University and at the Royal Military Academy Sandhurst in England. These had certainly molded the man. I had received a call from one of his staff that he was due to arrive and would appreciate a formal greeting. We organised this and the red carpet was laid out; I stood by the entrance to greet him. His car pulled up, a very tall and impressive man got out, smartly dressed in a Savile Row suit, sporting a rather incongruous pith helmet. "Your Majesty, welcome to The Observatory," said I with a small court bow. He raised his pith helmet in a polite doff, nodded acknowledgement, and shook my hand.

> "How do you do, delighted to meet you, my father spoke highly of your hotel."

What made this exchange most notable was that he had the most plum-in-the-mouth English accent I had ever heard. I had never heard the vowels rounded and rolled out so perfectly in all my life. Professor Higgins in *My Fair Lady* would have sounded positively 'cockney' by comparison. King Tupou V enjoyed the formality and his Oxbridge and Sandhurst education had turned out the ultimate English gentleman in the King of Tonga. [60]

Presidents who stayed with us included General Fidel Ramos of the Philippines, who supported Cory Aquino in ousting Ferdinand Marcos and Imelda, with her 3,000 pairs of shoes. Ramos was therefore a national hero. My wife was from the Philippines, and her uncle was a Senator, so she was delighted that President Ramos and his wife had chosen to stay with us. He was a very pleasant man and it was hard to imagine what he might have faced had the coup failed against Marcos, who had ruled for twenty years as a ruthless dictator. [63]

We hosted Xanana Gusmao, the first President of East Timor and his successor, Jose Ramos-Horta. Mary Robinson, President of Ireland, stayed with us, much to the delight of our Irish staff. One of my favourites in my 'best lunch guest' category was Archbishop Desmond Tutu of South Africa, anti-apartheid and human rights activist. We hosted a small lunch for him and we loved his great wit and humour. He joked that *"When the missionaries came to Africa they had the Bible and we had the land. They said 'Let us pray', so we closed our eyes. When we opened them we had the Bible and they had the land."* [64]

This was not the first time he had told this joke, but we had not heard it before and all laughed uproariously. He was a very impressive man. A controversial guest was Dr Hanan Ashrawi, the Palestinian legislator, activist, and scholar. These guests were recipients of *'The Sydney Peace Prize'* of which we were proudly a sponsor. Our sponsorship was questioned when the prize was awarded to John Pilger, the Australian journalist and BAFTA award-winning documentary filmmaker. I received a very aggressive call from a Zionist newspaper, telling me that we should not be supporting those who were so obviously anti-Semitic. I tried to explain that we simply offered accommodation and did not select or nominate any participants. He threatened to have the Australian Jewish community boycott the hotel. Initially I was concerned, as well as annoyed, but on taking counsel from a respected and influential friend who happened to be Jewish, I ignored the threat and we heard nothing more. We continued to sponsor the prize.

In 1997, as Hong Kong was handed back to China, Christopher Patton passed through, taking a breather following the handover of England's last outpost of its empire. Shortly afterwards we were to welcome Ms Anson Chan, Hong Kong's new Chief Secretary. The eternal sea of the world's business and politics never stands still. [65]

Chapter 7

#goodguysn'badguys #ladieslovablen'loathsome #besttenantever

Although JBS might have been gilding the lily somewhat in claiming that The Observatory was near the Opera House and the Sydney Harbour Bridge (neither could be seen from the hotel), he was however correct in his observation in regards to the business community and politicians: they did indeed prefer our discreet luxurious style.

One thing I have learned is that no matter how humble the origin, once a person reaches a position of power a luxurious lifestyle swiftly becomes the accepted norm. The Observatory Hotel had very quickly established itself as one of the most elite establishments in Sydney and soon became a regular haunt for people with a taste for the good life: local 'pollies' and foreign dignitaries alike.

In 1995 a young English politician stayed with us. Tony Blair was Leader of the Labour Party, then in opposition. He was impressive and far removed from such traditional 'cloth cap' Labour leaders as Harold Wilson, whom I had met in England. He was young, approachable, chatty and very down to earth. He was travelling with his wife Cherie. Having done my research, I knew she was the daughter of an English actor Antony Booth. He was the socialist son-in-law who was famously referred to as the *Scouse git* by Alf Garnett in the '60s sitcom, *Till Death Us Do Part*. Knowing the satirical contents of the show it was hard to imagine the wife of a future English Prime Minister with such a man as her father. She had read law at the London School of Economics, graduated with First-Class Honours and later became a QC. [66]

Having achieved all this, I am still not sure that the apple fell so far from the tree. One afternoon I was in the lobby when Mr Blair returned from a meeting with Paul Keating. He was in a jovial mood and chatted as to how he was enjoying his stay, after which he returned to his suite. Not long after a taxi pulled up and a rather irritable Mrs Blair stepped out, paid the driver and came into the hotel. I greeted her and told her that her husband had just gone up to their suite.

> "He's here is he? I have been chasing him all over Sydney. I even went to Kirribilli House (the Prime Minister's residence) to see if he was there. For goodness' sake!"

She was far from happy and I would have liked to be a fly on the wall once she got to the suite and confronted him. I amused myself thinking of the comedy scenes as she went round Sydney demanding *"Have you seen my husband?"*

I could never imagine Denis having a go at Maggie Thatcher. Cherie was indeed an independent woman; quite fiery and certainly a woman I would not wish to cross. When I watched the movie *The Queen*, I thought Helen McCrory got it just right with her portrayal of Cherie Blair.

Two other notable British politicians stayed with us, unbeknownst to each other thankfully. Ken Livingstone had, against all odds, became the first directly elected Labour Lord Mayor of London. (He later lost to the Conservative candidate Boris Johnson). Michael Heseltine, later Lord Heseltine, was an MP in the House of Commons. To quote from *GLC – the Inside Story* by W. Whitehouse:

> *In 1991, the Conservatives very timidly broached the idea of creating strong local leadership via their Secretary of State for the environment, Michael Heseltine, but this was met with opposition both from local politicians and MPs, too wary of their style being cramped by the competition they feared this political move might create. The recent abolition of the Greater London Council had left the Conservatives with the bitter taste of humiliation due to the antics of Ken Livingstone and his cronies and there was no inclination from the head of the party whatsoever to hand any power back to what they feared would be left-leaning local authorities.*

These two had a history. With this in mind I took some mischievous pleasure in allocating them to suites opposite one another. As it turned out they did not come to blows. I did however have an interesting chat with Ken Livingstone over a drink in the Globe Bar, when he told me of his plans to introduce a toll on cars entering London. Knowing London I just could not comprehend how this would be possible, with so many points of entry to the city. It was not as simple as our toll system on the Sydney Harbour Bridge, but he was adamant it was possible. I thought he was dreaming. A few years later I was in the UK and drove into London and discovered that he wasn't. It cost me £5! In 2011 it increased to £10, substantially more than the Bridge toll here in Sydney.

Most of the contemporary Australian Prime Ministers, along with numerous ministers, stayed at the hotel during their time. They did not leave me with any great impression although Paul Keating was the most colourful. As I write this, we are regularly shocked at Donald Trump's tweets, yet how quickly we have forgotten Keating's acerbic tongue. Apart from catching the headlines for breaching protocol and putting his hand on the waist of Her Majesty The Queen, and being called 'infamous' and 'the Lizard of Oz' by the British tabloids, Paul Keating had a great turn of phrase and regularly shot down his opponents with such withering barbs rarely heard before or since in Australian politics. He called Mr Howard "a dessicated little coconut" and said of another politician that arguing with him was "like being flogged to death with a warm lettuce." [67] My personal favourite is the immortal "He is simply a shiver looking for a spine to run up."

Mr Keating once invited me into his suite for a chat. The approachability of Australian leaders was something that always surprised me, after experiencing the very formal protocols in British politics. He was aware that I was National President of the Australian Hotels Association and he chose that minute to have a go at us about local tourism issues and what had always been an eyesore in Sydney, the Cahill Expressway, which cuts the city off from the Harbour. It was Sydney's first freeway and the problem was that it ran on an elevated roadway on the top deck of a two level steel railway station across the front of Circular Quay. It blocked what could be a wonderful view and pathway up into the city from the Harbour.

> "I have offered Carr (the Premier of NSW) the money to pull it down but he doesn't listen. You should be pressing him on it!"

I was totally taken aback; even through the AHA, could I have any influence on such matters? I was flattered to imagine he thought I had. In truth I think it was more about what Paul Keating could do, but I was happy to accept the kudos, even though we never got anywhere - the Cahill Freeway stands in place still.

Regulars at hotel events were the likes of Gough Whitlam and his wife, Margaret, both very imposing figures. He was a colourful and famous ex Labor Prime Minister and she had represented Australia in swimming at the 1938 British Empire Games. Gough was famous for, amongst many other things, his quote at the time of being sacked as PM by the controversial Governor-General Sir John Kerr in 1975:

"Ladies and gentlemen, well may we say 'God Save the Queen', because nothing will save the Governor-General."

I always thought it daft that this was what he was remembered for, when he had been instrumental in far more memorable policies, such as ending the White Australia policy in 1973 with a series of amendments dismantling the racist old immigration law, and many other polices to modernise the somewhat hidebound Australian society of the 60s and 70s. [69]

On the other side of politics, I became very fond of Lady Sonia McMahon for her sense of fun and genuine support of the hotel. She was the widow of a long past Prime Minister, Sir William McMahon, a great philanthropist and Sydney socialite and would bring other notable ladies with her: the very elegant Lady Susan Renouf, socialite and ex-wife of Andrew Peacock, and notable Liberal, the Hon Bronwyn Bishop, a somewhat controversial, long term politician and later the Speaker of the House of Representatives. I found her a fearsome woman in comparison to the other two ladies, although on most occasions I like to think my charm won her over. [68]

She took me to task about our soup spoons. "Patrick, I am surprised that a hotel such as yours cannot even provide correct soup spoons." I attempted to explain that it was not incorrect to use a spoon shaped as a desert spoon, as this was the correct cutlery used before the Victorians introduced the round spoons to assist the masses to understand the different cutlery to be used. I felt I had got away with it, only for her to shoot back, "Don't give me that rubbish, the original soup spoon was larger and deeper."

I always felt she had aspirations of becoming an Australian Maggie Thatcher. When I suggested this to John Howard, with whom I had lunch prior to him becoming Prime Minister in 1996, he rather vehemently replied "That woman will never be Prime Minister!"

I couldn't help but feel he encapsulated the Liberal Party's view that women should not be encouraged in politics. By the time I had lunch with him again he had become Prime Minister, and would be the second-longest serving Australian Prime Minister prior to his defeat in 2007.[70]

To my great regret the only PM I did not meet in person was the recently departed Hon R J L Hawke AC. The one thing I discovered about him was via a phone conversation. He imparted this gem of information when he called to ask the price of a two-bedroom suite for a weekend for himself and Blanche d'Alpuget. He confided that he snored like a bear, and Blanche required her sleep. It has never ceased to amaze me at how open and natural Australians are; I could never in a million years have imagined a British politician ever telling me such intimate details.

The politician I was particularly fond of, more than any other, was Natasha Stott Despoja, leader of the Australian Democrats and - as a Senator at 26 - was the youngest woman to sit in the Parliament of Australia. Coincidentally another one of our favourite guests was Ian Smith, one of Australia's most influential political lobbyists. Many thought what a lovely couple they would make, as neither appeared to fit the usual mold of those involved in the cut and thrust of politics. We were therefore delighted when we read in the press of *'Natasha's engagement to the dashing and lovable Ian Smith.'*

A more well-suited couple would be hard to find. I was deeply touched when Ian took the trouble to attend my retirement farewell event.

Another successful politician I got to know from the left of the political spectrum in the NSW Parliament, representing the electoral districts of McKell and Port Jackson for the Labor Party, was the rather feisty Sandra Nori. I confess to being on the right of politics and have in every election both in the UK and in Australia voted that way … except once.

A casino and high-rise development was planned for Darling Harbour, which was close to the hotel, including a heli-pad. I had enjoyed a few helicopter rides in my life so I knew that the engine revs to a deafening level and in an area surrounded by tall buildings the noise would be exacerbated. This would seriously impact our guests and I looked for ways to object.

To slightly misquote Shakespeare, *politics makes for strange bedfellows*, and so it was in this case. Sandra Nori of the Left was our champion; she ran such a strong campaign that the plan never got off the ground, let alone a helicopter. That year I voted Labor, the first and only time, and Sandra and I are good friends to this day.

My final politician was a delightful man, not my usual descriptor for such as he. Tim Fischer, former National Party leader and deputy prime minister, who sadly died as I wrote this, from acute myeloid leukaemia. He was exactly three months younger than I, throwing our common mortality into sharp relief.

I met Tim on a couple of occasions and soon learned of his passion for trains. Being Regional Director for Orient-Express, who operated the world's most famous train, I felt comfortable in my knowledge. Tim Fischer was soon politely correcting me on the details. I simply stopped trying and let him tell me all about the train. His knowledge of where, how and when they ran was encyclopaedic. He was indeed a great man in both stature and politics, and well-liked and respected.

Our regular business guests were not always as dull as one might imagine. One such was the entrepreneur, investor, and stockbroker, Rene Rivkin, who had been the youngest member ever of the Sydney Stock Exchange. He was famous for his trademark large cigar and gold worry beads. He'd sit in his favourite quiet corner of the lounge, running his beads through his fingers, puffing away when smoking was permitted, chatting into his phone beneath the watchful eye of Sidney Nolan's rather depressing portrait of Billy Budd hanged from the yardarm.[76]

As is often the case with high flying entrepreneurs, not all was as it seemed. In 2003, following a long-running investigation by the Australian Securities and Investments Commission, Rivkin was found guilty of insider trading, resulting in a sentence of nine months' periodic detention on weekends. He died in May 2005.

Another high-flyer who stayed with us was Alan Bond (I had met his extroverted wife Eileen in Melbourne). He'd become a public hero after bankrolling challenges for the *America's Cup* yachting prize, and winning in 1983. They broke the longest winning streak in the history of sport. This brought him fame and fortune, especially in his home state of Western Australia. He bought the Channel 9 TV network (for a billion dollars from Kerry Packer, who bought it back three years later for a quarter of the price) and a brewery, built hotels, and founded Australia's first private university, Bond University. In 1987, he purchased Vincent van Gogh's renowned painting, *Irises,* for $54 million - at the time the highest price ever paid for a single painting. However, the purchase was funded by a substantial loan from the auctioneer, Sotheby's, which Bond failed to repay. This was the start of the unravelling.

When I met Alan Bond, he was a shadow of his former self and it was hard to imagine him ever having been married to the feisty redhead I had met in Melbourne, Eileen 'Red' Bond. He had recently been released from Karnet Prison Farm, having served four years in various West Australian prisons after pleading guilty to using his controlling interest in Bell Resources to deceptively siphon off A$1.2 billion into the coffers of Bond Corporation. It has never ceased to amaze me how ex-prisoners and bankrupt businessmen could still somehow manage to find the cash to stay in luxury hotels, such as ours. He died in hospital in 2015.

As well as the black sheep, we also hosted some very nice and very interesting 'suits' who weren't bankrupt or found guilty of crimes. John Singleton was a real character and a true entrepreneur. He stayed from time to time, and was a regular Galileo guest where he would have his breakfast and meetings. He always arrived whilst I was having my own breakfast and would call across a cheery good morning from his window table on the other side of the restaurant, as if we were the only guests in the room. Occasionally he would chat, ignoring anyone who might overhear him. He was like Jack Nicholson in the movie *As Good As It Gets*. He always wanted the same young person, Sinim, to serve him his coffee. If she was off duty or busy elsewhere he would call across the restaurant, "Patrick, what have you done with Sinim, where is she? No one else has a clue about making coffee!"

He was a very nice guy and warm and friendly to all the staff. When I mentioned I was getting divorced, he said "Patrick - you will learn. Next time just find a woman you don't like, buy her a house, and be done with it." This from a man who'd had six wives.

I'd heard it before but I still laughed. John was very successful in advertising and radio, although at times he showed off a rather eccentric side to his character that probably detracted from just how brilliant he was. He is well known as a larrikin in Australia for his love of a good time, and the public and media knew him as 'Singo'. He once bought drinks for the entire Rosehill racecourse in Sydney after his horse won the Golden Slipper.

The richest suit to visit the hotel was Kerry Packer. A well-known smoker, he had come in for a business lunch to one of the first Sydney restaurants to ban smoking - Galileo. He was a gruff, large man and not full of conversation. He and his guests had a good lunch, and at the end of the meal caused us to have a crisis of conscience. The waiter told the head waiter, who told the F&B manager, who tapped on my door, rather distressed. "Excuse me Mr Griffin - Mr Packer has just asked for a packet of cigarettes. Obviously he wants to smoke - what should we do?"

Mr Packer was an Australian media tycoon. The family company owned a controlling interest in a television network and a leading publishing company amongst other things. He was best known outside Australia for founding World Series Cricket. He was the richest, rudest and possibly the most influential man in Australia, worth around $6.5 billion. And I was being asked to tell him not to smoke.

We'd had long discussions in the hotel on the subject of smoking in the restaurant and I had been adamant that - no matter who - we must stand by our principles. In this case, however, I also liked my job. The restaurant was almost empty; could a back down be justified? I took advice from Shakespeare, with 'discretion being the better part of valor', and 'gave permission' to allow Mr Packer his cigarette, much to the relief of all the staff in the restaurant. At that point I had to dash off to a meeting, or so I said. I did not wish to be observed as the coward who had buckled to the power of Mammon.

We always tried to meet our guests' many and varied demands, so senior staff would have a daily 'arrivals meeting' to check off that day's guests. To alleviate the tedium, we'd make the odd wisecrack, and when someone read out the guest name of Whistler, I piped up, expecting a good chuckle, "Is he bringing his mother?" Silence. Puzzled response: "No, he's travelling alone, why?". I was aghast at the lack of art knowledge. What the hell were the schools teaching? A fortnight later, someone from the meeting said, "Last night I got your joke about Mr Whistler! Very funny!" Thinking they'd run off to watch a documentary or read a book on the artist, I was even more taken aback when he said "I saw it in the Mr Bean film! It's a painting isn't it? Whistler's Mother!" Who would have thought of the educational benefits of low brow slapstick comedy?

Another notable name that appeared on our arrival list one morning was that of the very wealthy Sir Evelyn de Rothschild, the British financier and a member of the Rothschild family. He was a product of Harrow, where Winston Churchill was educated, and Cambridge, and was - to me - a terrifying figure of man with even less humour than Whistler's Mother, and who epitomized the English ruling classes. He was a philanthropist, as well as serving as Queen Elizabeth's financial adviser. A man of strict formality and with a back straight as a ram rod. It was with this in mind that I briefed the staff on our daily 'arrivals' meeting, on the formalities of dealing with such a man. "Yes sir, no sir" was to be the order of the day.

On being advised of his approach I rushed to the entrance, preparing my formal nod and greeting. There I found the now famous Michael, who was then a doorman, greeting Sir Evelyn with "G'day Sir Evelyn, how's ya day?"

I was mortified. Here was the Savile Row-suited gentleman, complete with starched detachable collar and tie, standing at the kerbside, having 'g'day' shouted at him. I immediately tried to rectify the welcome with a rather Basil Fawltyesque fawning and nodding, as I welcomed him and escorted him to his suite. As it turned out, I learned a lesson in just how effective the Aussie warmth and sincerity could be. The following day, there was Sir Evelyn standing at the desk chatting to Michael like an old mate. No jacket, braces on display, sleeves rolled up and - had he not been wearing a shirt with a detachable collar - he would most certainly have abandoned his tie. This was a far cry from the same man I had witnessed castigating people back in England. Given a few days I think Michael would have talked him into wearing a pair of boardies and thongs.

The family who were to become very special were the Tennants. I first met Christopher Tennant, his wife Andrea and two children, Andrew and Flora, when they stayed with us in the late 1990s. He was an aviation entrepreneur, a very charismatic and courageous man with a keen nose for business.

They were a lovely family whom I gradually got to know quite well due to their regular visits. A very relaxed, gentle man, always friendly. The staff all grew very fond of them and there was nothing the staff would not do for him. He was quite an aristocrat, but would have hated anyone knowing it. He was the son of Sir Iain Tennant, Knight of the Thistle, who was cousin of Lord Glenconner, by his wife, the former Lady Margaret Helen Isla Marion. Christopher had even been a Page of Honour to the Queen, although no-one would have guessed it when meeting this unassuming man. He had left Eton without great deal of academic success - a modest set of 'O' levels. A situation to which I could relate.

He obtained a licence to fly helicopters and it was to prove a hobby that was to change his life. In the 1980s he founded a company called Lynton Aviation, provided aviation services to rich and famous pop stars, executives and sportsmen. I read later how courageous he was:

In 1979, he was diagnosed as suffering from a serious kidney disease which meant he had to be on a dialysis machine twice a week. With his usual drive and determination, he set up an office in the London Clinic and carried on as before. However, his condition showed no improvement and in 2000 he decided to sell the company to the BBA Group for $55m. ....Soon after the sale had been completed, he had a kidney transplant and for two happy years he and his family travelled the world.

This is what brought him to The Observatory.

While visiting friends in Australia, he was offered one more challenge - to bolster the profits of Hawker Pacific. With his accustomed drive and energy (and sheer hard work) he turned it into one of the most successful aviation companies in Australia. It was, for Tennant, a remarkable double achievement.

With his family, he spent the English winter in Australia and returned to England for what is known as 'The Season'. He had even arranged to have his beloved red Aston Martin shipped out for use while he was here and we stored it for him when he was back in England. He told me I should drive it so as to keep it ticking over, and to my regret I did not take him up on the offer.

One day I had a call from him to meet him for a coffee. When we sat down I noticed he had a set of the hotel plans with him. He must have got them from Charlie Dodsworth, the chief engineer. With his charm he could get anything out of anyone.

"Patrick, you know I love it here and we spend months with you, but I am now getting pressure from Andrea to find a house, as she wants to have a more normal life and cook meals for the kids. I'm sure you get the picture. It would even be cheaper to rent a house, but I love it here and I love the team you have who look after me;

it's the little things from bringing the car up to keeping the suite the way I like it. But I need a kitchen."

He then rolled out the plans of the hotel on the table.

"Look - with this corner suite, it has all we need and is adjacent to a room service pantry and store that I gather could be adapted to a kitchen. The door from the suite could be built through this wardrobe in the lobby, which really isn't needed as both bedrooms have their own."

He had thought through everything and the changes were already drawn onto the plans.

"I have estimated how much the work would cost and I'm happy to pay. You'll then have the benefit of a suite with its own kitchen for guests when I'm not here. And of course it would please my wife so that I can keep staying with you."

He had costed everything and there was no questioning the design. I could not help but feel it was a bit of a set up in conjunction - with a little inside from Charlie! - but it could work. I agreed in principle, subject to my bosses agreeing, which they did. We didn't ask for any planning approval for another kitchen, however, the needs of our guests came first - especially guests like the Tennant family.

In 2002, we were saddened to learn he had developed cancer. We thought that with his wealth and influence he would find another kidney donor, but I was to learn that he had refused another transplant, having already had one chance, and wanted someone else to have the opportunity. He died on 12th June, 2003, in London, aged 52. Andrea, his wife, wrote a lovely letter to me expressing her thanks for looking after Christopher, and the family, and thanked a member of the housekeeping staff who was able to attend his funeral. There was one more thing: we had given Christopher a special blue bathrobe, monogrammed with his initials CJT, and we were touched to read in Andrea's letter that he had asked to be buried in it. I saw Andrea and the children only once again some years later, and the staff welcomed them back as if they were family. Michael, my old chief concierge, posted on The Observatory Facebook page in 2019 that he met Andrea recently on a visit to Sydney. She is currently living between homes in London and Malibu, with the family now grown up and doing well. It never fails to gratify me to see the warmth of relationships that still exist between staff and guests. In the photo Andrea doesn't appear to have changed one bit, whereas Michael - maybe just a little? [77]

The airline industry in Australia has had its ups and downs, with companies like Ansett, Compass and Kendell Airlines coming and going. Qantas was left with a virtual monopoly in the late 90s. It was therefore with great excitement Richard Branson announced in 1999 that he would launch an airline in Australia called Virgin Blue. Much like Christopher Tennant, Branson was another aviation entrepreneur, amongst other things, but on a much larger scale and known for his extroverted, headline grabbing personality. We all agreed if anyone could make it work, he could.

He was famous for his rather tongue-in-cheek humour. My nephew Ben once told me the urban legend handed down at Stowe public school which he had attended some years after Branson. The school wanted to build another house to accommodate young women who, in 2003, were to be accepted into the elite institution at £12,000 a term. According to the story, Branson offered to pay to build the house on the proviso he had the naming rights: "Virgin House". The board of governors politely declined his offer, preferring to call it "Queens", which brought an equally tongue-in-cheek response from my nephew, that it was an interesting choice for a school that had up until that time been for boys alone.

When Branson stayed with us, he held a number of board meetings with his Australian directors. I was always amused to see Richard Branson in his casual trademark jeans, open shirt and long hair, surrounded by the most well-groomed and formally attired group of suits. No doubt this is why when as he departed, he saw my suit and thrust into my hands a stack of files. Surprised, I gave them a quick look. They were all the papers relating to the feasibility and launch of his new airline. For a moment I wondered how much Qantas CEO James Strong and deputy Geoff Dixon might offer me for these documents. Another suited man snatched the papers abruptly from me. "Ours, I believe." [78]

The airline was a great success and grew to be the major competitor to Qantas who then launched their own low-cost airline, Jetstar, in 2003.

Not all the suits were men. We were delighted to look after Mrs Janet Holmes a Court, a businesswoman, philanthropist, and one of Australia's wealthiest women. She was chairman of one of Australia's largest private companies, Heytesbury Pty Ltd, whose fortunes she turned around after the death of her husband Robert Holmes à Court in 1990. She was not quite as wealthy, however, as Mrs Gina Rinehart. Heiress to Hancock Prospecting and now chair, she hates to be known as an heiress. She is one of Australia's richest people, and one of the most astute businesswomen in Australia.

We also hosted Mrs Rinehart's nemesis (thankfully not at the same time), Rose Porteous, a Filipina-born Australian, best known as the housekeeper who married the mining magnate Lang Hancock, Gina's father. On his death, Rose inherited his fortune, only to enter into a protracted legal battle with her step-daughter over the circumstances that led to Lang's death and the distribution of his estate. In all my years in the hotel industry Mrs Rose Porteous, nee Hancock, tops the list of *difficult* guests.

We had a call from her secretary one afternoon requesting the best suite for one night. The Presidential Suite was taken so we offered our next best suite. Mrs Porteous arrived with her assistant, who was permanently flustered due to the many demands made of her. Once checked in, she was escorted to her suite, and she was not overjoyed with it. Later that evening, I was in the Galileo Restaurant entertaining some guests when she arrived at the restaurant entrance. After less than a minute the maitre d' approached her. "Do you know who I am? I don't like having to wait."

He escorted her to a side table which she ignored and headed for a table more to her liking. "I am sorry madam, but that table is reserved."

"Well, find them another table. I am already here."

The maitre d' accepted the *fait accompli,* and offered her the menu. She ignored the menu and ordered a drink. She took out a cigarette and was in the process of lighting it as the waiter delivered her drink. "I am so sorry madam, but I am afraid we have a no smoking policy and I must ask you to put your cigarette out."

She started swearing and dropped the cigarette into her drink. Grabbing her handbag she pulled out her mobile and called her assistant. The conversation could be heard by the entire restaurant and I would now need to intervene.

> "Get me out of this hotel! If you can call it that! The staff are rude, and as far as my suite is concerned, it's smaller than my wardrobe [...] I don't care where. Find me somewhere. I am not staying in this place."

I was rising from my table to speak to her when I was beaten to it by a man having dinner with his wife a few tables away. He approached her table and in a quiet, controlled, but authoritative voice said, "Excuse me madam, but would you mind lowering your voice as you are rather disturbing the dinner of my wife and I."

With which he returned to his table, with admiring looks from other diners who had by now recognised the woman making the fuss. She fumed for a few moments more on her phone before picking up her bag and pushing the table violently away. She headed for the door and detoured past the man's table. Holding her phone as if she were about to strike him, she waved it in his face, "If you ever speak to me like that again, I will ram this down your throat." She stormed out of the restaurant.

There was a burst of applause from the rest of the diners. I approached the couple and apologised, offering him a bottle of champagne for his troubles.

> "Oh no problem, it was my pleasure, I happen to come from Perth. Anyone who builds such an ostentatious house as she did in Peppermint Grove and calls it *Prix D'Amour* should not be in such a fine establishment as yours."

She departed the hotel thirty minutes later, I believe for the Ritz Carlton in Double Bay. I wondered if I should call the general manager, Jenny Brown, a friend of mine, just to warn her a typhoon was heading her way. I didn't but many years later I spoke to Jenny who remembered her visit only too well. Mrs Porteous never returned to The Observatory.

Another rather notorious guest was Mr Dimitri de Angelis, who was not the most easy or likeable guest to deal with. One day he failed to arrive to take up his booking and it was no surprise to read a short while after in the *Sydney Morning Herald:*

A Sydney conman who duped investors out of more than $8 million and pretended to be friends with celebrities like former US president Bill Clinton, has been jailed for a maximum of 12 years. Judge Richard Cogswell spent two hours sentencing Dimitri de Angelis in the NSW District Court on Friday as he detailed the extravagant lifestyle he had fabricated. Justice Cogswell said de Angelis duped potential investors by showing photoshopped pictures of himself with famous people.

The photographs depicted himself with no lesser persons than Her Majesty Queen Elizabeth II, His Holiness Pope John Paul II, His Holiness the Dalai Lama, US Presidents George Bush senior, George W Bush and Bill Clinton, and Australian Prime Ministers John Howard and Kevin Rudd," Justice Cogswell told the court.

He represented to people that he owned fleets of luxury cars as well as mansions and luxurious homes in Sydney and Melbourne. Part of the proposition that he put to investors was that every one per cent in his company would be worth $6 million when the company went public. Justice Cogswell said de Angelis's company was actually "in financial crisis" but he was "very skilled" at deceiving his victims.

De Angelis pleaded guilty to 16 fraud charges last year. The former Qantas steward also rented Rolls-Royces, luxury holiday homes and offices to fool investors into thinking he was a wealthy businessman and that his recording company Emporium Music was a "foolproof scheme".

Those stung by de Angelis included Anne Keating, the sister of former prime minister Paul Keating, Sydney's former deputy lord mayor Marcelle Hoff, experienced businessmen and lawyers. Justice Cogswell said he acknowledged that Paris-born de Angelis might have narcissistic personality disorder and that he had had a tough childhood in France, having spent most of it in state care. He will be eligible for parole in May 2020.

I hope the new hotel owners will be on high alert for him!

One of our unusual guests was a man who was a regular but required a level of special attention. We believed he was bipolar, and when off his meds he would do all sorts of strange things. Once he threw $50 bills off his balcony window at passers-by. He would always arrive with a plastic bag, not a suitcase, would ask to buy shirts and ties from staff, and would leave them all behind when he checked out. Grant Raubenheimer, my deputy, recalled the guest always wanted the Presidential Suite every time he stayed. He would only deal with Grant as he thought Grant was the only one to give him a discount. When Grant quoted him $3,500 a night - the standard Presidential Suite corporate rate - he was delighted. As with most people, it is all just a matter of perception.

Chapter 8

#royalsinmusic #candidcamera #spathatlovedme

The Observatory become known as the place to stay for those who sought anonymity - or as much as you could expect when your face graced magazine covers and you were regarded as public property. Some of these guests were stars who'd been around for a long time. Others were what I call supernovas - they burn very bright for an instant and then are gone. Some may disagree with my choice of supernovas - my age may well have started to impair my 'star' judgement!

Angela, my director of PR in those early days, came into the office one morning. "I have arranged for you to have a photo with Tevin Campbell, he's in the foyer now." Before I could ask for more details, she was off, with me following along behind dutifully for the photo opp. Tevin Campbell? Never heard of him. Sounds Scottish. [71]

"Patrick, this is Tevin, could you just stand over here?"

A good looking young African American lad; American accent; big smile; arm around me; snap! "That's great, thanks Tevin." And he was off to his awaiting car.

"Who is he? What is he? I have never seen him or even heard of him."

"Come on Mr Griffin - you must have. He's a singer - he's had number 1 hits. Careful - you're showing your age!"

Others included a nice young man called Nicky of Westlife, an Irish group of lads, D-Ream and a group of rather attractive young women with the catchy name of Bananarama, so I wasn't complaining. Their - and others - lights have long since dimmed. [72]

Then there were those real stars whom one could never forget, and my favourite without a doubt was Olivia Newton-John, or ONJ as she was known. I had first admired her when she was on the Cliff Richard Show in England in the 1970s, along with Una Stubbs and Hank Marvin and The Shadows. My wife at that time was not a fan, but that didn't stop me avidly watching the show each week. It was therefore a thrill that she started to stay with us regularly.

First she came with her husband Matt Lattanzi and their daughter, Chloe, who over the years I saw grow up from a rather mischievous child. Once I caught her and a friend rolling our expensive vases down the corridor in a game to see how far they could go without crashing into the wall. I told her off and threatened to tell her mother; she grew up into a very glamorous young woman.

ONJ was one of the nicest people I had met. She was always friendly and greeted me with a kiss on the cheek. I often wondered what my ex-wife would have thought now that I had become so familiarly acquainted.

One day when ONJ was in the swimming pool, she noticed a young girl who was obviously going through chemo, an experience she knew of only too well herself. The girl had been brought in by her parents for a treat to the hotel's day spa, and she was excited to see Olivia. After *Grease* everyone loved *Sandy*. The girl was very hesitant and it was obvious that she wanted Olivia's autograph, but didn't want to interrupt her. Olivia saw this and simply swam over to her, got out of the pool and as if they were friends, sat down beside her and started chatting. They must have chatted for nearly an hour. I found it wonderful; without doubt she had brought happiness to the girl and gave her encouragement to face the traumas ahead. Usually stars don't do this unless a camera is there to record the good deed. This wasn't Olivia's style, and I will always love and respect her for the joy she brought to that little girl.

ONJ stayed with us many times and I can truthfully say that in all that time she was kind, warm and friendly to all. Well - nearly always. She was having a game of tennis on the hotel's court across the road, when a young man started taking photos of her. When she noticed, she was furious and stormed over to the fence and laid into the young man. "How dare you just snap away, taking photos without my permission. Even worse - you ruined my serve!" With which she turned and continued to play, the young man rather sheepishly slank away. Obviously not a shameless *paparazzo*. ONJ is indeed an Australian icon.[73]

I met another icon at the launch of *Vogue*. The event was held in a large wharf building on the harbour, attended by hundreds of the fashionable set. The champagne was flowing and the speeches had started. They were rather longer than I would have wished, but there were plenty of interesting celebrities and A-listers to observe. As I stood there towards the back, I noticed the late arrival of a diminutive young woman in a tight long pink dress who squeezed in front of me. I would not wish for anyone to think of me as licentious, but I couldn't help but notice, due to the tightness of the pink silk following the curve of the body, this young woman could not possibly be wearing any underwear. Just as I was wrestling with the thought, the speeches ended and everyone applauded.

The young woman in question stepped back and in doing so her high stiletto sank deep into my toe. I let out a yelp and instinctively brought my hands up. In doing so I created a Benny Hill moment and my hands landed on her bottom. In a split second she turned around with gushing apologies, "I am so sorry, I didn't mean to tread on you. Are you OK?"

My embarrassment at the brief manhandling was compounded as before me was the smiling and rather beautiful Kylie Minogue. I realised that I had just touched what was probably the most famous derriere in the world, and Kylie was the one apologising. When we did in fact meet again, thankfully for me this was never mentioned. Kylie and her sister, Danni Minogue, stayed at the hotel from time to time. At these times she was not the sweet little songbird but looked like a very impressive young business woman. She and Danni both had their acts together commercially. [74,75]

The Minogue girls' musical style was not of my generation. I enjoyed their music but preferred that of some of our other guests in those early years: Phil Collins [79] was and still is at the top of my list, followed by 70s greats Thelma Houston [82]and Chaka Khan[81]. Then there was Randy Crawford [80] who stayed, whose *Rainy Night in Georgia* was my romantic favourite back in the day. It was historical to meet Helen Reddy, the Melbourne girl whose song *I Am Woman* launched the second wave of feminism and became its anthem. They were gracious lovely women.

I had also been a fan of Cilla Black since my teens. I knew the words of *Anyone Who Had a Heart* and *You're My World* off by heart. Her down-to-earth Liverpudlian accent with catch phrases like *"Lorra lorra laughs"* had endeared her to her many fans. I had these thoughts in mind as I stood excitedly at the door for her arrival. She swept in. It was the middle of an Australian summer, it was 30 degrees Celsius, and Cilla was wearing a floor length mink coat. I put my hand out in welcome and all I got was "I hope you have put me in a nice suite!"

Where was the Liverpudlian smile and greeting? Where was everybody's sweetheart? During her stay, her mood and her approach were aloof.

I admit I was never a great fan of Tom Jones' music but he had remained at the top of his game, especially with those original fans who were now 40 years on and still throwing their underwear at him on stage. I preferred his theme song to James Bond's *Thunderball*. He was a genuinely warm person, with that wonderful Welsh accent. I had arrived just in time to greet him, as I'd been to pick up my son, Tim, from Scots College. He'd been doing his cadets, so was still in the uniform which included a kilt. He hated wearing it and was not enthusiastic about the cadets as they only had wooden rifles. As I stood chatting with Tom Jones, and PR waited to get a photo of him, Tom noticed Tim hovering behind me. "Who's this?"

I introduced my son. "Nice to meet you, that's a nice kilt, do you know the tartan?" said Tom.

Tim, I discovered, hadn't a clue. Neither, for that matter, had I. To help save face Tom followed up quickly with "That's the Black Watch if I'm not mistaken." We agreed with relief. [83]

> "Come on, let's have a photo," he said. He was a really nice guy, happy to sign autographs and pose for photos with whoever asked. And with the age demographics of The Observatory skewing baby boomer, there were many requests.

Neil Diamond and Elvis Costello stayed with us, as did Ronan Keating who had survived the boy band era to become a star in his own right. He was a fresh faced young man and when I saw him sitting at the bar, my first reaction was *Is he old enough to drink?* He had a large, very expensive cigar in hand, but was not enjoying it as a cigar aficionado might be expected to do. After a few puffs he placed it in the ashtray and did not pick it up again. It remained there until he left, when a young female member of staff, obviously a fan, tidied up, and discreetly retained the cigar as a keepsake.

It was thrilling to welcome the very elegant Marina Prior, the soprano who starred as the first Aussie Christine in the premiere of *The Phantom of the Opera* opposite Anthony Warlow in Sydney.

My most memorable musical interlude was the very individual, very *different* Nigel Kennedy. He was born in Brighton into a musical family. His grandparents were Australian, and he was a musical prodigy. At the age of 7, he became a violin pupil at the Yehudi Menuhin School of Music, one of the greatest violinists of the 20th century. As Kennedy's talents became recognised, his persona was out of step with other classical musicians. He developed a punk image and had a *mockney* accent, instead of the rather *posh* accent he'd been brought up with. The establishment rather disapproved, but he opened up the classics to his younger fans - no one could ignore his incredible talent. To add to it, he became an ardent Aston Villa supporter.[84]

The Observatory became his home in Sydney. He always had the same suite, where the temperature and humidity had to be tightly controlled, much to the concern of the chief engineer, Charlie Dodsworth and later Janusz Zaklikowski. It was not his own comfort he was concerned with, but that of his violin, a Stradivarius Cabriac, a beautiful antique string instrument worth over $3,500,000. We all lived in fear of any accident that might befall the violin whilst under our roof.

He was always entertaining, if occasionally difficult to handle, especially when he insisted on lighting up a joint at breakfast.

Whenever he arrived I would go out to say hello. He never shook hands, but gave me the fist-bump greeting. I found this amusing but not as much as the staff did, who watched me trying to be hip and stifled their laughter. The knuckles were accompanied by "Or'right Pat" or "Wotcha Griff", in his humorous mockney accent.

One morning I happened to glance at the security screen that covered the lift lobby on the third floor. Opposite the suite in which Nigel was staying I noticed a mass of people standing around, with some even sitting on the floor. I assumed the lifts had got stuck and the guests were now trapped on the third floor. The concierge checked but the lifts were fine. I went to investigate and as the doors 'pinged' opened on the third floor, I was greeted by fifteen pairs of irate eyes glaring at me, as if my mobile had rung during a funeral. People were sitting in the lobby chairs, on the floor, propping up walls, all as silent as church mice listening to the strains of a violin playing unbelievably sweetly through the door from Nigel Kennedy's suite, as he practiced for his performance at the Opera House. I didn't dare call the lift again, so I joined my guests and we enjoyed a very upfront and personal performance from the maestro. Eventually there was silence, and, not wanting to miss anything in case he continued, everyone stayed put. The door of his suite opened and a head popped round the door and said, with a cheeky smile, "Or' right then - was that OK?" and disappeared. His audience breathed out as if someone had released the pause button, and we all departed about our business.

Not all our guests shared the same admiration for Mr Kennedy. Ernesto, our cheerful breakfast man who greeted all our guests each morning, told me the tale of Madeleine Albright, politician, diplomat and the first female Secretary of State in U.S. history who served under President Bill Clinton. She was quietly enjoying her breakfast, when Nigel and friends turned up, having been drinking heavily the night before after his last performance at the Opera House. He and his friends sat at the table next to Mrs Albright and, as he made himself comfortable, there was an enormously loud sound of breaking wind, much to the hilarity of Mr Kennedy and Co. Mrs Albright, as the diplomat she was, politely excused herself from the table and immediately left the room.

The daily hotel reports provide the eye-witness 'Adventures of Nigel in Sydney'.

1) Some guests were playing tennis across the road and came to the concierge to complain that someone was throwing soap at them. Mr Kennedy was hiding on his balcony and Michael Anderson, the Chief Concierge, went out and told him off from Kent Street.
2) I was coming to start my breakfast shift. Went to the front office to collect my float, on the way back to Galileo I saw a body on the floor next to the fireplace. Nigel Kennedy was sleeping! I asked him Nigel you should go to bed. His only answer, No. It's nice and warm here.
3) One day early in the morning the garbage truck driver came to Galileo and said

'I'm trying to empty the garbage bins in the loading dock but there is a car and someone's sleeping in it'. Nigel Kennedy had once again failed to make his bedroom!

4) Turning up after a late night on the tiles, driving a convertible Saab without much of a front end left....and the taxi he T-Boned followed him to our front doorstep.
5) One morning Mr Kennedy lit up a huge joint before breakfast right outside Galileo entry in the foyer. I knew PLG would

be along shortly so we ushered him up to Observatory Hill. So that was his 'spot' from then onwards.

For Ernesto and his team, it was 'just another day at the office'.

There's a lot of drama behind the scenes in a busy hotel. With a hotel like The Observatory with a name and reputation to protect, our team was outstanding with their discreet professionalism, which maintained the atmosphere of a calm and peaceful haven that our guests expected. To this end, it was very much like watching a swan glide across a lake. Above the water, to those watching, all is serene and graceful. But we were paddling furiously underneath.

The hotel's day to day operations ran smoothly, thanks to The Observatory's skilled people, from the doorman to the kitchen staff. Most of the furious paddling was caused by the misbehaviour of our guests. Our staff protected the guests and their reputations from themselves.

As part of hotel security, the duty log is completed by the manager on duty, confirming that the various checks are done, such as checking fire systems and boilers. It also includes notable events that occur during their shift. Some were concerning, some were amusing and some were just unbelievable.

- **4.00pm** - Lady patron enters the Globe Bar for afternoon tea - asked for two cream teas, assuming she was being joined by a friend. Tea is served and an argument ensues between the lady and her invisible guest David. Her voice became raised and she became abusive. Duty staff suggested that she and her 'friend' may wish to take their tea in a quieter corner of the lounge. She apologized for 'David's' behaviour, she and 'David' were happily re settled.

The mail when delivered was sorted by the porters and distributed to the relevant staff or guests.

- **10.00am** - Post collected and sorted - one letter had no name. Opened by th`e secretary, who was shocked to discover two polaroids of a very explicit bedroom action between a lady and gentleman. Enquiries made at the concierge who happened to recognise the envelope and the writing to that of similar letters that had regularly arrived that week for a female guest.

The woman was easily identified from the photos. It was decided that to save any embarrassment to the young woman, we should not deliver the letter as it had now been opened, and we would destroy it. We assume that it had been sent by her adoring husband, who I am certain would not have *dreamed* in a million years that anyone else would have opened it. It was rather difficult to look the young woman in the eye for the rest of her stay.

In 2000 Sydney hosted the Olympic Games. We accommodated the eminent American lawyer Robert Shapiro, who had become a household name in defending O.J.Simpson at his murder trial.

- **9.00am** - Request from Mr Shapiro, for a meeting room today. He had freely commented that with the dangers of the doping scandals that the purpose was to conduct a brief legal seminar for those athletes who may be interested. Arranged Boardroom 300. Please advise the concierge should there be any request from outside guests.

A number of athletes turned up, among them Marion Lois Jones, a world champion in track and field athletics and a former professional basketball player. She won three gold medals and two bronze medals at the Sydney Olympics, but was later stripped of the medals after she admitted to taking steroids. Obviously she did not heed Mr. Shapiro's advice.

- **3.00pm** - Call from a guest who departed this morning - on arriving home he opened his suitcase to find a snake inside - asked if we had lost one - he didn't seem worried. Had a call an hour later saying he had spoken to Ansett Airlines, who told him that yes, they had in fact lost a python.

I am full of admiration for the night staff and the issues they faced. During the day there is always a full team of managers, heads of departments and all the support that might be called upon, but the night staff were comprised only two or three at most. Of course it was the night shift that tended to have the more unusual events to deal with, whether it be through the imbibing of excess liquor or a full moon. The morning reports often made for an interesting read.

- **8.00pm** - Call from the room attendant, asking me to go to Room 118 occupied by very regular guest Mr ****, seeking advice as to what he should do in regards to 'turn down'.

- I attended, on entering the room I discovered …

1) A bright canary yellow PVC sheet spread across bed
2) A number of shoulder length PVC veterinarian gloves, in various fashionable colours
3) Numerous unwrapped condoms strategically placed about the room
4) Selection of pornographic videos, and
5) A tube (drum) of KY jelly lubricant,

I instructed staff to leave the room and treat it as a DND

Which of course means do not disturb, so staff would not enter the room. The night manager also added a wry post script:

OK, who told the wackos that I was back on night duty?

We had CCTV monitors which recorded events during the night, resulting in quite a collection of unique and potentially lucrative candid camera moments. To the staff's credit, nothing ever leaked.

- **1.00am** - Alarm on rear South fire exit, checked camera and found two people in laneway with what appeared to be a TV and video recorder and placed in the car. Fire door closed behind them and they could not reenter the hotel. Thought it might be a break in. Went to investigate and met the people coming through the main entrance and into the lift (guests from 210!) Guests called down minutes later claiming someone had entered their room while they were out and stolen their stuff! Went to their room and found TV and video also missing, and in addition they claimed jewelry and cash was missing along with an expensive watch! I advised them I would contact the police. Returned to the office and reviewed CCTV, and took lock reading. Guests had returned to their room at 9.23pm confirmed by CCTV and no record of leaving. Police arrived. Book 'em Danno! Guests departed with the police who will get back to us today.

Whilst in Asia on one occasion, I found a vendor selling fake but very good looking Mont Blanc pens. I could not help but purchase several to use at reception for guests signing in. I had been very impressed when I first saw them used at George Rafael's hotel in Munich (now the Mandarin Oriental), except that his pens were genuine. Most guests however had no idea and were simply impressed at such extravagance.

- **6.00pm** - Noticed a pen was missing - reviewed the security tape, and surprised to see Mr **** (*very well-known and wealthy businessman*) sign in, looked at the pen with interest, looked about him and then discreetly placed it in his top pocket. He then nonchalantly left for his room. Not happy! Could not believe that a man of his wealth would pinch our pen. I called him in his room and much to his surprise, I apologised and suggested that he may have *inadvertently* taken our Mont Blanc pen on signing in. He was most apologetic and confessed but he had done so without thinking! I explained how easy it was to make such a mistake when his mind was obviously so full with high finance issues etc. He returned the pen.

A few years later, he was found guilty of various financial irregularities and subsequently served time in one of our State's fine institutions proving that a leopard never changes its spots.

- **11.30pm** - Table of 3rd floor lobby found broken along with flower vase and flowers - From the camera it appears that a husband wished to take a photo of his young, rather 'buxom', bride posing on the antique pedestal table beside the arrangement of flowers. Just as she was draped across the table in a seductive pose, the table collapsed under her weight. In sheer panic they looked about to see if they had been observed and I assume suspecting not, they vanished into their suite - Await instruction - do we charge? (GM's Note - We didn't)

It was not unusual for a guest, always for some reason male, to step straight out of a shower or whilst getting changed, to absent-mindedly step outside their room to pick up a newspaper, or shoes left outside or to push their dinner trolley outside their bedroom door, only to find the door had closed behind them. This was not an easy situation for the guest to resolve without drawing attention. The lifts operated on a key system and the only floor to be accessed without a key was the hotel lobby. The only other alternative was to head to the fire escape. Once in the fire escape the only way out was to the street, all doors being designed for egress only. It was always interesting as to how innovative some could be when finding themselves in such a predicament. One guest was reported as appearing with two 'wet paint' signs appropriately positioned, whilst another utilised the dinner plates from his trolley.

A very well known Aussie TV celebrity found himself in just this predicament, when putting his room service tray out in the corridor. He of course was in his birthday suit. We had a great chuckle when viewing the CCTV footage the next morning as he ducked and weaved through the hotel, stark naked, before eventually making his way down to the day spa, where, from the refuge of the lift, he called to the staff to pass him a bathrobe.

In the following days a number of photos circulated amongst the young staff who were most impressed by the man's very fine *gluteus maximus*. These photos were confiscated, and kept under lock and key. The man will remain nameless as he went on to become a household name in Australia. I leave the reader to make their own deductions from the photo included.[85]

- **1.00am:** I heard a banging on the inside of the centre lobby fire escape door - eventually to his good fortune I discovered a gentleman naked (as always a gentleman), very embarrassed and attempting to cover his modesty with an A4 sign he had found in the stairwell reading 'IN the EVENT of

> EMERGENCY', not exactly the emergency we had in mind. He sheltered in my office until I found him a bathrobe. Escorted him back to his room. He was very grateful.

A well-known society lady had been hitting it hard one night.

- Mrs **** returned to the hotel in a taxi with hubby - possible disagreement - he was not happy? (she had left the hotel with her husband for a function earlier in the evening - looking very elegant.) Taxi driver called management for assistance - the lady attempted to get out but unable to do so, collapsed and lay prone on the pavement. I attended and assisted the husband to lift her but she was a dead weight and incoherent. Husband, not amused stating 'she's pissed, leave her' and left - I paid the cabbie, and with the porter's help managed to carry her inside. Husband had gone to bed. I decided to make her comfortable in an armchair in the lobby so as to keep an eye on her, concerned that in her state she may be taken ill. Husband later came down and collected her.

The following morning there was of course no mention of the events the night before, the only surprise being that she was able to make it down to breakfast at all - albeit very late. Some photos from these crazy nights are included, but the subjects cannot be identified, in keeping with our discretion policy. [86, 87]

I was always proud of the level of diplomacy that my team displayed. Brendon Fellows told me of this classic example.

> "There was an awkward moment I had with a guest today. I was escorting the guest to their room. She had a large suitcase I was carrying. As I followed the young woman into the lift, I put the bag down to select the floor number. As I did so a loud buzzing started to resonate from the bag. I looked down at the bag and

then at the guest. She was very red faced, so I said to her 'toothbrush?' to which she replied 'toothbrush'. We didn't have much of a conversation after that as she was quick to get rid of me once we reached her room, I'm guessing to deal with her misbehaving 'toothbrush'."

We were very pleased when a member of a royal family from the Middle East chose to stay with us. With his entourage, he took over two floors of the hotel for ten days, a great revenue earner that brought the month in over budget. I was even more delighted when he wished to extend for another week or two. I assumed this had to be a reflection on the excellent facilities and service we offered. I was brought back to earth with a thump however when I learned that the prince allegedly had succumbed to a less than desirable social disease and found it desirable to delay his return home to ensure his indiscretions would not be discovered by his wives.

Our staff were the souls of discretion. We prided ourselves on our ability to recognise our regular guests. It helped being a small hotel and computers helped even more. In an instant we had the guest's customer history at our fingertips. One gentleman loved the hotel and was a regular, however there were the odd occasions when he would arrive with a different *wife*. To avoid any embarrassment, we agreed to his request that he should always be treated as a first time guest, however often he might visit.

Another guest, Mr X, arrived with a woman partner in a rather impressive sports car, and flamboyantly tossed the keys to the porter requesting it be parked. That morning was rather busy and it took longer than usual. A short while later an irate woman came in and asked for the room number of her husband, Mr X. Obviously not the lady who'd arrived in the sports car. Our quick-thinking receptionist advised the woman that we had no

Mr X and would not be able to give out information on a guest in any case. The woman challenged this, declaring she knew her husband was here as she had seen his car parked outside. On overhearing this exchange, the front office manager retreated to the back office and called Mr X advising him of the escalating situation. With a note of panic in his voice, the guest asked if he might exit by a back entrance. It was arranged but his wife was making it quite clear that she would remain in the lobby until her husband appeared.

A few minutes after his escape from the rear of the hotel, the woman who was his wife had established her observation point from the comfort of the lobby. Mr X calmly walked back into the hotel through the front door. Upon seeing his wife, before she could say a word he challenged her as to what she was doing in the hotel and who was she waiting for? A little taken aback, she asked him why he was there when he was meant to be in Melbourne? He explained with irritation that he had had to delay his flight to collect some papers from an office nearby, and had used the convenience of the hotel to leave his car for an hour. His confidence in acting out this scenario would have impressed any Hollywood producer, but as they departed the wife looked far from convinced.

The first woman who had arrived with Mr X appeared later rather sheepishly in the lobby with two cases, one which she left with the concierge for Mr X to collect at a later date. Whether he convinced his wife we shall never know, as the last we saw of Mr X was a fast retrieval of his bag on his return from Melbourne the following day.

While royalty and rock stars always caused a flurry amongst staff at The Observatory, it was when a sporting celebrity stayed that there was always a extra interest, whether the person was Australian or not.

We were fortunate to be the only Sydney hotel to have its own tennis court. It actually belonged to the Millers Point Community, however we became the custodians and maintained it perfectly. It was a beautiful little court at the front of the hotel, carved out of the rock of Observatory Hill. It came complete with its own timber clubhouse. [88]

Many guests used it, including Olivia Newton-John who enjoyed a game, but it was particularly exciting to see the trademark moustache of John Newcombe, who one day turned up to play. I watched him play with his usual style, the only audience to watch his game that day. How different it was to the previous occasion in 1971 with a capacity crowd at Centre Court Wimbledon, when I was fortunate to have a seat, courtesy of my then wife, to watch John Newcombe play Stan Smith of the USA. I confess I supported Stan, but that didn't help him as Newcombe won the trophy for the third time.

Other tennis greats who came to the hotel included Pat Rafter, Lleyton Hewitt and the brilliant doubles team, known as the Two 'Woodys' [89]

In 2002 Lleyton filmed a humorous TV commercial for Sorbent toilet paper in the hotel's Drawing Room. The commercial was screened during the Australian Open tennis competition, and Sorbent sales increased markedly, grabbing a 28% share of the Australian toilet paper market. The commercial was created by Clemenger Communications and Wikipedia states - incorrectly - that it was shot in Melbourne.

There were of course the swimmers who were attracted to the hotel's magnificent pool, Hayley Lewis and Kieren Perkins among them. It was rather hilarious for 'the largest subterranean swimming pool in the Southern Hemisphere' to host a shoal of medal winning swimmers, Hayley Lewis, Glen Housman, Andrew Baildon and Elli Overton wearing not their streamlined speedos but their uber-kitsch Chux Superwipe and GLAD Wavetop Tie Bag costumes at the launch of National Foods sponsorship of 1994 Commonwealth Games.[90] Oh dear. The things we do.

Cricketers came and went: Mitchell Johnson the brilliant left-arm fast bowler, the legend, Allan Border, captain for many years of the Australian team, and one of the greatest of all, Sachin Tendulkar, captain of the Indian national team, regarded as one of the greatest batsmen of all time. I was in the lobby when he departed, alongside a famous Bollywood film star, Hrithik Roshan. Tendulkar joined me for a photo and as he turned to leave, "Do you like cricket?" Readers will know I am not a great fan of the game; it was ruined for me on the fields of my prep-school when a boy. So, naturally, I lied. "I love the game!" [91]

What else could I say? Much to my surprise, he lobbed a cricket ball across the lobby in my direction. With more luck than judgement, my hand shot out, more in self-defence than anything else, but I caught the ball! "Good catch!" he said. I smiled nervously, amazed at my success. The ball was signed, a prize I still display with pride today.

We hosted Dermott Brereton, professional Aussie Rules football player, regarded as one of the greatest players of his generation, although I still could not understand the game. We had our share of 'revheads', including Peter Brock, otherwise known as 'Peter Perfect", "The King of the Mountain", or simply "Brocky", one of Australia's best-known and most successful motor racing drivers, and David Coulthard, known as DC, a British (Scottish) Formula One racing driver and winner of thirteen Grand Prix. [92]

Just to mix it up, Bondy's mate John Bertrand turned up, and yachting enthusiasts would know he was the guy who skippered Australia II to victory in the 1983 America's Cup, ending 132 years of American wins. Jayne Torvill and Christopher Dean stayed, simply known as 'Torvill & Dean' the British ice dancers and former British, European, Olympic and World champions. They brought *Boléro*, the classical orchestral piece by the French composer Maurice Ravel, to the top of the music charts. [93]

My favourite celebrity guests were the adventurers, the people who had done something extraordinary. It may have been by design or by accident, but to me they were the most courageous. They were the 'stars' of my childhood and it was a privilege to meet people who had defied the odds and survived great challenges.

In my early hotel days at The Cavendish in Eastbourne I had met Norman Jackson VC, a real war hero. Then in the 70s at the De Montfort I met the Robertson family whose book *Survive the Savage Sea* was made into a film. They survived for 38 days aboard their small dinghy in the Pacific Ocean, battling storms, hunger, thirst, danger and death, after their yacht sank following an attack by killer whales. Around the same time we hosted the paratrooper, Capt. John Ridgway who, with Chay Blyth in 1966, rowed across the Atlantic from North America in a 20 foot dory. After 92 days at sea, around 3,000 miles later, they reached Ireland. During this epic journey they had braved two hurricanes, vicious storms, huge waves, and whales bigger than their boat, not to mention fatigue, damage and lost rations caused by Hurricane Alma.

Now at The Observatory we welcomed Sir Edmund Hillary on more than one occasion. For my generation in England in the 1950s, Hillary and Tenzing Norgay were heroes. As a schoolboy I had avidly followed his Everest expedition. We all thought of Hillary as an Englishman, there was no mention of New Zealand. In those days everyone in the Commonwealth was British, especially if they were heroic adventurers. At the time the role that Tenzing played was not heralded in the same way as Hillary's: he was seen as 'only' a sherpa to aid Hillary. Thankfully we have tried to correct the old empire neglect. Hillary was, however, not the most outgoing of people. I suppose if you spend your life surviving in the rarefied air in the mountains of Nepal, small talk and chit chat doesn't rate very highly. [94]

I met another climber, who - although not *quite* in the same league as Hillary - was more interesting. A journalist I knew from a major UK newspaper asked if we might be interested in a sponsorship. He explained that there was a man who was suffering from multiple sclerosis who had set himself the task of climbing a mountain on every continent while he still could, to raise awareness of the disease. In Australia he was to climb Mount Kosciuszko, mainland Australia's highest mountain. At 2,228 metres an incredible challenge for a fit man, let alone one suffering from MS. I had no hesitation in sponsoring as this was truly admirable, particularly when I was told that he came from the English town of Kenilworth, the town where I had lived for many years and where I held my first general manager's job at the De Montfort Hotel. He would be travelling with his wife and would it be possible for me to greet them?

The morning of their arrival, the receptionist knocked on my door to tell me my guests had arrived, and I could see from her expression that something was amiss. "What is it?"

> "I am not sure if we have the booking correct, but they are waiting for you. I'm sure it's OK."

I was completely puzzled but I didn't want to keep my guests waiting. In the lobby I was met by the journalist, who looked uncomfortable as he shook my hand, "I'm sorry I had no idea ..." What was going on?

My guests were signing in, and my brain did somersaults. I saw two women at the desk. I greeted one of them, then the other one turned around and instead of the rugged mountaineer I had expected, I was looking at a man in a wig and a dress. Being uncertain as to how to address 'her' I was pleased when a hand was offered with a firm grip and a smile, "Hello Mr Griffin, I'm *****, I don't believe we have met but I gather you managed the De Montfort Hotel, which of course I know well."

The mountaineer had discovered that he identified as a woman and wished to be referred to as Ms. rather than Mr. His wife was in full acceptance. We were more than happy to have them stay as our guests. This was nothing unusual for Sydney, home of one of the most vibrant LGBTQI communities in the world. I was more worried about how his straight-laced English upper class readership might handle his story back in England. Anyone walking out in public dressed in this manner in Kenilworth would have made the front page of the *Kenilworth News.*

They were a lovely couple. He was even more to be admired in my eyes; even with the challenging disability of MS and his attempt to climb a mountain, he was at one with his own gender identification and sexuality. (I can't help but hope that he wore sensible heels for the ascent.)

Compared to this man, my other hero might even seem to be less adventurous. I admired Edward 'Buzz' Aldrin - not Buzz Lightyear as a friend's child asked me recently. This was the real Buzz, who I watched with bated breath on a flickering black and white TV as he stepped onto the moon in 1969. I met him at The Como in Melbourne and again at The Observatory. He was a hero to me, although I cannot say he was the warmest of individuals. He was rather grumpy and even declined to sign the 'Golden Book'. I suppose his signatures were sought after by collectors who would sell them for a high price. [95]

Other astronauts stayed with us, due to our relationship with the Sydney Observatory perched on the hill overlooking the hotel. We had a visit from Sally Ride, the first American woman to go into space on the shuttle Challenger in 1983, and K. Megan McArthur, an astronaut and oceanographer, who was the Mission Specialist aboard STS-125, the final shuttle mission to the Hubble Telescope. [96, 97]

The other type of adventurers I admired were photographers, who could take me on an around the world from the comfort of my sofa.

American portrait photographer Annie Leibovitz was our guest, who produced iconic photos such as Demi Moore naked and pregnant on the cover of *Vanity Fair*, and a naked John Lennon embracing Yoko Ono. This haunting photo was of profound significance as later that evening, John was shot and killed outside his New York City apartment. I liked the photo of the actress Whoopi Goldberg in a bath of milk, who in her true comedic style had slipped at the moment the photo was taken.

The photographer who impressed me most was Patrick Lichfield or more correctly named 'Thomas Patrick John Anson, 5th Earl of Lichfield', a cousin to the Queen. He photographed the Royal Family but was best known for his society photos in the 1960s and 70s of models, rock stars and film legends. I had a call from his publicist who asked if I would host a small lunch gathering, for no more than ten, which I was of course very happy to do for such a celeb.

During lunch, Lichfield held forth on the subject of photography and had the entire table spellbound. He spoke of the new digital age of photography and how he had embraced it. I asked him about his famous Pirelli Calendar of models that had hung on my wall year after year. He told of a famous models he had to photograph in the desert outside Las Vegas and what a nightmare it had been: heat, dust and all the desert could throw at them, along with the models' temperaments. Now he was photographing models in front of a green screen and simply adding in a tropical beach, a jungle, a snow-capped mountain or a desert. So much easier and cheaper.

He told of the time he was taking photos of a particularly difficult Hollywood diva, whom he refused to name. Having spent all day trying to get it just right, he returned to his studio. He had to show her the results the following morning. He developed the film and made sample prints, and was back in her suite first thing. She took the photos out of the envelope and laid them on a table. She occasionally picked one up to examine more closely.

After an eternity of expressionless silence she turned to him with a large warm smile, "Perfect. Absolutely wonderful. You have managed to capture me exactly. I love them."

He was surprised at her reaction; she was never as enthusiastic as this. When he returned to his studio he looked at the photos again. What might have garnered such a favourable reaction? He looked again. Ah. He had printed all the photos back to front, resulting in a 'mirror' image! She'd been looking at a photo that was identical to the image she saw every time she looked in a mirror. From that day on he always reversed his portraits of women.

He believed that photos in the 90s were all touched up; people were made to look thinner, musclier, without blemishes. No photo was a true likeness anymore, according to him. He said he refused to photograph people who had had too much botox, as he felt any character in the face had been lost. "Might as well photograph a dummy."

My father had been a very keen photographer and I wished he had been alive to witness the age of technology and to hear Lichfield's tales. I put the photographer on my list of most interesting lunch guests. Just twelve months later he died at the young age of 66 and was buried in the family vault in Colwich, Staffordshire, England. [98]

At the top of my lunch list was Alan Whicker.

I had sat glued to the TV screen in my youth, watching this man with his distinctive nasal delivery, who'd been lampooned most notably by Monty Python. He appeared in a starched collar, tie and blazer wherever he was, on a beach or in a palace. He interviewed millionaires and monks, cowboys and comics, with or without money, from the notorious, despotic Haitian dictator 'Papa Doc' Duvalier, to Peter Sellers, Joan Collins, writer Harold Robbins and the Sultan of Brunei, all of whom subjected themselves to his courteous but penetrating style of questioning.

I was excited to meet the man, and we clicked. I hosted a small reception for him, and thought that was it. The next day, however, he asked if I would care to join him for lunch with an old friend, Len Evans, one of the most influential men in the wine industry and credited with putting Australian wines on the world stage. Len was described as *'an English-born Australian promoter, maker, judge, taster, teacher and drinker of wine'*. I knew of him but had never met him, so I readily accepted the invitation. We drove up to the Len's vineyard home in the Hunter Valley, a beautiful place more in keeping with the Dordogne in France, than the open spaces of New South Wales. Len lived up to his reputation; he was lots of fun and a real Aussie larrikin.

Over lunch, Alan's own sense of fun came to the fore. I had watched him on TV over the years: charming, articulate, always polite and the epitome of a perfect English gentleman. I asked him, "When did you know you had reached the pinnacle of success?" He thought for a moment then, looking through his trademark horn rimmed glasses, said in his perfect English accent,

"When I got my 'fuck off' money"

I had never even heard him say 'damn'! Here was a doyen of BBC broadcasting swearing like a trooper.

"Sorry?" Had I misheard?

"It was when I realised I had sufficient money in the bank that when the BBC asked me to go out to some godforsaken place to interview some crazy despot, I could turn around to them and simply tell them to fuck off."

I was still laughing when we arrived back in Sydney hours later. My mother would have been horrified, along with most other English viewers who were enthralled each week by Mr Whicker, the epitome of the English gentleman. How impressed she would have been to read the invitation he sent to me to stay with he and his partner, Valerie, at their home in Jersey. How I regretted not taking him up on his kind offer, as he died in 2013. [99, 100]

My friendship with Len blossomed and he often took me along for lunch in some of the better restaurants in Sydney, always picking up the bill, if there was one. You could be sure the bill always included a bottle of Penfolds Grange. God bless you Len.

Our next guest was ironically the aforementioned impersonator of Alan Whicker. The sketch satirised "Whicker's World" and became "Whicker Island" - a tropical island paradise where all the inhabitants have Alan Whicker suits, glasses and microphones. Of course it was Sir Michael Palin, the English comedian, actor, writer and television presenter. Originally a member of Monty Python, he had since the 80s became well known for his travel documentaries. He had a very different personality to Alan, but always had a smile that signalled the humorous adlib that would pop out. He was warm, relaxed and friendly, in an open neck shirt and jeans. His only jacket was a rather crumpled casual one. [101]

Sir David Frost had the style of Alan Whicker, and was better known around the world. I had met him forty years ago, and in those intervening years David Frost has gone from being a comedian to one of the most respected television hosts and journalists of his time. He interrogated the biggest names of the 20th century, including John Lennon, Henry Kissinger, and George W. Bush but his most famous interview was with Richard Nixon in 1977, when he attempted to get a full confession from him about his knowledge of the Watergate scandal that brought down his presidency. He didn't confess but David did record an apology to the American people. He then packaged and sold the interview to nearly every country in the world, and achieved the largest audience for a news interview in the history of television.[102]

Strangely, his chat with me was never made into a film. We did fit in a photo opp, and I was amused with the instructions he gave as to how best to present myself. "When they take your photo you must laugh, as your facial expression looks so much better, just try it." We stood there waiting for the photographer to take the shots. I had no idea how difficult it would be to stand there and appear sincere, laughing maniacally at nothing, until the instant the camera shutter clicked. This might explain why he always seemed to have a fixed pose in all his photos. I am still trying to perfect this piece of invaluable advice from one of the world's greatest interviewers.

What made this re-encounter with David Frost significant to me was that I had met him at the start of my career, a young 21-year-old assistant manager at the Castle Hotel in Norwich. Now I was meeting him shortly before my retirement. He died too early at the age of 74.

Hindsight is a wondrous thing. In the early 1990s, we had rather a nutty professor stay at the hotel. He'd talk about what was happening to the planet and a strange thing called global warming. We had great respect for him as a scientist, but thought he was over the top with his doom and gloom predictions. Boy did we get it wrong. The scientist was David Suzuki, a Canadian academic, science broadcaster and environmental activist and of course he was right. I can hear the news right now in 2020 reporting that the Australian bushfires have burned 5.9 million hectares (15 million acres), destroyed over 2,500 buildings (including over 1,300 homes) and killed at least 22 people. A billion animals have lost their habitat, and in Indonesia they're suffering worst floods in decades. Ecological disasters around the world are now scientifically attributed to global warming. David Suzuki must be shaking his white-haired head in despair as he hears our leaders continue to deny there is any such thing as global warming. [103]

The last guest of this special group wears many hats; adventurer, TV presenter, and also an environmental activist and conservationist: Sir David Attenborough, whose unique voice and style was mimicked even more than Alan Whicker's. Sir David was rather reserved. On farewelling him, I said effusively, "Sir David, I do hope you have enjoyed your stay. I have been an avid fan of your work and what you did to bring nature into our homes, thank you."

His response was not quite what I expected. He glared at me and replied, "What I *did*? I assure you I will continue to do so. I'm not dead yet you know!" I was rather lost for words and could think of nothing that might lift me out of the hole I had dug myself into. He has indeed continued his work and I am still a great admirer of his ongoing series *Blue Planet*. [104]

We hosted several authors in my time. The first was in our early days at The Observatory - and it wasn't the best experience. Judith Krantz was described as 'a Jewish-American novelist who writes in the romance genre', a 'thinking girl's Barbara Cartland'. She was warm enough on her arrival, but when she departed the hotel, I asked her how she had enjoyed her stay. She snapped back "Well let's say your hotel will never be featured in any of my books!"

I never got to the bottom of this stinging rebuke. She wouldn't expand on her comment and neither could the staff shed light on what might have prompted it. We never did appear in one of her books, but I am happy to include her in mine.

Among the happier authors who stayed were Thomas Keneally, most famous for *Schindler's List*. Tara Moss stayed, a Canadian-Australian documentary maker and presenter, former model and prolific author of crime fiction with eleven best sellers to her credit. Matthew Brace, unlike Judith Krantz, *did* include us in his book *Hotel Heaven* and what a great read it was. We became good friends.

I got to know Colleen McCullough, best known for *The Thorn Birds* which was made into a television miniseries in 1983, with a cast of stars including Richard Chamberlain, Barbara Stanwyck, Christopher Plummer, Jean Simmons and Australia's Rachel Ward and Bryan Brown. Rachel Ward and Bryan Brown were married in real life and, being Sydney based, were often to be found in the hotel. *The Thorn Birds* is special as it was the first Australian program I'd seen, and I was glued to the TV from the first episode.

The publicist who booked Colleen into the hotel had warned us that she could be very difficult and feisty. It was therefore with a little trepidation that I approached her to enquire about her stay. She was in the same suite that Judith Krantz had hated, and I really did not want to jeopardize the opportunity of an inclusion in one of Colleen McCullough's novels.

I found it hard to believe she had such a reputation. She was warm, friendly and funny, especially when I told her of the significance of *The Thorn Birds* to me. She told me that she had been under a lot of pressure to write a sequel, which she never did.

This friendship led to her returning to the hotel, when she and I would often chat over breakfast. She was aging and her sight was going but she loved the comfort and old-world charm of The Observatory. I was to meet her twice more away from the hotel when our paths crossed in other hotels when we were travelling. On her last visit to the hotel, she gave me her latest novel and on the fly-leaf had inscribed, *"For Patrick L Griffin. Dear Patrick, May we always keep meeting this way! How about Hong Kong next time? Warmest regards, Colleen McCullough."* A truly great lady and a brilliant author.

It was early after opening that we realised very few people used our much-lauded subterranean pool. This became an ongoing headache. We could have saved the money it cost to build and simply advertised a pool with nice photos in our brochure, telling people it was closed for maintenance if they asked to use it. We could have settled out of court with any disgruntled guests, and still come out ahead. The 'Health & Leisure Club' contained only men early in the morning doing a work out before going off to work. For the rest of the day it was empty, the beautiful costly pool shimmering with hardly a ripple. We needed to find a way to attract more guests and get some return on the health club.

I had no idea what to do. Our 'big idea' that was to change everything came about by chance.

We had joined an American marketing organisation called API, so we could tap into the US market. Each year they would hold a Travel Mart in different locations around the world. In 1997, I went to the luxurious Phoenician Hotel in Scottsdale, Arizona for the event. I remember it well as Princess Diana had died in Paris and it filled all the US TV channels 24 hours a day. I sat watching TV in my room on a free afternoon, and read the hotel information folder. There was a list of the hotel's facilities and things to do. One suggestion was to visit their spa. *The Phoenician Spa rises in celebration of the individual spirit, nurturing and contemporary in its approach to iconic service, relaxation and overall well-being. At its essence is a collection of exclusive offerings, transformative in nature – affecting peace, purity and strength well beyond the spa experience.*

Typical American hype, I thought grumpily. As I became disheartened by the constant reruns of Diana's death, however, I thought 'why not?' As a fifty-something conservative Englishman I had a dim view of what awaited me: overweight and limp wristed men in bathrobes? Plump blowsy women with blue rinse hairdos? It was with some trepidation that I entered the Spa; in England spas and saunas had rather a questionable reputation. A very smartly attired young woman greeted me with a warm welcoming smile. "Hi there, and how can I help you?" Her friendliness seemed genuine. Sigh of relief.

> "Er, well I'm not sure, I haven't been to a spa before." I suddenly felt rather silly and very provincial.
> "You're English. Well, we have a number of treatments but maybe you would like one of our massages."

She gave me a card listing the many and varied treatments on offer, with extraordinary names, sounding downright dangerous. I decided to go with what appeared to be the one that would hurt the least and that I might survive. *A Phoenician aromatherapy treatment* that offered me *the ability to reduce anxiety, ease depression, boost energy levels, speed up the healing process, eliminate headaches, boost cognitive performance, induce sleep, strengthen the immune system, reduce pain, improve digestion and increase circulation*.

All for only $150. A snip for this miracle cure. I removed as many clothes as I felt was necessary, leaving my underpants on under the bathrobe, hoping this was sufficient to prevent me being arrested for indecent exposure. In a small room I was asked to lie on a high massage table. I was feeling very exposed and rather uncomfortable as a young woman asked me to remove the bathrobe, and delicately placing a towel over my waist, said, "Do you wish to keep your shorts on? That's fine."

This was even more unsettling and, with the tense state I was getting into, it would be impossible to 'reduce anxiety'. I lay face-down looking through a hole in the table at a bowl of floating rose petals. The young masseuse got to work and after the initial pain she settled down to a steady gentle massage. I started to wonder what sort of masochists would enjoy a set of fingers and thumbs pressing their flesh almost to the bone, and realised just how low my pain threshold must be. The time passed in a wonderful blur of massage and scents. After it was finished I was led to a relaxing room, and I lay on a padded lounger. The lights were low and the sound of a small waterfall took over my mind. I was out to the world. I did not come to for nearly an hour and lay there convinced that what I had just been through was nothing short of miraculous. I felt amazing! Everything they claimed would happen had indeed come to pass.

As I got dressed I looked around me at all the happy, relaxed people. None had been pumping away on what I regarded as medieval instruments of torture, otherwise known as 'a gym'. More importantly, I thought of how much we were prepared to pay for just lying on a benchtop in a small room. This was a goldmine.

As soon as I returned to Sydney I started my research. There were no hotels at that time promoting a 'spa'; all had 'Health & Leisure Clubs' and none offered a swimming pool as part of their club. I also discovered that not one of the Orient-Express Hotels had a spa, which made me a little nervous, as JBS was averse to spa baths. Perhaps he opposed the whole spa concept?

I met with Kendra, our H&L club manager. She confirmed that spas were taking off, mainly as extensions of cosmetic companies to flog expensive creams and lotions. Next I spoke to Charlie Dodsworth, chief engineer, who knew every nook and cranny of the hotel. We found a few storerooms off the gym, and some massage rooms that had never been used. Gradually we worked out a plan. Not everyone was enthusiastic, especially some of the male members of the gym, but if we wanted to make any money at all we needed to do something new.

We knew nothing about spas or how to set one up, so I started to look at the spas currently being operated in Sydney. It was the late 90s: Aveda, Elemis, Dermalogica. I started to call around. All seemed interested, so we'd meet and I would explain my experience in the USA and ask how we could replicate it at The Observatory. They just didn't understand what I was after. The local brands were only interested in display space where they could market their products.

I had almost given up on the idea when I received a call from an American woman from a company who understood what I was after. She had been consulting with them but her contract would finish the following week. Would I be prepared to hold off until then? I was delighted to agree.

The following week I sat down with Deborah Mangum. She was classically American, large infectious smile, blonde, attractive and - most of all - confident. She had grown up in Maryland and attended the University of San Francisco and she knew exactly what I was talking about. I took an immediate liking to her.

I was very nervous about telling the head office of our plans, so I didn't. If it worked we could get the glory. If it didn't, we would bury it so fast no-one would notice. I managed to get Scott Downs, our financial controller, on board and we found money from every corner of the budget. We scored a top up from head office for a general redecoration of the Health &

Leisure Club. The one great advantage with being on the other side of the world was that we rarely had visits from London.

Charlie set about moving walls, installing doors and creating treatment rooms. Some were no larger than a broom cupboard, but who's to notice when you've got your head in a hole looking at a bowl of rose petals, with low light, soft music and sweet aromas? Deborah designed the services and new uniforms: gone were the polo shirts and gym shorts, in came medical-styled tops and trousers. In no time the place was transformed. We kept the gym so the chaps were happy, and the spa guests visited later in the day anyway.

With the magnificent pool, the whole spa concept presented so well it took off like a rocket. Soon London was asking questions, but who could argue with our success? We were the forerunner to many Orient-Express properties opening their own spas; soon other Sydney hotels followed. I can proudly say that The Observatory team was the first.

Deborah continued to introduce services which never ceased to surprise me. One day she appeared in my office with a new concept she had seen in the US: Stone Therapy. My first reaction was - knowing she had been to San Francisco - did she say 'stoned therapy'? Is this something to do with marijuana?

> "It's about using warm stones positioned along the back and they melt away tension, ease muscle stiffness and increase circulation and metabolism. They can even relieve chronic pain, reduce stress and promote deep relaxation."

I was looking rather sceptical, and asked "What sort of stones?"

> "Normal basalt stones."
> "What are these stones going to cost?"
> "The rocks and the training, about $10,000."

I nearly fell off my chair. "$10,000 for rocks! In England we had beaches full of them. We could pick them up by the bucket load for nothing." In her usual calm and confident way, in her soft American accent, she went on to explain how special the basalt rocks were, with high silica and iron content making it hold heat longer than most stones.

Of course she talked me around. The clincher was, "and I don't know of anyone else doing this treatment as yet - great publicity!" And so it was that the spa produced more publicity than anything else and introduced us to a new untapped market.

Australia didn't only produce bronzed muscular male sports heroes. Women worked just as hard at their physiques, and this was evident by the number who started visiting the hotel and using our spa, both for exercise and for treatments. We provided a far more pleasant female-friendly environment, rather than the usual sweaty blokey gyms.

Pink, the American singer, songwriter, and actress, had an athletic stage performance that would challenge any sportsman and she loved our spa. Models too, like Elle Macpherson, Kate Fischer, Belinda Green, Jennifer Hawkins, Deborah Hutton, and the ageless Lauren Hutton. We pampered the very elegant and charming Sarah Murdoch, British-born Australian model, actress and television presenter, who happened to be the wife of Lachlan Murdoch, heir to media baron Rupert Murdoch, and Linda Evangelista, the Canadian supermodel model, one of the most accomplished and influential models with 700 magazine covers. They all visited the hotel and our spa, the covert innovation that we had introduced on a shoestring budget. Since then of course the spa business has grown like Topsy; there seems to be one on every street corner and stone treatments are on every menu. You can thank me later.

Chapter 9

#nighttoremember #birthsmarriagesn'deaths #crazyrichasians

Hotels are a home away from home, and domestic events occur every day. Death was something commonplace, and was one of my first experiences way back at the start of my career at the Grand in Eastbourne as readers will remember. Births, however, were less so. I assume there were no doubt many conceptions on site, and on occasion we even received a note from a very happy couple thanking us for providing the atmosphere, comfort and occasion for such an event. But rarely the actual births.

Just before Christmas in the early 2000s, an event occurred that made me glad the night manager was Ron Morris, one of the best night managers I have been fortunate enough to work with. On reading his morning report it brought about a congratulatory round of applause from the day team and proved to me yet again that all the training in the world is no substitute for common sense and a cool head.

02.00 Call for a late reservation.
03.00 Guest initially checks in alone - later returns with lady (his partner) who was obviously heavily pregnant.
04.05 Guest calls down requesting an ambulance as his wife was giving birth. Ambulance called. Was going to the room when Mr **** came running down the stairs very distressed and advised

me the baby had arrived and should he cut the umbilical cord. Advised him to return and stay with his wife. I called Emergency with a request as to what action we should take. I tried to relay the requested details of age, how long etc unable to ask the guest as phone off the hook. Fortunately the ambo crew arrived and I took them to the room. Attempted to comfort distraught husband. 04.55 All left the hotel in the ambulance. Advised mother and baby OK.

The father called the hotel later in the day to thank Ron and the hotel for all their help - the baby was a little boy. The significance of this event was not missed by the PR department and already the story was taking shape for the up and coming edition of the hotel's January newsletter. Putting the facts together:

- It was just before Christmas
- A late reservation - was there no room at the other 'inns'? A baby boy was born
- We were The Observatory was there a star visible above?

Unfortunately the story had a very different outcome to what we all had hoped was a joyous event. We received a call from the mother's parents, who advised us that their daughter had only recently been released from jail and it was due to a cocktail of drugs she had taken that brought on an early labour. The baby had been taken into care by the Department of Community Services as their daughter was not able to take care of him. His grandparents were now to care for him and were happy to do so. There was palpable sadness in the hotel when we heard of this.

That other milestone event in our lives, the wedding, might be regarded as stock in trade for a hotel but the proposals were memorable. We had a 'mariachi band' employed to sing beneath the fiancee's window, a guitarist strumming a love song written for the proposal, and a ten metre banner unfurled on the hotel's tennis court across the road. The most remarkable was a proposal set up for a TV reality event, filmed in secret and unknown to the young woman involved. At the big moment he went on one knee for the proposal, the camera and crew appeared from hiding and - much to the disappointment and embarrassment of the man - she declined. The suite was not used that night, nor was a refund requested. We never learned if there was a happy ending to that story.

Another prospective husband had bought his girlfriend a very expensive diamond platinum engagement ring. He requested that the ring be frozen in a small block of ice, to be served in their favourite cocktail at which point the young woman would discover the ring. The cocktail: The Midnight Kiss. The recipe: Vodka, tonic water, cranberry juice, four basil leaves and ice.

Apart from our concern about the freezing of such a valuable ring and how this might safely be done, there were the more mundane issues of food hygiene and health and safety regulations. But the guests' desires were our top priorities, so we did it.

The evening came, the ring was safely encapsulated in the cube of ice and the 'Midnight Kisses' was placed before the couple, carefully ensuring the cocktail with the ring was in front of the young woman.

The waiter looked on as sip by sip they consumed their cocktails, waiting with anticipation for the moment the ring was discovered and the excitement that would follow.

They appeared so intent on their conversation - had the ring been forgotten? The last drop had been sipped from the young woman's glass - and yet no reaction? Anxiety was turning into panic. Had she swallowed it? Where was it? The man gave a nervous glance at the waiter. Had the ring been stolen? Just as we were all descending on the table, the young woman raised her glass and the decorative basil leaf slipped away. Hearing a little 'ding' she looked down and, at first puzzled, she then squealed. The diamond glittered in the light of the candle, to the joy of the man and the relief of the waiter. The stress and fear of that evening was never to be repeated, although it was often requested.

When it came to tying the knot it was more traumatic for the hotel. Over the years I had arranged weddings with all sorts of themes, from Grand Regency with period costumes to Roaring Twenties in the style of the Great Gatsby. I'd seen some extraordinarily lavish affairs where fortunes were spent, but none matched the scale of an event we hosted in 2006.

Our banqueting department arranged many wedding receptions, and although it was routine for our staff, we aimed for the client to feel that their reception was to be the highlight of the hotel's calendar. I was called in one time to meet wedding planners from Colin Cowie, who had coordinated receptions for such celebrities as Michael Douglas and Catherine Zeta-Jones, Charlie Sheen, Jennifer Lopez, Oprah Winfrey and Kim Kardashian. They were very cagey about whose wedding it was for, but it had to be someone big. Every member of the staff was laying bets on whose wedding it might be.

When it was confirmed that the hotel was to be the base and would not actually host the wedding, things quietened down but we still waited with some excitement. We had a meeting and under the strictest agreement of secrecy we were advised that the bride was the actress and model Cathy Chui Chi-kay.

I looked at my organising team: I had never heard of her, and from their expressions, neither had they. The groom, Martin Lee Ka-shing, was the son of property mogul, Lee Siu Gei, who founded Henderson Land Development, one of the wealthiest men in Hong Kong.

It was the most lavish wedding I have ever seen in my career. The extraordinary detail in the press reports that followed signified the importance of this Hong Kong society wedding. The Observatory played a cameo role, hosting a small reception in the Drawing Room. When the planners saw the blue carpet it was deemed unlucky for the bride on such a day and so, twenty four hours before the event, we removed it and had a preferred red carpet laid. Always amazing what can be achieved when money is no object.

We were advised to watch for the Chinese *paparazzi*, who would do anything to gain access to the hotel. They had two aircraft with separate flight plans logged at Hong Kong airport in an attempt to put the press off the scent.

When the wedding guests were checking in, we knew they were the most glamorous society elite that Hong Kong had to offer. I even saw a Rolls Royce fully decked out in Gucci livery. The hotel lobby became a showroom for every major fashion house: Gucci, Coco Chanel, Tom Ford, Yves Saint Laurent, Giorgio Armani, Vivienne Westwood, Christian Dior.

The Hong Kong press breathlessly reported the event:

Martin Lee Ka-shing and actress/model Cathy Chui Chi-kay exchanged their vows in the Australian city's Royal Botanic Gardens under a white marquee decorated with pink peonies, with a view of the Sydney Opera House.

Despite heavy rain in the morning, the 24-year-old bride dazzled more than 100 guests on her arrival in a white wedding gown, spectacular 50-carat diamond necklace and a diamond wedding ring estimated to weigh about five carats. 'The necklace is a gift from Lee Ka-shing. "I saw a princess wearing this style. I drew a sketch and he got it made", Chui said. The groom's brother, Lee Ka-kit, and friend Brian Li, son of banker David Li Kwok-po, were best men; Chui's younger sister Daisy and cousin Cecilia were bridesmaids.

The groom's father, who took his private jet to Sydney, would not comment on rumours that wedding gifts worth HK$400 million had been given to Chui's family or that the wedding cost HK$100 million. "It's a small sum that you are talking about but I don't think it costs that much ", said Mr Lee, whose US$11 billion net worth puts him at 37th on the Forbes rich list.

The ceremony was preceded by a lavish welcome dinner on Thursday night that Chui attended in a gold Escada gown reputedly worth HK$150,000. Yesterday's events included a lunch and a cake-cutting ceremony, followed by a reception last night at the city's State Theatre. At the welcome dinner Chui expressed the hope of starting a family soon and repeated it at last night's reception: "I love children and I hope we can form a happy family."

Chui's family emigrated to Australia when she was five. She returned to Hong Kong as a teenager and started working as a model before going to England to gain a degree at University College London. The couple will spend a month travelling around the world.

A later report by *China Whisper* in 2012 said "Some have compared Chui and Lee's wedding to that of Prince William's marriage to Kate Middleton, calling that royal wedding "frugal" in comparison."

It was regarded as "A Century Wedding" by the media.

Private jet (Gulfstream) for groom and family to fly from HK to Syd - $62M

Private jet for 150 guests to fly from HK to Syd - $183,000

Accommodation for 150 guests for 4 days and 3 nights in Observatory Hotel, the Rocks - $833,000 (We wished!)

Pre-wedding party - Overseas Passenger Terminal (Ocean Room), Circular Quay - $20,000

Ceremony in Royal Botanical Gardens - $43,000

Reception in the State Theatre - every seat bought for 3 days/nights - $74M

Wedding Planner - Colin Cowie - $333,000

Tips for family/friends acting as helpers/ushers etc - $166,000

Bride's jewellery - $3.3M

Bride's dresses - $192,000

Bride's hair and makeup - $83,000

Red envelopes (ie cash – a Chinese custom) the groom's father gave to all his workers (who weren't invited) because his son was getting married for 1050 people - $1.75M

Property - 2 units in Hong Kong - $17M

More property - $17M

Red envelopes for the Bride's family (in Chinese custom, the groom's family pays for everything for a wedding) - $17M

Total $117,000,000 Australian dollars or $700,000,000 HKD

After such a wedding one could only wish the couple a wonderful future of happiness and joy. Thankfully, it appeared so, as the press reported ten years later:

No expense was spared to celebrate former actress Cathy Chui and billionaire husband Martin Lee's 10th year anniversary and the

100th-day celebrations for their fourth son, Preston, on Saturday night (Jan 16). The guest list included the power couple's network of tycoons and celebrities such as Joey Young, Emily Lam-Ho and Michelle Reis, and the surprise guest for the night was none other than former Boyzone member Ronan Keating.

As a gesture of appreciation for Cathy, Martin has purportedly gifted her with a multi-million-dollar mansion in Beverly Hills in Los Angeles, USA.

Crazy rich Asians indeed.

We also unwittingly played a part in the saddest of human milestones as well.

I had in my early days at The Grand Hotel become accustomed to guests dying. I was young, they were to me very old, and I had no emotional attachment; it was just part of life. I did not think that as I got older and - having now experienced a number of near and dear cast off this mortal coil, I could be emotionally moved by a guest's departure from this earth.

One day a very charming couple checked into the hotel. They were warm and cheerful and said how pleased they were to be staying with us. As they went to their room the wife asked "Do you know if there is a church nearby?"

I said there were two, St Brigid's Church and the Anglican Garrison Church just down the road. With this information she entered the lift.

That evening the couple had dinner in the Galileo Restaurant, enjoying the best champagne and finest food and wine on the menu. The staff later commented on how lovely they were and how affectionate they were to one another, assuming this was a special anniversary. The following morning the wife left the hotel alone and as she did so, asked first reception and also the concierge about the churches and confirming the communion times.

An hour or so later she returned and went to her room, noticeably not acknowledging a greeting from the concierge and a question whether the service was to her liking. Shortly after that she called down and requested an ambulance for her husband. The ambulance team was escorted to the room. The husband was lying still on the bed, hands on his chest. The wife seemed sad but surprisingly calm. The ambulance team then started to try to resuscitate him only to have the wife intervene. "Please don't do that - it is not what he would want."

The body was removed and it was only later we learned of the true tragedy. The husband had been diagnosed with a terminal brain tumour. The couple were without doubt devoted to each other and, unable to get assistance in Australia, had travelled to Mexico, purportedly for a holiday to obtain a drug not available in Australia. He wanted to choose his own moment to die, not wishing to deteriorate or face the likely trauma that lay ahead, for himself and his wife.

I have dealt with a number of suicide attempts in my hotel career, but nothing like this. We were devastated by the lengths they had to go to, due to the punitive laws on euthanasia in Australia at the time. His wife could not be by his side at the time of death, as would have made her guilty of a crime. This explained why she took the trouble to establish the time when she was to attend communion at the local church. It was heartbreaking to imagine her emotional suffering as she left the hotel that morning, having said goodbye to her loving husband for the last time. I pray that she can take comfort in the memories of their last evening together.

It was the only death to occur at The Observatory, and was without doubt the most tragic of the many deaths that have dealt with during my long career.

Chapter 10

#hedonismrules #lifesaboxofchocolates #G&Tcolonials

'*Join the Navy to see the world'* they said. On the North Sea crossing from Holland many years ago I learned that sea travel didn't agree with me. Anyway, as the ditty continues, all they saw was the sea!

As a child, with my friend and hero, cousin Tim, we would admire a model sailing ship that stood in the nursery at Tachbrook. We made up adventure plans, sailing the world to faraway places, dreaming the way children did before the world was shrunk by airlines and the internet.

These dreams had tempted me to attend a naval academy at the age of twelve. Although crushed at the time by the colour blindness which ended that career before it started, it was really a godsend. That genetic quirk was part of the fate that meant that rather than travelling around the world in a hammock, sea sick and working like a *jolly jack tar*, I instead flew to all those faraway places at the pointy end of the plane, and slept between the finest Egyptian cotton sheets in some of the grandest hotels in the world. And I was paid to do so. I saw places unimagined in the nursery as a child at Tachbrook.

The Orient-Express company ensured we all met regularly at one another's hotels, to learn from each other and to set company policy. Head office and JBS were in London, and I regularly returned to the UK, which enabled me to also catch up with family and friends. With no OEH hotel in London it gave me the opportunity to try out some of the rather special places that, as a young man, I had longed to stay in but could only gaze upon in envy as I drove past seeking more affordable accommodation.

I liked the Dorchester, and inside it was very similar to The Observatory having had the same interior designers. The Savoy was rather dated and most suited as the set of a 1940s movie. Claridges was probably the grandest of hotels when it came to reputation, having been the home of several exiled royal families and heads of state who spent the second world war there. Surprising then, when chef Gordon Ramsay took up residence in the restaurant. Being so well known for his foul language, no doubt Claridges' discerning guests would have been appalled.

The Ritz was where I usually stayed when in London, but when they were fully booked, I tried The Connaught Hotel in Mayfair. It had a reputation for being run as a private home, with the highest standards and a superior attitude. It was very traditional in all aspects and did not take too kindly to the arrival of modern technology. In 1999, the first thing I noticed on arrival were discreet signs informing guests that 'no mobile phones may be used in public areas'.

The hotel existed in a bygone era, which suited the guests. At breakfast one morning, an elderly man was seated alone at a nearby table, sipping his tea and ladling out spoonsful from his own personal pot of Fortnum & Mason's Thick Cut Whisky Orange Marmalade. Another very elderly, very dignified man entered the restaurant, and - as if there were no other guests in the room - spoke loudly across the restaurant to my neighbour. "Good morning m'Lord."

"Morning, Sir Geoffrey."

> "I'm devastated at the news." By now he was sitting at his table on the other side of the room. All the guests were listening intently.
> "Why is that?" Both oblivious to any other guest.
> "Dusty's dead, Dusty Springfield - breast cancer." There was a pause. "She was a lesbian you know. Shame, lovely girl."

With which both turned to their breakfasts. I looked around the restaurant to see if anyone had found this exchange as amusing as I had. Everyone just read their papers and ate their toast. Such was the Connaught. It remained locked in the past until it closed for a £70 million renovation in 2007.

I know you'll forgive me for feeling a little smug as I looked back to my days with De Vere, when I thought a corporate meeting at the Connaught Rooms followed by dinner at the Mirabelle in London's Mayfair were the ultimate treats. My OEH corporate meetings now took me to places far more exalted.

Le Manoir aux Quat'Saisons was a hotel with a two Michelin star restaurant, run by chef Raymond Blanc in a small village in Oxfordshire. In the late 70s when he announced he was opening an upscale restaurant in this tiny village in the middle of nowhere over fifty miles from London, we all thought him mad.

My brother Chris, his wife Jill and I went there for dinner on one occasion. The place was packed and everything, from the decor to the service and the menu, was superb. The wine list was the size of an encyclopedia, and the sommelier's knowledge was indeed encyclopedic to match. I nervously turned page after page, looking at the price rather than the wine. Eventually, settling on a reasonably priced Bordeaux, I enquired if the sommelier agreed with my choice. He helpfully gave me a description of my selection, and by the time he had finished I knew everything there was to know except the colour of the grape treader's socks. "Yes we will have that one, sounds very nice."

It was gratifying to go back as a fellow colleague of OEH and meet Raymond. The hotel had expanded since my last visit, with more rooms and beautiful kitchen gardens. How envious we were at the size of his kitchens and the number of staff; the place had become world-renowned. Raymond was truly eccentric and a lovable character. He was so French he made the average Frenchman look English.

A rather more exotic location for our meetings was the Copacabana Palace in Rio de Janeiro, just across the road from its famous beach. An extravagant and magnificent building, it has hosted many of the world's rich and famous, such as Marilyn Monroe and Princess Diana. Built as a casino before gambling was outlawed in Brazil in 1923, it became one of Rio's most luxurious hotels. Inspired by Hotel Negresco in Nice and The Carlton in Cannes, Copacabana Palace was beautifully decorated with Carrara marble and Bohemian glass. In 1933 it became famous as the set for the movie *Flying Down to Rio* starring Fred Astaire and Ginger Rogers, which had actually been filmed in the US.

It was a must-do in Rio to take the cable car up to Corcovado (which means 'hunchback') and visit Cristo Redentor, the statue of Christ with outstretched arms, gazing over Rio. The mountain rises straight up from the city for 710 metres, and at night the brightly lit 38 metre statue is visible from nearly every part of the city. I was up there with my old friend Nick. We took the classic photo that all tourists take in front of the statue, with our arms similarly outstretched, and it was the most magical photo of my travels. The mist had crept in and enveloped the statue behind us. Fortunately the serenity was not disturbed by the soldiers armed with submachine guns, who remained just out of the picture. [105]

On the beach opposite the hotel, vendors wandered up and down hawking their wares and bronzed bodies soaked up the sun. The women wore bikinis made of dental floss, tourists looked on admiringly, drinking from ice-cooled coconuts. Countless games of football and volleyball were being played on the sand. My friend of old, Paul White, by then president of OEH and fanatical Ipswich supporter, arranged that management play our own company game of football.

Even though I was in goal, I was bruised and aching for days due to the enthusiastic competitiveness of the younger managers. I did receive a gold medal, which I liked to think was for valor - but we all received one simply for participating. [106]

On one of our trips to Rio we travelled via Argentina, and Buenos Aires became one of my favourite cities. The wide avenues, the colourful houses of El Caminito, the streets paved with cobblestones where artists sell their paintings, caught my heart. I still have a painting I bought of tango dancers performing on the sidewalk. And, of course, the Cementerio de la Recoleta, the most quirky of all final resting places. Housing magnificent mausoleums where presidents, Nobel Prize winners and Eva Peron are entombed, it's now a tourist attraction like no other. Streams of tourists follow guides, crocodile-style, down narrow passageways.

One of the grandest and most aristocratic of hotels, The Alvear Palace Hotel, was sadly not one of ours, but I was fortunate enough to stay there. I have never seen tables so ladened with silverware: from the heavy gage silver cutlery to the ornate salt and pepper shakers, the butter dishes and vases with fresh flowers, every piece was magnificently presented.

There was, however, something OEH did own in Buenos Aires. *La Cabaña* had been a favourite restaurant of Eva Peron, and JBS had taken to it. Its neighbourhood had become run down, so he bought the interior and all the artefacts and stored them with the intention of recreating a steakhouse brand in one of our hotels. This plan was shelved when a new location was found in the fashionable Alvear District, and the restaurant reopened in its home town.

A group of us were invited by the general manager, Maximilliano Pazo, to dine there one evening. I am a meat lover, and Argentina is famous for its steaks. We were all hungry after a day of sightseeing, so I ordered an appetizer and a steak as a main dish, to share with a fellow initiate to the restaurant. My local colleagues were amused at our ambitious choice. When *Round of Offals* arrived we understood why. It was the appetizer but could have easily fed a family of four for a week: the plate was laden with sweetbreads, kidneys, pork sausage and blood sausage. And that was just what I could recognise.

We bravely struggled through the mound of meat. Then the main dish arrived. *Great Baby Beef (1000 Grams, To Share) With Grilled Vegetables and Soufflé Potatoes.* It was the size of a concrete breeze block. As we munched our way through I just kept reminding myself of the Atkins diet. Atkins claimed that eating steak could prevent or improve serious health conditions, such as metabolic syndrome, diabetes, high blood pressure and cardiovascular disease. With this meal, we should live to be at least 100 then. [107]

Other company trips took me to OEH properties such as Charleston Place, our hotel in South Carolina. Charleston still had the *antebellum* feel found in Margaret Mitchell's *Gone With The Wind*. I loved it there. It was so different from other American cities, where brashness was the order of the day. One afternoon I was on a bit of a shopping spree, and I struggled with my bags. The shop assistant kindly took the bags from me and asked, in a wonderful southern accent, where I was staying and offered to take all my bags to the hotel, so that I might continue with my shopping unencumbered. I was nervous that I may never see my purchases again, but sure enough there they were in my room on my return. Never before or since have I experienced such service. [108, 109]

In New York, the OEH team met at The Twenty One Club on 21st and 52nd Street, which we'd owned since 1995. The famous Prohibition-era speakeasy was now a restaurant and a New York institution. It had a secret vault, known for storing the private wine collections of rich and famous patrons, past and present. The list read like a who's who: Presidents Kennedy, Nixon, and Ford, Joan Crawford, Elizabeth Taylor, Ernest Hemingway, Mae West, Aristotle Onassis, Gene Kelly, and Gloria Swanson. It was particularly popular in the 1990s with suits and was used as a location for films such as *Wall Street* and *The Associate*. In 1998 we met our new boss, Simon Sherwood, a very dynamic young man, who presented his re-branding vision for the future. It was obvious that there were changes in the wind, with a far more strategic focus on company development. He appointed the highly professional Pippa Isbell, as VP PR. She was brilliant, a breath of fresh air and she became a close friend. I felt the new team would certainly bring Orient-Express into the modern technological age that would be essential for the company to grow. [110]

We also dined at Restaurant Daniel, located in the former Mayfair Hotel on Park Avenue, the original site of Le Cirque. As we were about to tuck into our meal a man approached and greeted us, welcoming us to New York. At first I assumed it was the restaurant's owner. My mistake! Everyone stood up and I realised it was Jesse Jackson, the civil rights activist and politician. I remember seeing him in the press photos, standing next to Martin Luther King Jnr on the balcony on the day of the fatal shooting at the Lorraine Motel in Memphis, in 1968. Someone at the restaurant had mentioned who we were and he simply wanted to say hello, but it rather made my evening.

Another company conference was in Cape Town at The Mount Nelson Hotel with my old friend Nick Seewer. We followed with a visit to our property in Johannesburg, The Westcliff, overlooking the jacaranda trees around the zoo, before flying out to stay at our three Gametracker Lodges in Botswana. We called them our 'Big Five' in Africa, although this description was more correctly applied to the animals which I was glad to see: African elephant, black rhinoceros, Cape buffalo, lion and leopard.[111]

At the Khwai River Lodge we learned that shortly before our visit a guest had been killed by getting too close to a hippo. The hippos kept me up half the night with their endless grunting and groaning.. Due to the lions prowling around, after dinner, guests are escorted to their luxuriously appointed tent-style rooms by local spear-bearing tribesmen, a nice touch of theatre I thought, but necessary. Recently one of the kitchen hands had been mauled by a lion while walking home, and died. He had not removed his bloodied apron after work.

My favourite lodge was Savute in the Chobe National Park. It was surrounded by herds of giraffes, zebras, and elephants, hundreds of them. They'd removed the baths at the lodge as the elephants, in the dry season, would scent the water and trample through the enclosure. The manager was once on the lavatory minding his own business, when an elephant's trunk snaked through the window in search of water. The manager grabbed a can of insect spray and gave a quick squirt up the trunk's nostril. The trunk disappeared back through the window as the manager ran the other way, trousers around his ankles.

Wooden and wire fences were soon knocked down by the elephants. The staff discovered that the best way to keep them out was to dig a shallow ditch and bury old car tyres in it. It appears that elephants tread with great care and test the ground before they put down a foot; when they felt the ground soften they would back off. We also discovered the bleached skull of what was once a majestic beast, and learned that elephants have six sets of molars in their lifetime. As one tooth wears out another pushes forward to replace it. Eventually the loss of teeth leads to the death of the elephant. Amazing what one learns as a hotel manager. With Nick's help, I took my children, Tim and Charlie, on safari to see these magnificent animals in the wild. They loved it and it was an unforgettable experience.

In Europe, apart from The Cipriani in Venice, we met at Reid's Palace, in Madeira, a beautiful volcanic island, green and rugged with high cliffs. The hotel was in the most beautiful setting, in verdant gardens perched on a cliff, overlooking the Atlantic. The brochure states that 'you can wander down to our sea level platform and jump straight into the azure ocean'. I rather protest about their misuse of the word *wander*. While the view was spectacular the path was more suited for a mountain goat. The Portuguese are a hardy lot. [112]

In 2003, we returned to the Iberian peninsula, having just taken over The Ritz Hotel in Madrid. The name alone defines it, and, although a little tired, it still epitomised the grand Ritz era. Liveried staff stood in every corner, and a team was employed full time just to maintain the very plush carpets. In my wood-panelled bedroom was an enormous canopied four poster bed, with heavy tapestry drapes. The bed was also raised on a dais. As I lay there looking up at the canopy above and surveying the room, I felt like I was lying in state. At any moment I expected to hear organ music, and for the bed to silently glide through the panel behind me into a cremation oven. [113]

My morbid thoughts were invoked after a visit earlier that afternoon to the famous Museo del Prado to see its European art, dating from the 12th century. As I walked through the gallery from one room to another, all I could notice was how brutal the paintings were: stabbings, decapitations, torture, bodily mutilations. So much for Biblical paintings. Each room was more gruesome than the one before. By the end I was quite depressed at the inhumanity of it all and the terrors inflicted in the name of religion. I'm sure it's exceedingly brilliant artwork, but to me it deserved an X rating. Give me the calm beauty of Constable's hay wain, Van Gogh's irises or Monet's water lilies any day.

Flying about the globe was indeed exciting, particularly in business class and even better with an upgrade to first. Surely the fuselage was thicker and the seats much safer there? I was starting to become a little nervous that my sheer quantum of air miles meant that I was increasing the odds of being in a crash. A well-travelled colleague reassured me with conviction that one faced the same risk on each flight - there's no accumulator effect. I wasn't sure if that made me feel better or worse.

In spite of these ghoulish statistics, my only truly white-knuckle flight was courtesy of Thai Airways once on the way to London. The flight path took us via India with a refuelling stop in New Delhi. We were requested to disembark as they refueled and as we waited to reboard the aircraft I noticed an elderly couple attempting to get the attention of a flight attendant in the lounge. "Two gin and tonics, please!" It was mid-morning so the attendant politely said they needed to wait until they were on board. I found myself sitting across the aisle from them in the upper business class cabin. They were very British, from the old colonial set that had remained in India long after Britain lost its empire. The lovely Thai attendant came around with a tray of champagne, but the lady made a further request for their gin and tonic. It was explained that the bar had not yet opened and they would have to wait until we were airborne. All this was repeated by the wife back to her deaf husband in a voice audible to the entire cabin.

The plane was just reaching altitude and levelling out when we heard a loud bang. The engine pulled back and the wing dipped. Outside the window a few minutes later I noticed fuel was pouring from the wing and we could hear various alarms sounding in the cockpit. This was accompanied by a buzz of activity amongst the flight attendants, with muted but animated phone conversations. We passengers looked at one another with varying degrees of panic. The captain then announced the plane had some technical problems and he was returning to New Delhi. As we circled down the fuel continued to pour out. I was debating whether to pray or scream hysterically. My nails were dug deep in the armrest, and it appeared that we were all in the same state. Well, not everyone. The elderly memsahib across the aisle was buzzing her call button and as a rather flustered attendant came by, she grabbed her arm and firmly requested.

"Could we have our gin and tonics now?"

The attendant tried to keep calm but explained thatwe were facing a big problem, and we had to return to the airport and must listen out for the captain's emergency announcements. The woman looked grumpy and frustrated. Her hard of hearing husband asked "What did she say ?"

"She says we can't have our gin and tonics!"

Extraordinary how a touch of humour can ease a situation; all of us who had heard this exchange smiled, it had somehow put things into perspective.

When we landed I learned that an engine had blown and - having just taken on a full load of fuel - the plane was too heavy and needed to dump fuel to land safely.

We were advised that we would need to stay in a hotel and await news of when we would be continuing on to London.

Having never visited India before I was happy to make the most of it. We arrived at the hotel and a nice young clerk allocated me a room. As an afterthought he added "...and you will be sharing with Mr Williams." I explained that I was not happy with sharing my room with a complete stranger, and as a business class traveller I expected the airline to give me a room of my own. His reply stumped me. "Oh Mr Griffin I am sure you will be most comfortable, it is a very nice room and a very big king size bed!"

With all my bluster the very best I could negotiate was a twin room but my room-mate would remain. Mr Williams turned out to be an extremely left-wing school teacher from Melbourne, with rather questionable hygiene habits and an unwillingness to communicate with his rather right-wing room mate. With only one key between us we had a fraught three days until a replacement plane could be found. As we had no visas we were required to stay in the hotel. Under the circumstances I chose to ignore this. So after a bowl of cornflakes and some toast, both of which had a distinct flavour and aroma of curry, I found a taxi and headed off into New Delhi. My driver was wonderful; his taxi was an old Morris Oxford complete with all knobs and fascias in Bakelite and a smell that reminded me of cars in my childhood. I was surprised to find the weather cold, something that I had never associated with India. Eventually we were on our way again, and Mr Williams and I arrived in London where I headed off to my conference and he went off to visit the tomb of Karl Marx in Highgate Cemetery no doubt.

All our company conferences combined the business of learning with networking. The mix of fun and education bonded us as a group, and we all admired the unique collection of luxury hotels. Whether in a city, with the Ritz, on a mountain top, with Machu Picchu, out in the bush with Game Trackers, or beachside in Rio, even cruising up a river, or on a train, there was nothing homogeneous about Orient-Express. I was certain there was no better company and certainly no better job than the one I had for the final chapter of my career.

Please don't imagine that I never actually worked; the hours were long and the pressures in dealing with our high-end guests were intense. We also needed to continually find the guests who would fill The Observatory Hotel and pay the room rate that would produce a profit.

Australia's population was, and is, small. Australians were also not keen to pay the prices needed to maintain a luxury hotel such as The Observatory. Being close to Asia, where wages are low and luxury hotels are relatively cheap, the Australian market had high expectations and shallow pockets. They knew quality and expected good service and, while happy to pay for it in the USA and Europe, somehow did not see it this way in their own country. It was therefore essential for us to attract overseas guests who were accustomed to higher prices and prepared to pay for comfort and service. This task was not easy when the hotel was not part of a major branded global chain.

We realised that we needed to have a greater global marketing presence, so we joined a group of like-minded hotels, individually owned, with the aim of exposing us to more markets as well as a referral base: *Small Luxury Hotels of the World*. It was an interesting concept, born out of a regional group, *Select Hotels*, that Richard Rosebury had developed. It worked to some degree, but lacked the serious organisational skills required. I was on their Board for a while, but it was just a two-man business team run with limited capital. We attended a few conferences that were really more geared to networking, but the business generated was negligible at that time.

We then joined two other organisations that actually *did* generate more business; they did things in a style that appealed to the customers we wished to attract, and - most importantly - the agents who placed business with us.

The first was *Leading Hotels of the World*, a New York based company. Membership was by invitation only, which brought prestige. The chairman was a classic Swiss hotelier, and I wasn't sure what to expect. We were visited by two men, an American and a venerable Swiss hotelier of about eighty, who came to check if we were acceptable to join such an elite group. They were rather intimidating. The elder man, on inspecting the bed and having enquired as to the thread count of the sheets, suddenly posed the question "How often do you turn the mattress?"

I had no idea. "Once a month?" It seemed like a reasonable answer.

"Show me how you can tell. I assume you do personally check?"

I was beaten, and explained that I had trust in my housekeepers to do the checking. He shook his head. "You should place a mark on the corner of the mattress, and then you can tell."

I was being checked out as much as the hotel. He was truly old school and as we had dinner I grew to like him more and more. They did not make hoteliers like this anymore; he belonged to a different age. Would others think this of me in years to come… or did they already think that?

I discovered that he had run a hotel in Switzerland in Weggis on Lake Lucerne. It was the Beau Rivage, the very hotel at which I had stayed with my parents in 1957 at the ripe age of eleven. I recall the sky was so clear there you could see millions of stars. My father had convinced me that if I was quiet enough, I could hear the 'blip' of the recently launched Russian Sputnik as it flew overhead, and I believed him. I told this story, after which we got on like a house on fire. Shortly after The Observatory was accepted as a member of this august group, which did indeed produce business for the hotel. The brand 'Orient-Express' was well known but people knew it for the famous train and not for the individual hotels.

Our new association under the banner of being a *Leading Hotel of the World* worked well and gave me a wonderful opportunity of combining work and play in my travels. The first of a number of annual gatherings I was to attend was in Monaco, home of Prince Rainier and Princess Grace, city of casinos, mega yachts and of course the Grand Prix.

I flew into Nice with my wife and we were met and taken to a helipad for the transfer to Monaco to the Hotel de Paris, a sister '*Leading*' hotel to The Observatory. While waiting, another couple sat beside us. We travelled in fours in the helicopter. The man was talking on his mobile, held at arm's length in the air, connected by an earpiece. I assumed he was having difficulty with the signal or maybe, as was the fear at the time, afraid of developing a brain tumor. He was shouting away for all to hear, and as I listened to his voice it struck me. *The name is Bond, James Bond.*

It was indeed Roger Moore and his wife who we were to share our helicopter with. I didn't recognise him at first as he looked a little older than the Bond I had last seen on the screen. His hair was receding and a sandy orange colour. His wife at that time was more Miss Moneypenny than Pussy Galore. I thought of all the smooth comments I could make as we winged our way to Monaco, but could get nothing out. For the ten minute trip I sat silently content that I had flown with James Bond, and had not been shot down by Blofeld.

The room at the hotel was exquisite. The reputation of *Leading Hotels* was evident in the gifts left by suppliers. A bottle of Dom Perignon; an engraved silver spoon, with a curved handle. I still have it and still have no idea what it is for; perhaps an affluent version of the teaspoons usually used for cooking up heroin? I also still have the Hermes wash bag, although the expensive products have long since been used. I couldn't find the room safe, however, and I was just about to ask at reception when I noticed the huge bank vault behind the desk where tiaras and necklaces were being deposited by women in mink coats. I decided I would just leave my passport in my pocket. Apparently crime in Monaco did not exist, probably because there were more policemen than residents in this small principality.

We attended a few business events (yes we did work!) The gala dinner that followed was beyond anything I had experienced, and hard to imagine the menu could ever be surpassed. The chef was none other than Alain Ducasse, the executive chef at the Hotel de Paris and a three Michelin starred chef, regarded as one of the world's greatest. I kept the menu as a souvenir. It listed seven courses and the finest matching wines. The guest of honour was Prince Rainier and his son Prince Albert, who I learned played football with my friend and colleague, Hans Maison, who had taken over the Windsor Court in New Orleans from Philip Wood.

Other *Leading Hotel* conferences followed, in New York and Berlin, the latter memorable not for business but for the fact I managed to track down Ursel Langer, the German *au pair* from my childhood (mentioned in Part I). I hadn't seen her since I was ten years old. I stayed at the Hotel Adlon, now rebuilt following reunification, on Unter den Linden near The Brandenburg Gate. The hotel had been a favourite with Herman Goering and other Nazi party members. The interior had been designed in a way that retained the impression of those days: with corridors of faux stone blocks that echoed as I walked, I had a weird sensation of ghostly jack booted steps behind me as I went to my room at night.

In 2000, the *Leading Hotel* annual event was held in Marrakech. I had never visited before and images came to mind of Humphrey Bogart and Ingrid Bergman in Rick's Bar, and all those wonderful quotes...

Of all the gin joints in all the towns in all the world, she walks into mine.

We'll always have Paris. Play it, Sam.
It doesn't take much to see that the problems of three little people don't amount to a hill of beans in this crazy world.
Here's looking at you, kid.

After Shakespeare's *Hamlet,* I don't think there are any lines more often quoted than these. I realised that we were going to *Marrakech* and not Casablanca - but how different could they be? We stayed at the famous La Mamounia Palace Hotel. Winston Churchill had said to Franklin D. Roosevelt in 1943 that "It is the most lovely spot in the whole world," and he chose to stay there because the views from the roof were incomparably "paintaceous." The hotel was renovated in the 1980s but much remained the same. In the Middle East, in terms of style and history, Shepheard's Hotel in Cairo had been the only hotel to compare, until it burned down in 1952.

As I checked in, I was impressed by the architecture, the columns, the arches and the painted wooden doors. The porch, dating from the 1920s, has remained intact and I imagined Churchill and Clem standing where I was standing now. Having registered I wandered into the splendid 1920s style "Salon of Honor" where I found Nick Seewer from The Mount Nelson in South Africa. Nick and I found ourselves often together at events, as we shared the same interests and sense of humour.

As OEH developed and younger GM's joined the company, I discovered Nick and I were known as 'Statler and Waldorf' after the pair of elderly Muppet characters known for their cantankerous opinions and penchant for heckling. I don't think we were cantankerous but we did tend to have opinions at meetings. I was never sure whether to be flattered or offended. [114]

Nick and I went out for dinner that evening in Marrakech, and it turned into a rather late night. When I eventually got to my room I realised just how beautiful was the unique Moroccan style, with deep colours matching the wood and *tadelakt*, creating an elegant contrast with the white bedroom. It was so different from the bland bedroom format that had become the norm in most luxury hotels.

The turndown came with a three-tiered plate of various exotic sweetmeats beside the bed, with a small dish of bite size pieces of Turkish delight. I opened up the windows to let in the cool night air and looked across the lovely gardens: date palms shone in the moonlight and a tall minaret pointed a finger up into stars in the clear night sky. I felt a little disappointed to be there on my own with no one to share this romantic moment with me.

I felt like I had only just fallen asleep when I awoke with a jolt from my dreams. I shot out of bed; it had been a grave mistake to leave the windows open. Dawn was breaking and the minaret that I had so admired in the moonlight was now an object of hatred. It was blasting out the call to prayers through massive speakers that would be more at home at a Rolling Stones concert. What had happened to the gentle singing of a turbanned mullah who should have been atop the tower? This was no dawn chorus. I believe in respecting other cultures, especially when I am a guest in their country, but I wish I had been prepared for this early start to the day. I would have reconsidered that second bottle of wine.

I went down for breakfast and was soon joined by Nick. He sat down, looking a little worse for wear, and was intent on removing something from his ear. "What's the problem?" I asked.

> "Were you awoken by the loudspeakers this morning? I tried to sleep through them but they drove me nuts. I had kept my earplugs from the airplane, so I grabbed them and stuck them in my ears."
> "I wish I had had a pair!"
> "Well they worked for a while, then I felt something sticky. I had grabbed the Turkish delight at the side of the bed! Now I can't get it out of my ears!"

A mistake so easily made.

We had our business session in the morning and then Nick and I went off too explore Marrakech in the afternoon. We were joined by another OEH compatriot, the elegant, softly spoken John Volponi, a most urbane American chap. He was the general manager of the Inn at Perry Cabin in the US, on the shores of Chesapeake Bay, a short drive from Washington DC. The hotel was new to the company having been acquired by JBS from the English fashion designer, Laura Ashley. It was to be used as the setting for the movie *Wedding Crashers*, starring Owen Wilson, a couple of years later.[115]

We gleaned some information from the hotel's concierge and the three of us set out on our tour of the walled medieval city that dated back to the Berber Empire, with maze-like alleys where thriving souks (marketplaces) sold traditional textiles, pottery and jewelry. There were snake charmers, a great tourist attraction, and the stalls were crammed with things that none of us could identify. It wasn't long before we were picked up by a local 'guide' and no matter how hard we protested, he stayed with us with such dogged determination we gave in.

It wasn't such a bad idea in the end; as we wound our way through a labyrinth of alleyways we would most likely never have found our way out again. We ended up in one shop selling beautiful hand-woven rugs, obviously an arrangement set up with our trusty guide. We were fell upon by the shop owners. It was going to be hard to escape. They were most welcoming, warm and friendly, and offered us tea. Nick and I were about to refuse when John, for fear of offending, accepted. It was now quite obvious as to whom the keen salesmen would direct their pitch; they discarded the two Englishmen and focussed on the polite American. A rug was laid before him, politely rejected as too large. A smaller one was rejected as it was oval, then a square one, a rectangular one, and so it went on. Nick and I were full of admiration for John's creative reasoning in rejecting each rug politely. We positioned ourselves by the door, but John was trapped behind the ever growing pile of rugs before him. Eventually we went to his aid. "John, I am sorry but we must get back to the hotel. Maybe you could return tomorrow when we have more time?"

The expression on John's face was one of pure gratitude. Assuring them of his return, he made his escape.

We did in fact have dinner booked for that night. It is one that I recall with mixed emotions. We were - again - taken through little alleyways. Our escorts knocked on a door which was immediately thrown open by a smiling man who gestured for us to enter, "As-salaam alaikum." He greeted us with a bow.

The door opened onto a magnificent courtyard of date palms and fountains. This was known as a 'a riad', a small palace. We were escorted up to the roof, open to the stars, laid out with rugs, cushions and low tables. It was a setting straight out of 'The Arabian Nights', and I was expecting the sultana Scheherazade to appear at any moment.

At this point the evening became a little less delightful. Sitting on the floor wasn't the worst thing, even though it was uncomfortable for my ageing joints; nor was it the tuneless music, that went on for the entire meal, which was not to my taste. The traditional meal was the source of my dismay.

The first course was described by our host as a sumptuous traditional Moroccan dish, b'stilla. It is pigeon meat cooked in a slightly sweet and savory pie. The problem was that the chef had forgotten to clean, pluck and bone the bird. I am always open to try something new and this I did out of courtesy to our host, but it was a challenge to extricate the bones, feathers and unidentified detritus surreptitiously from my mouth. I often wondered later what the reaction was when the staff found my spat out bones and feathers under the fine rugs - a burial ground of a long departed sultan? Never again would I eat b'stilla.

I can't even recall what followed, as I spent the rest of the evening picking out feathers and small bones from between my teeth. I was therefore thankful for the trays of sweetmeats that had been left as the turndown gift in my bedroom that night, and I also remembered to ensure my window was firmly closed.

We were due to depart the following day, and Nick and I could not resist playing a last schoolboy prank on John. We convinced the concierge to call John in his room. "Mr Volponi, this is Mustafa from concierge. I have a Mr Shehata and a Mr Azzam here wishing to see you, they have some rugs for you. I believe you met them yesterday?"

We couldn't hear the response but it sounded rather panicky. "That is no problem; they are happy to wait." There were a few more words and the concierge hung up. "I think your friend is a little upset."

Nick then called the room, "John, the bus is leaving in a few minutes, I think you need to get down." Trying to contain his laughter. "Yes, I think I see them, the two men from yesterday. They seem to have a few rolls of carpets with them [...] OK, I'll try. [...] Come down and we'll get you out." As he hung up we both broke into gales of laughter. The concierge was also smiling broadly.

John's head very cautiously appeared out of the lift. Trying to edge along the wall without being seen, he eventually reached us. As he looked around, we burst out laughing again. He looked at us with relief. "You bastards." It was a great moment; John eventually forgave us and we have remained friends.

I would have liked to return to Morocco and Marrakech, especially La Mamounia Palace, but then we had 9/11, the 2011 Marrakesh bombing which killed 17 people, and the rise of ISIS, so I have never been back.

Nick and I even found ourselves in scrapes when we were trying to be good. Following one of our management meetings in London, Simon Sherwood felt it would be a good idea to do a company promotion in Paris. We had not done one before and the French were becoming a larger part of our market in the European hotels, as well as at La Samanna in the French West Indies. We also had the Hotel de La Cite in Carcassonne managed by the amiable Jacques Hamburger and our new luxury canal cruises, *Afloat in France*, as well as the Venice Simplon-Orient-Express. [113]

The event was held in a university somewhere off Rue Saint-Jacques, in a government office area. The street was one of those beautifully tree-lined boulevards that make Paris so special. Following the presentation, and wishing - as always - to be in the good books, Nick and I, along with John Rogers, another likeable Englishman who managed La Residencia in Mallorca, volunteered to pack up a number of the displays and take them back to the hotel. The displays folded up very cleverly and fitted into a bright yellow container, similar to a wheelie bin. Once packed, we headed back in the direction of the hotel hoping to find a taxi willing to take the three of us and our cargo. It was about 9.00pm, the streets were deserted, as they are in government districts of that type after hours. We took turns trundling our wheelie bin down the cobbled side street towards the boulevard. The noise was deafening. The wheels rolled over the cobblestones like a tumbril, echoing in the empty street. At last we reached the boulevard that would hopefully lead us back to the city where we might find a taxi. We were all in good spirits, laughing at the three of us dragging this bright yellow wheelie bin through the streets of Paris.

We turned into the boulevard, which was just as deserted. Not a car, not a soul in sight. Surely Parisians don't go to bed this early, we joked. We hadn't gone very far when suddenly we saw - about thirty metres ahead of us - a line of riot police in full black protective gear, stretched from one side of the street to the other. There must have been a hundred or more. With an uncanny resemblance to Darth Vader, their shields and batons glinted in the street lights. We stopped in our tracks. Do we make a tactical retreat? They might think we were trying to hide something by running away. Nick muttered "Just keep walking."

They watched us approach, looking like they were prepared to charge. But no one moved. I whispered, "Anyone speak French?" Thankfully Nick did. We advanced closer to this wall of terrifying men in their black body armour, shields and batons at the ready. To allay my fear, as we three Englishmen kept moving forward, I mumbled Henry V's exhortation at Agincourt.

Once more unto the breach, dear friends, once more;
Or close the wall up with our English dead….
...good yeoman,

Whose limbs were made in England, show us here
The mettle of your pasture; let us swear
That you are worth your breeding;...
Follow your spirit, and upon this charge
Cry 'God for Harry, England, and Saint George!'

Where the bloody hell was King Harry when you needed him?

Just as I thought we were about to meet our very own Waterloo, the line parted in the centre and without a word being spoken they peeled back, creating a gap through which we could pass. It then closed behind us. We kept moving, grateful for our good fortune. King Harry was right; there was now a definite feeling of euphoria.

And gentlemen in England now a-bed
Shall think themselves accurs'd they were not here,
And hold their manhoods cheap whiles any speaks
That fought with us upon Saint Crispin's day.

My English pride came before a fall. It was not St Crispin's Day, neither was this Agincourt. From a side street poured about twenty more police, surrounding us.

"Arrêtez! Les mains en l'airs!"

We froze. One searched our wheelie bin, others patted us down. Not a word was said until one officer started asking questions. Nick obviously gave all the right answers in French as we were then waved on with an air of irritation. We never learned what this had all been about. Perhaps they were expecting a demonstration, but we saw no mention of anything in the press or on TV the following day. At the time we thought it all hysterically funny. No doubt a similar scenario in our terror-conscious environment today would have run very differently.

I found myself in Los Angeles on a number of occasions, and had a love-hate relationship with the city, but I was fortunate to stay at some wonderful hotels when I attended my last *Leading Hotels* conference.

I loved the Bel Air in Hollywood, with swans floating in the waterways, ever since I was invited to stay in the mid 1990s by good friend Frank Bowling. He was a gifted and graceful hotelier. Another fave was The Beverly Wilshire, now forever linked in my mind with *Pretty Woman* and Julia Roberts. It was then run by Radha Arora, now President of Rosewood Hotels. Radha was always noted for his sartorial elegance, and was the protege of Terry Holmes at the Ritz in London, where I first met him. My favourite hotel was the Peninsula Hotel, managed at the time by Ali Kasikci, another great hotelier. Two things stay in my mind about this hotel: the sheets were the most comfortable I have ever slept in, and the rooftop pool with its cabanas, had the best panoramic views of Los Angeles.

The Beverly Hills Hotel on Sunset Boulevard is the most over-the-top hotel I have every stayed at in. It is pure Hollywood. The second you see this 'Pink Palace' of extravagance with its iconic sign you know you are going to have a memorable experience. It is one of Hollywood's brightest stars, 'the ultimate beacon of glamour', to quote their own publicity material, and as you enter you don't doubt it. It was impossible to get away from the pink candy stripe design or the massive tropical leaf motif. This was LA.

My bedroom was plush with padded furniture and all the comforts one could desire. What caught my eye was the large candy stripe hatbox in the bathroom containing every conceivable promotional product. Apart from the usual nail brush, toothpaste, toothbrushes, soaps and loofah, there was an array of cosmetics that could have filled an Estee Lauder counter. Had I attempted to bring it back home with me I would have had to pay excess baggage and duty.

I set off for a cocktail in the Polo Lounge. It would be impossible for me to describe it, so I will use the hotel's own description:

> Where else but the Polo Lounge could you have a candy-striped ceiling and make it look effortlessly cool? This iconic room, once described as 'Hollywood's commissary' has a history as fabled as Tinsel Town itself.

I was alone in the bar, apart from the very charming Pepe, with whom I chatted and who loved Australia and wanted to visit. I happily gave him my business card and offered him a job. He never did come to Sydney, but a Christmas Card arrived on my desk for the next ten years signed by the charming *Jose 'Pepe' De Ana - Polo Lounge - The Beverly Hills Hotel.*

He showed me to my table and explained that this was the best place to sit, to quietly watch the doorway in the mirror to see who was arriving. I was onto my second glass before anybody entered. A very frail elderly man tottered in. At first I didn't recognise him, but he sat quite near me and ordered a drink and I heard the gravelly voice. It was James Coburn, whose ultracool persona had propelled him to stardom in films such as *The Magnificent Seven* and *The Great Escape*. In the latter film he played an Australian POW attempting an Aussie accent, without much success.

When his drink arrived he had great difficulty holding the glass. It was tragic to see this in a man who had been so deft with his knife throwing in *The Magnificent Seven.* We spoke a little and he was very pleasant. He died a few months later.

I headed off to a dinner appointment with Lorraine Flaks, our US sales director, and a couple of travel agents. We met at

Spagos, Wolfgang Puck's restaurant. I had eaten at his restaurant when he first started out. I arrived early and was shown to our table, to do some people watching. Nearby was an elderly, rotund, balding man with a glamorous woman, very much younger than he. I wondered if she was his niece, but the body language was all wrong. He gave her a small box, which even from where I was sitting could see contained a large diamond ring. I wondered if this was for favours past or expectations for favours in the future. In any event she was affectionately delighted. She had to be an actress and from what I had seen, a good one. Very Hollywood.

Lorraine arrived with our other two guests. As the conversation flowed, I noticed another familiar face. I was getting used to the large age discrepancy that was the norm between my fellow diners, and in the case of this man he might almost have got away with it. With another lovely young woman sat the man who used to set every woman's heart racing and caused hysteria among his fans. Fifty years ago. The years had not been kind to Tony Curtis. He was shorter than I thought, and even with the evident 'work' he no longer matched the image of the heroes he had played in *Spartacus* or *The Vikings*. I could barely see the vestiges of Joe from *Some Like It Hot* with Jack Lemmon and Marilyn Monroe.

As the host, at the end of the meal I took the check when it arrived. I was glad I was still seated, and that it was on the company tab. It had reached the proportions of a small mortgage. Knowing how Americans are about tipping, I left what I felt was a most generous tip of 10%, which when calculated on the bill was a sizable amount. It was what the entire meal might have cost me back in Sydney. As I sat waiting for my receipt and credit card, the waiter came over and with genuine concern asked, "I hope you enjoyed your meal sir, and everything was to your liking?"

"Delicious, thank you, charming service."

A moment later another waiter came over. "Was everything alright with your meal, sir?"

They really are going over the top with service, I thought. Having reconfirmed we had loved the meal, he left. A third man walked up: the maitre d'. "How was your meal sir, I do hope the service and food was to your liking?"

I was starting to become bewildered at this excessive concern. Were they that keen to have me return?

As we were nearly out the door, Lorraine asked, "What was that all about?"

"I have no idea."

"Did you tip them?"

I explained my generosity and how much I had left them.

"Ah", Lorraine said knowingly. "At a place like this they have expectations for a little more than that. About double or more."

"Oh. Sorry. Do you think I might still be able to get a table in future?"

"I doubt it."

I was always taken by surprise at the tipping culture in America. Menus appear cheaper, but once you add all the taxes and the tips in, it's not as cheap as it looks. Then again, hospitality staff are so poorly paid in the US - the minimum wage is about 60% lower than in Australia.

With *Leading Hotels of the World* I met many good people and it took me to some great places, but, in truth, apart from positioning, we did not gain much in the way of new customers.

I mentioned before that two organisations helped our marketing, and the second one provided the better return on investment. In 1988 a company emerged providing marketing services and programs for independent luxury travel agencies, then known as Allied Percival International (API). They were a great success as they dealt with the agencies servicing luxury travellers that hotels such as ours wanted to attract. Matthew Church was the very dynamic and creative head of this organisation.

They held an annual convention which enabled hoteliers to have direct access to the travel agencies. Initially numbers were small, and I first attended a convention at The Phoenician in Scottsdale Arizona, and next in Hawaii at a hotel belonging to the unnamed chain I regard as my nemesis in the industry. Where my philosophy was to build on the positives of individuality and personality of the staff, this chain trained each employee to conform in word, thought and deed like robots, and with about the same degree of sincerity and personality.

I checked in, my credit card was noted and handed back, and I said, "Thank you."

"That is my pleasure sir," came the reply, polite and with a smile.

A porter appeared who took me to my room and handed me my key. Me: "Thank you."

"That is my pleasure sir," came the reply.

Later that evening a very pleasant room attendant came to turn down my bed. I declared, "Thank you."

"That is my pleasure sir."

I headed to the bar and ordered a glass of wine, which the barman placed before me. "Thank you," I asserted.

Sure enough: "That is my pleasure sir." For five days in residence, every time I used the words, "Thank you", I got the same reply, "That is my pleasure sir".

I decided not to say 'Thank you' but just nod and offer a grateful smile - thinking my words were a trigger for these auto-bots. That didn't work. "That is my pleasure sir" still came as the automatic reply. I do not say it wasn't courteous, but it became monotonous and most certainly did not sound sincere. I eventually asked the barman why everyone used the same response. "It's our training, we have to say it." The last few words of his statement got me - *we have to say it*.

I pushed him and asked what would happen if they said something different, something they wanted to say. "I would probably be fired." I thanked him for the chat, and "That is my pleasure sir" came the reply.

To me, this conformity is at the root of what is wrong in the hospitality industry today, as major chains become the norm. By all means, let them set standards of service consistency, produce identical building styles and interior design and dress staff globally in the same uniforms if they must. But with the staff themselves, let them maintain a degree of individuality rather than training them to be robots. Is there really a need to standardise all verbal communications? Select the right staff, with the best attitude, and trust them. I think managers might be surprised at the result - it delivered for us in spades at The Observatory.

As API grew, they changed the name and rebranded as 'Virtuoso'. The membership grew at such a rate it was no longer possible to find hotels large enough to accommodate both agents and hoteliers at their conference. In 2002 the Virtuoso annual convention had a new home at The Bellagio in Las Vegas. I walked into the convention hall in search of my small table, and the size of the event was quite daunting. There were new 'speed dating' rules; the hotelier sat at a desk and an agent would appear before you. You had three minutes to present your pitch. A bell would ring and the next agent would appear. By the end of the second day, you would be lucky to have a voice left. The next year it became worse as now it was the agents who sat still and the hoteliers moved from table to table, fumbling with their presentation folders. I would be faced with an expressionless agent who had tuned out hours before. As one agent grumbled, "If I see a picture of another hotel bathroom I will scream. Tell me something different about your hotel."

And so it was I laboured long and hard to find something that gave The Observatory a point of difference - in three minutes. Eventually it became a case of narrowing the field to those who actually sent business to Australia, and then making a personal bond with the agent. I learned that for a person to travel halfway around the world to our hotel, we had to sell the idea of travelling all the way Australia in the first place.

Australia had done some good marketing campaigns in America, although none was as popular as Paul Hogan's *Throw another shrimp on the barbie* ad. In fact, it was still remembered years after it ceased to be promoted. Remembered that is, until 2006 when Scott Morrison, as managing director of Tourism Australia, came up with a new slogan: *'So where the bloody hell are you?'* The language horrified the American and Japanese agents and did not go down at all well. I'd often get an agent castigating me over the use of such foul language. I was always amused at the double standards. Martin Scorsese's film *The Wolf of Wall Street* set a Guinness World record for the most swearing in one film: 'f**k' was used 506 times, an average of 2.81 times per minute. The Aussie campaign cost $180 million, got banned in the UK and was pulled in 2008. Scott Morrison went on to become Prime Minister of Australia.

The relationships developed with the agents were later cemented when the 'Virtuoso Symposium' was introduced. This event was held with a focus on a destination: a 'familiarisation tour' of a specific country, where again hoteliers from around the world would attend to develop their network. It would be utterly wrong to pretend I didn't look forward to these events, as the destinations would pull out all the stops to show off the very best they had to offer.

I had not been back to Hong Kong since it was handed back to China in 1997 so I was interested to see it in 2003. I had always enjoyed the 'white knuckle ride' into Kai Tak Airport, as the plane banked sharply and weaved in between the skyscrapers where you could actually see into the windows as families cooked dinner. I learnt from a pilot that it was one of the most feared and dangerous airports at which to land, when no computers could be used and all done manually, so it had earned the nickname Kai Tak - Heart Attack. Hong Kong was still suffering negative publicity following the outbreak of avian flu and so the government went over and above to impress. They succeeded, with the spectacular finale being a gala dinner at the Hong Kong Convention Centre overlooking Victoria Harbour.

The 'Virtuoso Symposium' events in Singapore and Cambodia were also memorable. Singapore was true to its international image, although Bugis Street was now Burgis Street, and without the transvestites and transsexuals who had made it famous in the 50s and 60s. The area had been cleaned up in keeping with the rest of Singapore, which was now one of the cleanest cities in Asia, if not the world. It was rather a disappointment. There's something engaging about Asian grittiness: the moss growing on the walls in the humidity, the slight grubbiness, the smoke and smells of the street vendors was missing. Bangkok on the other hand was *too* grubby, whereas Hong Kong I think had got it just right.

Singapore put on a great show. Sentosa Island, with a group of aging 50-something agents dying to recapture their youth and queuing up to do the Skyline Luge was something to behold. Some I might say were surprisingly good; their experience in electric wheelchairs may have given them the edge. I on the other hand diplomatically held back to allow the agents to win; that is my story and I am sticking to it.

After such exertions, I found my niche in a comfortable chair sipping my Singapore Sling in a corner of the Long Bar in the Raffles Hotel, following the time honoured tradition of discarding the peanut shells on the floor. I loved this elegant Colonial style hotel with its landscaped gardens built in the 1880s, when half the world appeared in my schoolboy's atlas as pink, the map colour for the British Empire, now long gone.

From here we headed to Siem Reap, where Orient-Express owned a hotel called La Résidence d'Angkor, recently acquired, managed by a delightful young Frenchman, Pascal Deyrolle. The hotel was set amongst lush trees on the banks of the Siem Reap River, and from my room I looked across to a few huts that were obviously the homes of local families, with children running around chasing chickens. It was a charming but sobering view of the real Cambodia - just a fence dividing my world of comfort and privilege from their rather more simple life. I hope from the squeals and laughter of the children it meant it was a happy one. [116]

Early in the morning we took a ride to the iconic Angkor Wat temple, about eight kilometres away. Many sunsets and sunrises are claimed as the most spectacular; for me, there was something very special about watching the sun rise over this temple. It was originally Hindu, dedicated to Vishnu, then in the late 12th century it was gradually transformed into a Buddhist temple. It is an extraordinary place, and I ran my hand over the numerous wall carvings, thinking of the stonemasons working here 800 years ago, and the worshipers wandering about much like I was doing.

Nothing could have prepared me for the dinner that night. I have eaten in some interesting places, from beaches in the USA to rooftops in Marrakech, but this one beat them all. We arrived by bus at a spot in the jungle. As we got off the air-conditioned bus the steamy tropical night air enveloped us, and we followed a path through the trees, lit by torch bearers in colourful traditional dress. Giant ice carvings were set either side of the path to cool us as we walked. In a clearing our dinner was served, framed by the beautiful ruins of a centuries-old temple, with burning torches lighting the scene. It could have been the set for an Indiana Jones movie. In the flickering light, surrounded by warm smiling staff from the local hotel schools in national dress, we drank cold champagne and were entertained by traditional dance and music. The spectacle was jaw-dropping. [117]

The staff's warmth and friendliness could not help but impress the most hardened of travel agents, who hopefully would send more clients to visit Cambodia. Apparently this is exactly what has happened, as the last report I heard was 'do not attempt to see the sunrise over Angkor Wat as you won't get near the place for throngs of tourists'. Sometimes success can ruin a place. I was fortunate to see it when I did in its fairly untouched state.

I spent a few days in Phnom Penh as I had been moved by the horrors of the movie, *The Killing Fields* and I wanted to see the place first-hand. I visited a school, S21, that had been used as a prison where unspeakable events took place, after which my driver took me out of the city along a raised dirt road through endless paddy fields to Choeung Ek about 17 kilometres outside Phnom Penh. It was such a peaceful, pretty place, and I realised that the pagoda at the centre was stacked with skulls of the murdered people. Around the area where pits had been dug to bury the dead, I saw bits of clothing still protruding from the mud. The eerie silence was overwhelming. I could not comprehend the suffering nor how such things could happen. I thought of the young people who had served our dinner a few nights earlier, and their parents and grandparents who were the victims or the perpetrators of this tragedy. I had to fight back tears. What had this quiet place witnessed?

The silence was suddenly broken by the shouts and laughter of children, the sound floating across the padi fields from a small school nearby. It almost made me weep with joy.

The journey back was silent, until I asked my driver what he remembered of it. His answer rather shamed me. "This place is for tourists. Cambodians don't visit. Things happen in life, and many bad things happened, but life goes on. We can't live in the past, we must forgive and try to build a better, more understanding country."

More than a million people were killed and buried by the Khmer Rouge during its rule from 1975 to 1979, nearly a quarter of the population: teachers, doctors, politicians and other educated Cambodians. If a parent was killed, then so was the entire family, so as to leave no one to seek revenge. Now busloads of "dark tourists" as they are now known come to see the mass graves and the pagoda of skulls, and it made me feel a little ashamed that I had been part of this grotesque and gruesome form of tourism.

I visited the region again when, having started to plan my retirement to Thailand, I purchased five acres of land on the banks of the Mekong River, opposite Vientiane, the capital of Laos. It was announced that our train, the Eastern Oriental Express, (E&OE) was to launch a new route that would take the train for the first time up to North East Thailand and across the Friendship Bridge at Nong Kai to Vientiane, the first train to do so. As I had some knowledge of the area I was invited along to assist with hosting a travel agent to whom we were promoting the trip.[118]

✧ ✧ ✧

In September 1993, Juan Antonio Samaranch of the International Olympic Committee announced the words that sent Sydney into a frenzy. *'The winner is Syd-en-ey!'* Sydney had won its bid to host the 2000 Summer Olympics, defeating Beijing by only two votes.

It was the middle of the night in Sydney but within minutes the phone was ringing with people wanting to book rooms - seven years ahead! We knew it was going to be big, but it turned out to be huge. What followed were offers of all sorts of incentives, all of which were put aside. There was however one American who turned up on our doorstep with what turned out to be an offer *I could not refuse*.

I listened to him at first with a great deal of suspicion. He owned a travel company with one business: providing major companies with packages to attend the summer and winter Olympic Games, wherever they might be. The deal offered to the hotel was the purchase of blocks of rooms with all meals. This was actually a bonus for us, because it filled in the revenue gap we'd have through loss of daytime restaurant business, if everyone was out at the Games. His packages were for several days each, with one group following the other for the entire period of the Olympics. Most surprising of all, he did not seek a discount. I said I would consider his offer but it all sounded far too good to be true. I set about contacting fellow hoteliers with whom he had done business during the Barcelona Olympics in 1992, and the winter Olympics in Albertville, France. All reports came back very positive; they wished they had given him *all* their rooms.

We then proposed what we believed to be an exceptionally good deal at excellent rates, taking into account the event was not for a few years. This was tentatively accepted and a contract drawn up, the draft of which had been agreed to by head office. I was not prepared for what came next. As the Olympics was such a special event and one that his clients paid a substantial price for, he felt it was important that we understood what was expected. To this end he *requested* - it was not really an invitation - that my wife and I attend the Olympic Games in Atlanta in 1996. I could not imagine Orient-Express shelling out for this sort of trip, but I was floored when he announced that *this will all be at our expense including flights, hotels and entry to the Games themselves.* I was about to immediately shake his hand but I paused for a second. Would the head office think this was some form of bribe, or corruption? I hid my excitement, thanked him and rather coolly said I would get back to him.

I did get back to him, and yes, my wife and I had a very pleasant trip to the Games of the XXVI Olympiad in Atlanta, albeit a little more eventful than planned with news of a major TWA air crash as we arrived and a terrorist bomb at the games as we departed. Oh how pleased I was that I became a hotelier rather than a deck officer on the high seas in Her Majesty's Navy, even if I didn't have a smart uniform. Oh well there had to be some sacrifices.

Chapter 11

#shoppingaround #islandslodgesn'lakes #trainsn'tantrums

For the first few years at The Observatory Hotel, Orient-Express was managing the property for its Japanese owners, the Nara Corporation. In the late 90s, Nara followed many other Japanese companies and withdrew from the Australian market. JBS and his son Simon agreed to buy The Observatory, along with two other Nara properties, Lilianfels in the Blue Mountains about two hours' drive west of Sydney, and Bora Bora Lagoon Resort in Tahiti. As these were to fall under my domain, I was rather excited at the prospect of trips to Tahiti. My enthusiasm was soon dampened by my colleague Willi Martin from the Park Hyatt in Sydney. He had a similar responsibility for a Hyatt property in Tahiti, and told me what a nightmare it was to get there from Sydney: it involved multiple flights, waits, layovers and boat transfers with limited timetables. I was therefore less disappointed than I would have been when Orient-Express requested that I focus on Lilianfels. JBS had also made it clear that it was not his choice to buy Bora Bora; having visited the place regularly in his navy days, he referred to it as 'Boring Boring'. So it came to pass that I oversaw just the two hotels.

JBS was keen to develop the Orient-Express brand in the Asia-Pacific region, but Simon, now President and CEO, did not share his enthusiasm. JBS was a visionary and loved a challenge, whereas Simon was far more cautious with a strong eye on the here and now, especially with regard to the bottom line.

In Asia, there was strong tourism demand and room rates were reasonably high in premium properties like those of the Orient-Express group. The operating costs, especially labour, were relatively low. The problem was that hotels that had been built prior to the global financial crisis in 2007 were not showing a return on investment. As *operators*, we would calculate the value of a hotel based on multiples of the bottom line, whereas *owners* look for a profit on their investment - and they would not negotiate. I learned why at my own personal cost some years later. Many hotels in Asia were paid for in questionable cash deals, which masked the transaction. Most western hotels are indebted to a bank for a loan, so if the money remained buried in bricks and mortar, owners seemed happy to simply leave it there. Far from reducing the price for a sale, they would often increase it as time went by until a buyer was eventually found. This was not the way of Orient-Express.

It took a number of years before the right deal came along which enabled Orient-Express to buy a small group of hotels, and then upgrade them to the company's standard. They had done this with the Pansi Group, resulting in a foot hold in South East Asia with hotels in Thailand, Laos, Cambodia and Bali.

In regards to my own domain, we were to search out properties in Australia and New Zealand. I was not confident that our search would result in much success in Australia, but had more hope we might find something in New Zealand. 'The land of the long white cloud' had managed to get the formula right when it came to smaller hotel properties, better known as lodges. They had set their room rates much higher and kept them there, producing better returns than we were achieving in Australia.

Simon was never keen, but JBS would send us off on inspection trips and we wrote numerous reports on our findings. On these trips I was usually accompanied by Ian Routledge, JBS's man in Sydney. We explored the Antipodes in search of the right properties for the OEH group. On other occasions Scott Downes my financial controller or, when he left, Stacey Gurrie accompanied me.

We had great fun on these adventures and some got closer to the finishing line than others. We visited Hayman Island, off the coast of Central Queensland, originally developed in the 1950s by millionaire Reg Ansett, founder of Ansett Airlines. I've mentioned that Sir Peter Abeles spent over $300 million turning it into a palatial resort. There were many problems in regard to daily supply and even water had to be shipped in. This one fell into the too-hard basket.

Other islands we looked at were Bedarra, Dunk and Daydream, although this last one kept getting blown away by cyclones. One of my favourites was Heron Island. It had stunning wildlife, birds that you tripped over as you walked about and crystal-clear water. I'm sure I caught a glimpse of Robinson Crusoe in the distance.

Another potential Queensland buy was Lizard Island, probably the best of the island resorts: a 1,013-hectare national park and right on top of the Great Barrier Reef. It was beautiful, popular and very expensive. We hesitated, and it was snapped up by another buyer. These trips could be tough but someone had to do it! [119]

One benefit of this trip at least was that we were able to poach the general manager, an incredibly talented young woman, Robyn Pontynen, to run Lilianfels in the Blue Mountains which had been going through some difficult times; I felt the manager had let the laid-back mountain life cloud his better judgement, and staff were running the place to suit themselves. Robyn, the first female manager in the company, faced a tough challenge. The staff, having had the run of the hotel, were naturally appalled at having to obey a new manager with new rules. The hostility Robyn faced was extraordinary. They made her run a gauntlet of disruptions to daily operations. One of them allegedly even interrupted the gas service to the hotel. The last straw was when the local police called me to tell me my manager - Robyn - was stealing furniture from the hotel. I had actually authorised her to take some old items to help her furnish her new flat. The informant was a staffer who was related to the policeman. So much for the integrity of NSW police!

Most managers would have just walked away. Not Robyn. She turned the operation around, eventually building a team of devoted followers. She was one of the most professional and successful managers I have ever dealt with. I've never seen such drive and commitment nor such a sense of adventure. Her holidays were not spent lying on a beach in Bali. She'd be off on a trip down the Amazon or trekking up mountains to see the gorillas of Rwanda and Uganda. Hardly surprising that she eventually left Lilianfels to manage the Kwai River Lodge in Botswana. I saw her again when I visited the lodge with my boys a few years later.

We continued to search in our hope to expand Orient-Express in the Asia-Pacific. We had high expectations of finding something that fitted with the brand on the Australian mainland. The Heritage Lodge in The Daintree Rainforest was interesting, with streams nearby containing some of the largest and most fearsome saltwater crocodiles I have seen, and at far too close quarters for my taste. Ian and I spent a few days in Tasmania and very much liked Cradle Mountain Lodge, set right on the edge of World Heritage-listed Cradle Mountain-Lake St Clair National

Park. There was much we would need to do, starting with the service. Having noticed there were no phones in the rooms, I asked the manager why. His reply? "No, not keen on them, if phones are available people will just be calling us and wanting things."

I was not impressed.

Ian and I were optimistic for a property in Perth, although JBS was more interested in Fremantle. Tim Roberts was the boss of Multiplex, who had built The Observatory, and asked if we might be interested in going into business to develop the Old Swan Brewery, an interesting character building dating back to the 1880s lying vacant on the banks of the Swan River. It was the time of the mining boom and it had possibilities. As we viewed it from a helicopter, with Tim at the controls, the view across the water to the Old Brewery with Kings Park as a backdrop looked impressive. The only problem was that it was not in the CBD, something I recalled from my Como days in Melbourne. They dismissed this issue as they planned a boat would drop guests off at Elizabeth Quay in a Venetian experience, but to me it was fanciful. Business at the time was good for hotels but the room rates were still low. On closer examination, with the number of rooms we could fit in, together with location and parking issues, it was a non-starter. It ended up as apartments with a cafe/restaurant and function centre.

I really hoped we would find something in New Zealand as it is a beautiful country. The first potential purchase was a hotel under construction in Auckland, on the quay on the waterfront. It was being built by an interesting man who entertained Ian and I royally. By the time JBS arrived, he was not keen on the chap and appeared to hate the property. Some years later he was to stay there, and I was surprised when he instructed me to approach the owners with a view to purchasing it. By this time Hilton had a fifteen-year lease on it, so no go. One property we looked at had a salmon run beside the hotel, and another was on a lake near Queenstown. It reminded me of Lake Lucerne in Switzerland, with tourist boats gliding through the still waters in the shadows of the mountains that rose out of the lake.

The best of all was a small property near Nelson on the South Island, The Lodge At Paratiho Farms. It had been developed by a very wealthy American couple. The detail was extraordinary and the money spent phenomenal, from the graded coloured stones that edged the car park to the technology in the bedrooms. The bathroom amenities surpassed even those of the Beverly Hills Hotel, and it was the first time I had encountered a bedroom where, when answering a call of nature in the middle of the night, rather than stumbling through the darkness searching for a light, as you step out of bed a soft light automatically brightens your way and on returning to your bed, it dims back into darkness. Wonderful.

All this travel I fear did not result in any purchases. Orient-Express ownership remained at just the two properties in Australia, The Observatory and Lilianfels in the Blue Mountains.

We did however meet with a little success if only by playing a minor part. Vincent O'Rourke, CEO of Queensland Rail, happened to hear Nick Varian, the Vice President of the trains division of Orient-Express, speaking at a conference and was fired up with the idea of developing an Orient-Express style train in Australia. Vince was very much an entrepreneur and a man of vision. Queensland Rail, in an attempt to make itself profitable, had been downsizing and staff had been laid off. To help placate the unions, with many staff who were skilled craftsmen but no longer required, Vince set them to work renovating old carriages, much in the same way as JBS had done with our own train, The Venice Simplon-Orient-Express.

Nick Varian was interested and we were asked to view the carriages and the feasibility of the route from Cairns to Brisbane. The carriages had been beautifully restored, certainly to the standard of our own, but better in terms of facilities as they had ensuite showers and even a viewing car, more in line with the Eastern & Oriental Express (E&OE). Their *Spirit of Queensland* already ran the same route as we planned to do, but it was not of the same style and, when Ian and I experienced it, we found it uninspiring. The decor was basic and the experience underwhelming. Music was piped through to the cabin, the source being a young woman in the bar car playing on an electronic keyboard. Her songs would be interrupted as we passed something of interest, with a sudden enthusiastic squeal, "Look over there to the right, a mob of kangaroos!" The train lacked the sophistication and romance that we offered, and even in my wildest imagination I could not see Hercule Poirot boarding such a train.

Much as we had done with the E&OE train in Asia we set about developing a new Australian train and this was to be called The Great South Pacific Express, (GSPE) at a cost of $35 million. [120]

The route was to run from Cairns down the coast to Brisbane and then on to Sydney, however there was the problem of the two different rail gauges. Queensland had adopted the narrow gage of 3 foot 6 inches, whilst New South Wales had the standard gauge of 4 foot 8 and a 1/2inches. This necessitated a stopover in Brisbane whilst a complicated lifting system raised the carriages up and replaced the bogies, the wheels. The narrow gauge was less stable so the train rocked rather more than was comfortable, and was not helped by the poor suspension. Finally, there was the matter of the drivers, who were used to carrying freight. As such they did not bother about Newton's first law of motion and what happens to the people on board when the train braked or accelerated. It was many months before the drivers learned to drive their locomotives with more of a deft hand with passengers in mind.

The train was eventually launched in 1997 with great fanfare. We had arranged for a special dining experience for local dignitaries in Sydney. Our own chef, Randell St Clare, was to prepare the dinner on board with Christian Bodiguel, the chef of the Venice Simplon-Orient-Express, who was here on a promotional trip. [150, 160]

This grand event nearly didn't happen. The night before it was due to take place, I received a call late at night telling me the train was on fire. Fortunately the security staff acted promptly and put the fire out before it did too much damage. At the crack of dawn we were on board, with the hotel's cleaning staff, engineers and anyone else we could rope in to assist. They did an amazing job, and it looked as if nothing had happened. I got home just in time to don my dinner jacket and return to welcome our VIP guests on board.

The preparation and service of a dinner for sixty guests, all to be served at the same time from a small galley on a moving train was not an easy task. Stress levels were high. The train pulled out of Mortuary Station in Sydney, an interesting point of departure. This haunted Victorian Gothic structure was built in 1880 to transport deceased people to the end of the line, literally, to their last resting place. It was buzzing around that the fire the night before was the result of dark forces. I hoped that this was not a sign of things to come. With everyone on board we snaked our way towards the Sydney Harbour Bridge, champagne in hand and all in a very celebratory mood. It was a wonderful way of travelling and all our VIPs were thoroughly enjoying themselves. Our destination was Lavender Bay where we would stop and enable the diners to enjoy their meal whilst looking out to a spectacular view of the harbour.

The meal was going well when I spotted my maitre d' looking flustered and signalling to me from the end of the dining car. I thought of ignoring him but the look of panic on his face made me think twice. I excused myself and headed to the galley. The scene was straight out of *Fawlty Towers*. Our chef was on the floor scuffling with the engine driver. Fortunately, the space did not allow enough room for real fists to swing but it was not for lack of trying. Visiting chef Christian Bodiguel looked on in total bewilderment, and the waitstaff stood there in a line waiting for the next course to be served.

I managed to separate the two combatants, and in no uncertain terms told my chef to get on with his business, whilst also trying to calm the engine driver. It appeared that in the middle of service the engine driver and his stoker had appeared in the galley and demanded dinner for them both. They received short shrift from the chef who was already on the verge of a heart attack. This led to a few strong words, and then an ultimatum from the driver that should they not get their meal then and there they would go on strike and abandon the train where it stood. I was fortunate to have David Hill, the Director of State Rail on board, who came to our aid. After a few placatory words and a couple of bottles of champagne to take home, some food was found and an uneasy truce ensued. The inaugural trip in Sydney was therefore a great success, and our driver brought us back safely. As a bonus, at Mortuary Station all our passengers and staff alighted alive and well and no-one required a coffin, much to the disappointment of one or two superstitious staff.

My conversation with David Hill was remarkable. When I told him of my background and training at the Grand Hotel in Eastbourne, he told me that he had been born in Eastbourne in 1946, into a poor family with four boys, and his single mum had been a chambermaid at the Grand Hotel! Not being able to keep all the children, she placed him and his twin brother in Barnardo's children's home in Barkingside, Essex. He migrated to Australia with his brothers from Tilbury Docks, London in April 1959 aboard the *SS Strathaird*. He told me of the tough times he experienced as a child, and some time later I saw an interview with him that reminded me how moved I had been when we chatted on the train.

> "I can only remember it as traumatic. The idea of nurturing and care and affection and love just didn't enter the equation back in those days. I can remember Mum gave us some coloured writing paper so we could write to her. The other kids stole our paper, humiliating us, tearing it up and running away. It was only much later I realised this cruelty was because they didn't have anybody to write to."

A tragic story, with a happy ending for David in Australia. What astounded me was the fact that he told me all about it. In England a man in his position would have attempted to bury his family background for fear of judgement. In Australia such things were not considered important and, if anything, he was proud of it. I like that about Australia.

The Great South Pacific Express ran successfully for a few years, although without great profit, and when a Labor government took over in Queensland, the new transport minister decommissioned the train in 2003 to save money. It had run up losses of around $12 million over four years. I felt this was a very short-sighted move as it brought a lot of kudos to tourism in Queensland. Obviously not a view shared by those who held the purse strings.

The magnificent carriages were left to languish in storage at North Ipswich for a few years until a settlement was agreed with

Orient-Express, and in 2016 they were shipped to Peru in South America.

In May 2017, Orient-Express Hotels, Trains & Cruises, now renamed 'Belmond', relaunched the Great South Pacific Express, also renamed and refurbished, as the Belmond Andean Explorer, South America's first luxury sleeper train. The train now travels from Cusco, climbing to 4800 metres on the Altiplano, before arriving at Lake Titicaca and then continues to Arequipa, a city with a UNESCO World Heritage site, stopping en route at Sumbay Caves, where it is possible to add on a visit to the Colca Canyon, known for its condors. It was far removed from its origins and a very long way from its original planned journey of the eastern seaboard of Australia as seen by its visionary creator, Vincent O'Rourke.

Chapter 12

#masterchefs #toomanycooks #foodforthought

By the time I had reached my position at The Observatory, the industry had changed greatly. Apart from advances in technology - computers didn't exist when I first started - chefs now had not only to be specialists in their chosen cuisine and style, they now had to be star media performers and public relations experts. It was no longer enough to simply be a good chef, and they couldn't hide their (understandable) bad tempers behind the kitchen wall any more.

Our first executive chef at The Observatory, Kit Chan, was a brilliant and innovative chef but was rather shy and reticent with the press. Mark Clayton, a young Englishman, was a good chef and we sent him to The Cipriani in Venice to learn the Italian style of cuisine that we wanted as our signature cuisine, but I don't think he liked being confined in this way. We therefore agreed to let our next chef try a more popular style of *Modern Australian*. Anthony Musarra was an Australian chef and did well, and the press started to take notice, especially when we started to host visiting celebrity chefs.[121, 122, 123]

These events grew and grew, and, as new chefs joined us, each brought something different and exciting to the hotel. After Anthony, our chef was Randal St Clare, a larger than life American from Portland, Oregon. He was a great performer and the press loved him. For the first time The Galileo was awarded a chef's hat in the *Sydney Morning Herald Good Food Guide*, the first hotel restaurant to receive one. Randal was followed by another Australian, Steve Grein, who after leaving us went to The Portman Ritz-Carlton Shanghai. He was a great chef but Randal was a hard act to follow. On Steve's departure, we sought to change our image, helped dramatically by our next chef. [124, 125]

I was friends with Tetsuya Wakuda, an iconic Japanese chef and restaurateur in Sydney. I had first met him when he had his restaurant in Rozelle, and later, when he wanted to move into the city, we talked about setting up his restaurant at the hotel. I thought it was a brilliant idea, but head office did not. At the time we were managing the hotel for Mr Nara, and it was deemed that it was our expertise that he was buying and would therefore have reflected badly on us to contract out the restaurant. This was especially risky as Tetsuya was Japanese, and Mr Nara ironically was rather an Anglophile. Tetsuya's food was some of the finest I have ever eaten, so when another highly recommended Japanese chef came forward I was more than enthusiastic.

We employed Haru Inukai immediately and what an impression he made! On his first day he came to my office with concern that the kitchen wasn't very clean. I was obviously worried that his first impression was not a good one. I immediately offered to call in a cleaning team. He said simply "No that is OK, I will deal with it."

I thought I'd best go and see for myself. I was surprised to see him, scrubbing brush in hand, doing it himself. The other members of his brigade stood looking on in amazement. Chefs do not clean kitchens! Haru, however, did and before long, the rest of the team were scrubbing away as well. A man who leads from the front - I liked him immediately. Another time, I was having breakfast when I saw a delivery truck passing by with Haru in hot pursuit waving a tray of strawberries. He caught up with the surprised driver and gave him a dressing down as to never ever leaving supplies on the loading dock without allowing him to personally inspect the quality of the items. From day one a new set of standards applied in his kitchen. Having enjoyed the style Haru brought to the hotel, I was sorry when he decided to leave to set up his own restaurant. It is always hard to hang to staff with such talent. [126]

Haru suggested we employ another Japanese chef and I was delighted when I discovered he had been the chef at a Michelin-starred restaurant in Tokyo. Masahiko Yomoda, or Yomo as we knew him, was a wonderful new addition and took the restaurant from strength to strength, staying there until my retirement in 2011. [127]

The chef and his kitchen are the engine room of any hotel, and if the food is not creative and top notch in a five-star property, you're in trouble. We were incredibly fortunate to have employed Eddie Teh in 1998 as Director of F&B, who gave us consistency when chefs moved on. Eddie was talented and creative, and he also had the ability to lead. I had seen over the years many maitre d's who ran what we now call F&B, ruling their restaurants with a rod of iron, but Eddie had a manner about him that meant the staff were only too happy to follow.

Overseen by Eddie and our chefs, we had many celebrity chefs 'perform' at the hotel, always with a great following. Amongst those notable chefs from OEH were Renato Piccolotto from The Cipriani, Christian Bodiguel from the Venice Simplon-Orient-Express and Garth Strobel from The Mount Nelson in Cape Town. They all drew crowds and were well received; when we had a visit from an international name we could have filled the restaurant three times over at whatever price we chose to charge. [128, 129, 130]

Charlie Trotter came from Chicago, where his restaurant had been receiving global rave reviews since it first opened in 1987. Such was his fame that he even made a cameo appearance in the 1997 film *My Best Friend's Wedding*, where he screamed at an assistant, *"I will kill your whole family if you don't get this right! I need this perfect!"* It was a good parody of another English celebrity chef, but I found him to be anything but an angry chef. I had not fully appreciated just how highly he was regarded until I was handed a note to give to Charlie. It was from a local butcher who had been requested to deliver some meat, but had not responded promptly until he discovered who it was for. I'm not in the habit of reading other people's mail but I read the scribbled note. It was extraordinary to say the least. I thought of the scene in *The Godfather* when the landlord has refused to lower the rent for an old woman, until he hears from the Godfather directly. Grovelling apology would be an understatement. Let's just say the meat arrived, for which there was no charge.

The reverence with which everyone regarded Charlie Trotter was never more evident than when I went to the kitchen to see how the preparations were going for the night's event. Through the 'pass', the hotplate that fronts the kitchen, I saw the entire kitchen team gathered round Charlie. On the hotplate was a plate on which were the main ingredients of the meat course. Charlie held a runner bean delicately between his finger and thumb. All eyes were on what he would do next. It was a tableau; no one moved, no one spoke. He gently lowered the bean and placed it at a particular angle on the plate beside the piece of meat, then stood back. There was an audible gasp of amazement and general nods of agreement. In all my life, I had never seen such attention paid to a runner bean, but everyone seemed to love it.

The meal was superb, the food and flavours and matching wines could not have been better. The dessert was intriguing: served on a glass house brick, beautifully presented, was ice cream. No ordinary ice cream - *wasabi* ice cream. However it did not taste hot or wasabi-like - and it was delicious.

The guests were raving about the meal; it was without doubt one of the best events we had held to date. After the coffee I went into the kitchen to congratulate the team, all were there with one exception, Charlie Trotter. I was told he had gone to the adjacent room, the Orient Suite, to relax and unwind. Now I have always understood how highly strung and temperamental chefs can be, so I entered the room with caution. The lights were out and I was about to leave, when I noticed a figure in the corner of the darkened room, curled up in the foetal position. I was about to say something but thought it better to withdraw quietly. I was concerned so I asked one of his team if he was OK, only to be told he was fine but he often did this as a way of destressing after an event.

Charlie Trotter was without doubt revered, groundbreaking and one of the leading chefs in the world at that time, yet I found him a quiet, unassuming, nice guy and held in extraordinarily high regard by most leading chefs in Australia. He returned a number of times to the hotel in the years to come. [131, 132]

Apart from his cameo in *My Best Friend's Wedding*, there were a number of documentaries made with and of him. He closed his restaurant in Chicago in August 2012, and was to die suddenly at his home of a stroke in 2013, aged 54.

Another notable chef we hosted was Marcus Samuelsson. Born Kassahun Tsegiels, in Ethiopia, and adopted and raised in Sweden. He was executive chef of Aquavit, in New York. He was the youngest chef ever to receive a three-star restaurant review from *The New York Times*. [133]

The first event was planned for 12 September 2001, and was a sell-out. Very early that morning I had a call from one of my staff at the hotel. *Had I seen the news? Turn on the television!*

What I saw horrified me and the rest of the world. Late night, Sydney time, on the 11th September, two airplanes had crashed into the World Trade Centre in New York. I was dressed and into the office by 6.30am, and everyone was in shock. Marcus and his team gathered in the restaurant and I said what I could in terms of sympathy - what can you say at a time of such a tragedy? Nearly 3,000 people died in the terrorist attack, and a number were known to the chefs who either had, or knew of, friends who worked at the Windows of the World, the restaurant at the top of The Trade Centre, and where I had enjoyed dinner a few years before. Having expressed my sorrows I announced that we would of course cancel the planned event and help in any way we could to get them safely home to New York as soon as possible.

I was rather taken aback when Marcus spoke up. "Thank you, we appreciate your thoughts, but we, me and the guys, have discussed this, we are professionals, and love what we do, and love being in Australia. There is nothing we can do right now back home, and these dinners will help take our minds off what is happening. We have all agreed we want to stay and do what we came to do to make this a great success. In any event we can't get back as all the planes are grounded."

All our team around the room started to cheer and applaud, in admiration for these American chefs. The same reaction came from the guests. After the meal, everyone raised their glasses in respect to Marcus, and all the chefs were given a standing ovation. [156]

Not all our guest chefs had such a round of applause. Ainsley Harriott is known for his smile, humour and cheery 'yeah bwoi' expression. This London born chef, presenter and entertainer, had a number of popular TV shows in England. When he came to The Observatory, we were rather excited as his reputation for being an entertainer had preceded him. He spent very little time in the kitchen directing the preparation of his menu, but left it to the hotel chefs to prepare his dishes. The staff were disappointed when he spent more time out with the guests, and didn't acknowledge them for their efforts. His fans at the dinner loved him, but the staff felt left out. [134]

Our greatest events with the biggest following and the most excitement took place in 2007 and 2008, masterminded by Eddie Teh, Chef Haru and Chef Yomo, building on the popular Japanese cooking show *Iron Chef*.

It had a cult following in Japan and Australia. Each week, one of four Japanese specialist chefs would face off against a challenger, in a frenetic culinary battle featuring a secret theme ingredient chosen by the flamboyant host, with the winner judged by a group of celebrities.

How Eddie and Haru pulled it off I have no idea, but they started a number of highly entertaining and complicated performances with the superstar chefs from the show. Everyone in the hotel got involved; we had cameras in the kitchen and screens on which to watch the excitement in the restaurant and bar. Each night a guest was invited to join the team in the kitchen, and an MC gave the commentary on ingredients and preparation, as it was done in the TV series. We had tried to get Takeshi Kaga, the actual Iron Chef host but by then he was in high demand. So we found someone even better. Haru had found a young Japanese woman, Tomo Ishikawa, an accountant by day but with a love of cooking, who turned out to be a natural entertainer and a great host. Everyone loved her and she changed my opinion of accountants and my perception of Japanese culture forever.

Other MCs included local celebrity and very popular TV presenter, John Mangos, along with Joanna Saville, the food, travel and tourism journalist, all of whom added an extra dimension to the evenings.

Finally, it came to the chefs who were to be the highlight of the event. In 2007, with our own Chef Haru Inukai cast as the challenger, his 'opponent' was Iron Chef French, Hiroyuki Sakai.

I was terrified as we had never tried anything so far out of the box as this event, but Eddie Teh assured me all was under control. With my deputy Grant Raubenheimer tasked with keeping me at bay, Eddie, Haru, Maître d' Nicolas Cleradin, and Sommelier Christian Baeppler set about pulling it all together. There are so many things that could go wrong in a commercial kitchen anyway, but add to this mix a full theatrical setting of lights, cameras and sound and it could be a disaster. One mistake and it would all end in tears. Handling the public relations for this event was Kim Salt, very professional and extremely talented. When I asked her what was plan B in the event there was a problem, she simply said, "There is no Plan B; it will work." She was right. The team performed brilliantly and the press and the new-born breed of food bloggers all wrote about it in rapturous terms. It was the greatest F&B success we had experienced. But with the benchmark now set so high - how could we top it? [135, 136, 137, 138, 139. 140, 141, 142, 143,144]

Calls were already coming in - *when are you doing it again?* Even before we announced the next date, we had people booking tables.

Always the worrier, I was nervous as to how we could do better than before. So often the remakes and sequels fail to meet the expectations raised by the original. I started to feel like a movie producer attempting to do a sequel to *Casablanca.* Haru had moved on to his new restaurant, and we had Yomo, our excellent new executive chef, but he was new and as yet not established amongst the 'foodies' of Sydney.

Eddie soon put my mind at rest when he outlined his plan. He had arranged that, alongside Chef Yomo, who had graciously agreed, Haru would return as a guest chef and together face off against, not only Iron Chef French again, but also Iron Chef Chinese, Kenichi Chen. [139]

I was delighted, but there was more. Our fame had spread, and the Head Chef from Restaurant La Rochelle in Tokyo, Toshiyuki Kudo, wanted to join the team. I doubt if there was ever such a gathering of Japanese chefs in Australia, combining the extraordinary talents of these five. The interest was phenomenal, especially amongst the Japanese community, both locally and in Japan. Such was the demand that we had to extend the restaurant into the adjoining Globe Bar, and charge a menu price of $500 a head. Rather a little more than the price of the seven course dinner I first served as a trainee at the Grand Hotel in 1963 of seventeen shillings and sixpence; $1.35.

We set a new standard in hotel restaurant entertainment. Apart from the food and wine, there was the presentation, the sponsors and even merchandising. We even published our own coffee table book of the event. I am always surprised at the variety of talents that come to the fore in a hotel. I have found futures traders, artists, tailors, musicians, and in this case a very talented photographer, Jan Barth. He recorded the event for posterity, and it is he who I thank for the photos of the event. I have included some, but in black and white it does not do them justice.

Over the years there were many dinners conceived and creatively executed by our chefs and managers, but none as stunning or unique as those run by Eddie Teh, who was given a great degree of latitude and used it to build a reputation for doing things a little differently at The Observatory. There were *Phantom of the Opera* dinners, where the atmosphere was set with dry ice fog drifting over the candlelit tables, reflected in the mirrored function room. My special favorite, *Dinner of the Czars* featured, possibly for the last time, caviar, which was to be banned in Australia due to unsustainable fishing in the Caspian Sea. Thankfully it returned a few years later. On this spectacular evening, Eddie and his team had really gone to town. It was like a setting for *Anna Karenina* and I hosted a small dinner party, including my elegant and charming friends, Lady Sonia McMahon, Lady Susan Renouf and Victoria Mather, travel editor for *Tatler* magazine in the UK. It may be that as a result of this event I found myself at the Ritz in London later that year being presented with the award for *Tatler's* 'The Best Townhouse Hotel in the World' by Carol Thatcher in 1998. [145, 146]

Over twenty years at The Observatory I ate very well, sometimes too well and perhaps too often. My favourite time though was breakfast each morning in the Galileo Restaurant. I have always believed that breakfast is one of the most important meals a hotel offers, not just because it is healthy to do so, but that it is often the last impression the guest will take away with them. It also gave me the opportunity to see our regular guests and to see how the team performed. I can truthfully say I was never disappointed by our team.

There were a number of highly professional staff who came and went from the breakfast brigade over the years. The most memorable team could be seen in action during my last ten years at the hotel, headed by Ernesto Faundez, a cheery welcoming young Chilean man, who was responsible for the smooth running of the breakfast service. He later was to confess a few tales of which I had not been aware.

"We had a very wealthy family from India arriving at the hotel. Booking notes said that they were on a very light diet and they specifically requested that all meals should only be prepared with extra virgin olive oil.

First morning they order hash browns with their breakfast. As you would expect we used to make them in house, fresh, and we cooked them in extra virgin olive oil. They didn't like them. The next day we made special hash browns and we used the potato gnocchi from the Galileo dinner menu and we cooked them in extra virgin olive oil. But they didn't like them either. The third day (naughty me) I bought some hash browns at McDonalds in Wynyard station and served these to them at breakfast. They loved them!

I didn't ask if McDonalds at that time used extra virgin olive oil!"

We would often have a chat as I ate my breakfast, and I would hear little tidbits about our guests.

"There was an American couple staying and after a few days they went to visit the rainforest. When they returned, I asked them how it was. They didn't seem enthusiastic and answered, *it was ok but it rained too much!* Maybe that's why it's called the rain-forest not DRY forest!"

As with all good staff, they get promoted. After Ernesto went on to greater things, the role was taken over by Sinim Ha, the favourite of many customers, especially John Singleton as I've mentioned. We had a melting pot of nations, with diminutive Lynn from Thailand and the quiet but efficient Magno from Brazil. One deserves special mention: Shelby Rejoice, a Korean woman with a lovely name whose skills astounded me every day.

Shelby worked in the restaurant but took on the role of barista during the busy breakfast service. Every morning over the years I had the same breakfast: fresh fruit, yoghurt and muesli, and I finished my meal with a flat white coffee. My day would not have been the same without this routine. What made it so special was that Shelby was an amazing coffee artist. Every morning when my flat white was placed in front of me, the milky froth on top would have a different 'drawing' on it, kangaroos, koalas or cockatoos and a little message like *G'd morning Mr G* or *Enjoy your day PLG*. It always brought a smile to my face and these little messages started my day off well. I hasten to add that these were not simply done for me but all the guests as well. It was the personal touch that I always encouraged and which set us apart in style and service.

I have always had a sweet tooth and there was no better place to sate my sugar cravings than in the small room where the patissiers worked their magic. I'd follow the smell of fresh baking and arrive at the moment a fresh batch of cakes or biscuits came out of the oven. I blame two women in particular for the extra kilos that I'd be better off without, so I am happy to name and shame them: Ewe Goralewski and Melissa McGeoch. As well as the biscuits, they both produced truly wonderful desserts and presentation pieces. I have always admired the skill of the patissier. Their talents have been recognised: when I last heard, Ewe was working at Dinner by Heston Blumenthal in London and Melissa was Pastry Chef at Hilton Sydney.

In my fifty years in hotels, the biggest problem and the basis of most discontent was usually the staff food. Staff could compare the beautiful food being served to guests, alongside what the chefs tended to throw together for the staff. I was determined to improve the situation, so I found a woman who could keep the skilled and hardworking staff nourished and motivated each day: Penchan Siriwatna. She was a Thai chef, manager, and friend to many staff over the years when she ran the staff canteen.

We had started by offering a positive work environment, and the staff meals came next. Our efforts worked, but it was not until this wonderful Thai woman joined us that things really settled down, and, from that day on, I rarely heard any complaints. I also made a point of eating with the staff most days, not only to show solidarity but also because I could get to know them. I could hear of any discontent or problems directly, and nip problems in the bud before they escalated into major issues.

F&B seems to be less at the heart of hotels today compared to when I started out in the industry, but it's so important. It helps to create atmosphere, and build reputation. It is a vehicle to drive the hotel creatively, try out innovations, and bring some fun into the hotel for both guests and staff.

At The Observatory Hotel, with a magnificent array of creative talent about me and giving them the opportunity to experiment and try something different, we succeeded in creating experiences that few other hotels, limited by their strict corporate formulae, were able to do.

Chapter 13

#starsthatsparkle #saintsn'sinners #milehigh

Back to the rich and famous. I had never thought that I would get to meet so many people I'd watched on the silver screen. I got off to a good start with Charlie Chaplin at the Grand Hotel in Eastbourne when I was seventeen. I would have been content to tell my grandchildren about him, but now I am rather spoilt for choice. I won't name all the celebrities who passed through but I will note the notables, who were either particularly delightful or particularly not.

One day Pauline Sidhom, my PA, tapped on my door. "Mr Griffin, your 11 o'clock is in the lounge and ready for you."

I had no idea who or what she was on about. "Sorry, who's that?"

"Oh come on. You know who it is. Priscilla."

By this time my director of PR, Kim Salt, was at the door. "Time to go."

An integral part of our success was our image. The smart young women in the public relations department maximised every opportunity. Whenever there was a special event or a celebrity in the house, they would milk it for all it was worth. Today we were getting press coverage by having Priscilla Presley as our guest. Of course, I knew of her and was old enough to recall the gossip at the time when Elvis was in the army in Germany and had fallen in love with a young girl, Priscilla Wagner. The King had met her when she was only 14 and he eventually married her when she was 21 in 1967, much to the disappointment of his fans.

Priscilla had gone on to carve out her own career in films, but most of all she had become quite an impressive entrepreneur as the business brains behind Graceland and the Elvis legacy. She was a multimillionaire in her own right.

As I approached, I saw a hand outstretched by a *very* beautiful woman before me. I shook the hand and it struck me that she was in fact 61 years old - older than I was at the time! It was hard to believe, she looked so young. When we spoke, the secret was out of the bag. Not a muscle in her face seemed to move. Kim ushered us into position for a photo. Snap! And the meeting was over. I thanked her and mouthed a few pleasantries to which she replied, although I wasn't sure what she said as I could not see her lips move very much.[147, 148]

Another lovely actor was Cate Blanchett, on the verge of becoming a superstar. She stayed with her husband Andrew Upton. Robyn Dalton, the author and producer was her friend and had mentioned to me just how grounded Cate was. At one time, she said that she would have been as happy to just stay in Sydney and have a normal family life. Robyn told me that Andrew had admired her from afar for a long time but was nervous about asking her out. Robyn claimed that she was the one who gave him the push that started the relationship that is now regarded as one of the strongest in show business. They were a charming couple, and as such a rarity in the film industry. [149]

Glenn Close was booked to stay with us and the first comment I heard from Reservations was "my God - the bunny boiler!" She had single-handedly made many husbands think twice about straying from the path of monogamy with her film

Fatal Attraction. At the time she checked in, she was a little aloof, and looked very 'unglamorous' for a star. I understood why, as she was playing the lead in the wonderful film *Paradise Road*, a movie about a group of women who were terribly mistreated and imprisoned in a Japanese camp in the Second World War, with wonderful music. Her appearance was therefore part of the 'method' of getting ready for the film. Another member of the cast was Elisabeth Spriggs, one of those wonderful English character actresses who pop up in so many films - in her case, anything from *Harry Potter* to *Sense and Sensibility*. Speaking of Jane Austen, we also hosted Jennifer Ehle who played Elizabeth Bennet opposite Colin Firth's Mr Darcy in *Pride and Prejudice*. [150, 151]

Gwyneth Paltrow stayed with her soon-to-be husband Chris Martin, the English lead singer of Coldplay. It proved to be an eventful visit. Chris Martin was, very charmingly, exceedingly protective of Gwyneth. On seeing a *paparazzo* hanging around the entrance of the hotel, Chris tried to chase him off, even to the extent of throwing money at him. This of course only made matters worse and provided a lot more photo opportunities. Later in the day a pizza arrived at the hotel and was delivered to Ms Paltrow's suite. This brought about a furious call to me from Chris, wanting to know who had placed the order using Ms Paltrow's name and who had placed a note to her with the pizza. Turned out an apologetic Ms Paltrow had placed the order herself - the note had been put in by the delivery boy who was a great fan.

A rather less demure woman was Courtney Love, actress and lead singer of the rock band Hole, who had been married to Kurt Cobain, lead singer and guitarist of the grunge band Nirvana. She had been nominated for an award for playing the lead role of Althea Leasure, the stripper and drug-addicted wife of Larry Flint in *The People vs. Larry Flynt*. I thought she played the role superbly and felt it unkind when a journalist commented, *she doesn't deserve it. How can it be acting when she is playing herself?*

Another actor whose on-screen character may be regarded as a little less than chaste was Kim Cattrall, best known for her role as Samantha Jones in the hugely popular *Sex and the City*. She was in Sydney for her book launch, and was every bit as sophisticated as her character. David Stanton, one of our concierges, had called the lift to the basement level where the offices were located. Ms Cattrall had just finished a Spa treatment on the level below and wearing her bathrobe nearly walked out onto the office level. David apologised for stopping the lift and she simply smiled at him and stepped back into the lift, giving a bigger smile and saying in her Samantha Jones seductive voice, "Come in, I like collecting men". [152]

I was very happy to host an American actress who started out with George Clooney in the long-running medical drama *ER*, Juliana Margulies, who went on to appear in *The Good Wife* and even *Snakes on a Plane*. Another guest from the 70s and 80s was the star of *Hart to Hart*, Stephanie Powers. [153]

It was a delight to welcome Cyd Charisse, a legendary performer and one of Hollywood's iconic dancing stars. I recall seeing her movies on TV on wet Sunday afternoons, dancing with Fred Astaire and Gene Kelly. She was one of those traditional stars who radiated elegance and style. I was furious when I heard that Joh Bailey, a rather over the top society snipper, made a comment to the effect that *he was asked to go to the hotel to style a Hollywood superstar only to find it was some old has-been*. Not what I would consider a very gallant remark.[154]

Local stars would pop in or stay with us. Deborah Mailman is a lovely First Nations actress and singer. One of her movies, *The Sapphires*, is to this day in my top ten list of films. Another of my favourite actresses was the wonderful Ruth Cracknell, one of Australia's most loved stars. She was approachable and always had a nice word to say to the staff. When I last spoke with her she had hurt her hand painfully (before coming to the hotel I hasten to add). I sympathised with her, and hoped it would be better by her next visit. Sadly she didn't visit again, and died a short time later in May 2002. [155]

Our star guests all had their own kind of glamour, some a little idiosyncratic but nonetheless highly engaging and attractive. One of these was the young woman who had carved out a modern day film and stage career in burlesque, Dita von Teese. [156, 157]

In a totally different mold were Judy Davis and Sigrid Thornton. I had first met Sigrid at The Como in Melbourne, at the same time as that other diva Dame Edna Everage. Barry Humphries by now looked like Oscar Wilde with his coat hanging across his shoulders and a black broad brimmed hat worn at a rakish angle. Along with Aussie regulars Rachel Ward and Bryan Brown, who I've mentioned, we hosted Geoffrey Rush, Eric Bana, Guy Pearce, Hugo Weaving, and Paul Mercurio. [158] Simon Baker is known for his lead roles in *The Mentalist* and *The Guardian* and had all the female members of the staff dewy-eyed. I couldn't quite see it myself.

Hugh Jackman was in his 'pre-superstar' days, who I will always remember coming down the stairs of the hotel, heading out to an awards event, wearing culottes - they didn't seem to come from either *Boy from Oz* nor *Wolverine's* wardrobe. One who has always been claimed by Australia, but who is a Kiwi, and actually born in Omagh, Northern Ireland, was Sam Neill. I had loved *Reilly Ace of Spies* back in England on TV in the 80s. Somehow he found out the number of my direct line, and whenever there was an issue about his favourite suite 313 not being available, he would give me a call. I didn't mind - it was rather nice to think that I was on the autodial of a film star's mobile!

All the Aussie film stars I met were well grounded and easy to approach. Rarely did they put on the *prima donna* act that one so often found with those from Hollywood. Maybe it was because they were on home turf and not surrounded by sycophantic assistants.

From the UK, I've already mentioned the charming Gabriel Byrne, and then there was Ralph Fiennes, or Mr Ralph Nathaniel Twisleton-Wykeham-Fiennes as his full name would state. He had unforgettable roles in films including *Harry Potter, Schindler's List,* and *The English Patient*, the latter written by Michael Ondaatje, who - according to my brother Chris - is a distant relative of ours. [159]

I met Ralph Fiennes before his departure from the hotel and he was softly spoken, very charming, and with a gentle handshake. I must confess that I was rather surprised to read a short time later this headline in *The Australian* newspaper:

Hostie tells of 'amazing' sex during Qantas flight

Having boarded a plane for Mumbai after leaving the hotel, apparently he had joined the 'mile high club' with a young flight attendant. What had made this rather more newsworthy was the fact that the young woman alleged it was an 'unprotected' encounter, and Mr Fiennes was in Mumbai to raise AIDS awareness for UNICEF. The young woman's services were terminated by Qantas.

Shortly after I read of his Oscar nomination for *The English Patient,* and heard from my friend Frank Bowling at The Bel-Air in Beverly Hills that Ralph was to stay there. I sent Ralph a note wishing him good luck, and I had not expected any reply but was delighted when I received a letter.

Dear Patrick,

Thank you so much for the card that awaited me as I arrived at The Bel-Air for the Academy Awards. It was extremely thoughtful and I was deeply touched to receive it. I have fond memories of my stay at The Observatory and I hope to visit you again soon

Many thanks, Ralph.

He was very much the gentleman. And he did indeed return to the hotel.

We had the pleasure of welcoming other notable English actors, including Rowan Atkinson aka Mr Bean, [160] Rufus Sewell, Ian McShane, the heart throb of *Moulin Rouge* Ewan McGregor, and without a doubt the most sartorially impeccable Englishman, Colin Firth. I was very happy to welcome my favourite Canadian actor who I admired in many movies, but most of all in *The Dirty Dozen* and *The Eagle has Landed.* More recently I was surprised to see him in *Pride and Prejudice*, and I do of course refer to Donald Sutherland. For younger readers, he is the father of Kiefer Sutherland. Another actor raised in Canada who had many hearts racing with his friendly charm was Matthew Perry of *Friends*.[161]

One time I received a very unpleasant call from a publicist from Fox Studios in Sydney where they were filming *Star Wars: Episode II - Attack of the Clones.* Natalie Portman and fellow actor Ahmed Best had visited our other hotel, Lilianfels, in the Blue Mountains. Ms Portman was very upset at what she felt was a less than welcoming attitude by certain staff members to her colleague, Mr Best, who was African-American. As a hotelier and a humanist, any suggestion of bigotry to me is anathema. We welcome visitors from all nationalities and cultures, and pride ourselves in the way we care for all guests. Such an allegation that one guest felt disrespected was a serious matter for me.

I apologised and assured them I would investigate. Such issues are not always easy to get to the bottom of, but it turned out the Australian laid-back nature and rather less than politically correct sense of humour were taken as being rude and offensive by the stars. I know that I had had to get used to this myself, and I know that it was in no way meant as malicious or offensive. We counselled the staff to be more sensitive in future.

I penned a personal letter of apology and called the publicist back with my findings, asking where my letter should be sent. By now things had settled down and our conversation became more relaxed and friendly. She appreciated my efforts and was more than happy with my explanation and apologies. I was then invited to be a guest with my sons on the set to see for myself the filming and to meet George Lucas and some of the actors. I was rather pleased with the outcome, as was my son Charlie who was keen to see the making of the film.

Having watched Luke Skywalker flying through space to battle the evil Empire and Darth Vader on the big screen we had high expectations of an amazing film experience. Instead, we were ushered into a corner of the set, like a warehouse, where they were setting up an action sequence where Anakin Skywalker was to do battle with the evil empire, as they flew a starfighter over whichever city, on whatever planet it was.

Charlie and I sat in 'directors chairs' in one corner. George Lucas was sitting at a small table with eyes glued to a laptop computer. In front of us was a large green screen behind a cherry picker also wrapped in green, on top of which was fixed a small spaceship that looked as if it belonged on a fairground ride. After a while the actors appeared: Hayden Christensen playing Anakin, and a woman dressed in the uniform of the enemy pilot. They climbed up a ladder to get to the spaceship; the woman got into the cockpit whilst Anakin perched himself on the wing, attached to a safety wire. There was lots of discussion until George Lucas gave the nod and the clapper board appeared - no longer with chalk writing but with digital numbers flickering. The pneumatic arm of the cherrypicker with the attached fighter started to rock and judder as the fearless Skywalker battled to hang on, attempting to take control of the ship whilst the pilot with flailing arms fought to defend herself.

This continued for a few minutes, without dialogue, dramatic music or other activity. It was simply a cherry picker fairground ride bouncing about with two people attached. This was repeated time and time again. I could see nothing different in each take. We sat for about two hours, during which Charlie, having been relieved of his gameboy, as I had been denuded of my mobile, sat perfectly well behaved, silent and extremely bored.

Eventually someone shouted "That's a wrap" and for some reason lost on me, everyone on the set started cheering and applauding wildly. The ladder was brought out and Anakin and his mortal enemy were ushered carefully down to earth where they embraced. With much back slapping and congratulations I assumed peace had been declared and all was well in the Empire. It was later explained that what we had watched was streamed straight back to Los Angeles where it was incorporated with computer technology into the movie. I never met Ms Portman and only spoke briefly with George Lucas. I wondered if that afternoon had been my punishment for what had happened at Lilianfels. I chose to take it as the hand of forgiveness and, like the Empire, we were all now at peace. Years later I watched the DVD and sat, still rather bored, waiting for the moment when Anakin bravely risked life and limb to save the Empire. There it was! And in a nanosecond gone. I kept attempting to pause it at the point where we had been watching the shoot, but my reactions were not fast enough to capture the moment that Charlie and I had spent an afternoon on. Nothing had changed since that day; Charlie was still just as bored, having discarded his gameboy for the far more exciting challenges to be offered on the computer.

I had one further venture into a galaxy far far away. I met Princess Leia. Carrie Fisher had truly been through some tough times of galactic proportions; I hope you'll forgive me for being somewhat unchivalrous by suggesting that she was a little closer to the shape of R2D2 than the beautiful scantily-clad dancer held captive by Jabba the Hutt as I remembered. She was with us to promote her book about the problems she had faced in life. I'm glad to say that she was fun, friendly and undoubtedly the loveliest of guests. I was sad to read that in December 2016 she died, and her famous mother Debbie Reynolds died the following day.[162]

I was glad to greet the very interesting Charles Dance, a man who always seemed to play the villain, even before he became more famous playing the villainous Lord Tywin Lannister in *Game of Thrones*. When I met him, I wondered if he had indeed just been playing himself all along. Not that he was unpleasant in any way but - somehow - his demeanor was - how should I put it? - exactly like his on-screen persona. At any rate he was nice enough to pose for a photograph and thanked me for a lovely stay. As long as he enjoyed his visit, as a hotel we can ask for nothing more.[163]

Another guest who stayed with us quite early on was an extremely talented musician, a composer, a good actor, an extremely funny comedian and only 5foot 2inches tall. I had watched Dudley Moore in my teens when he played opposite Peter Cook in the hilarious *Not Only...But Also*, and I loved his brilliant films *10* with Bo Derek and best of all *Arthur* with Liza Minnelli and Sir John Gielgud, who played one of the best butlers I have ever seen on the silver screen. In most of his film appearances Dudley showed off his virtuosic piano playing; he was extraordinarily talented. [164]

I had a call from the driver, as was usually the case, of his impending arrival. As the limo pulled up at the hotel entrance, I stood ready to greet him. The car door was pulled open. We stood there waiting. Nobody emerged. Eventually I stuck my head in the door and there he was lying back in the seat wearing an airline eye mask; on his forehead was a sticker that read 'Do Not Disturb', so I didn't. We waited a little longer as his cases were removed from the boot. As the lid was closed with a hefty bang he awoke with a start, raised a corner of his eye mask, and in his Derek and Clive voice said, "'Ello, 'oo are you?"

I was never sure if he was joking around or whether he had been genuinely asleep. Throughout his stay he amused everyone with his quips. He even sat down with the hotel's pianist Alex Nettleback and played the piano. It was a great loss when he died a few years later, in 2002, aged 66.

If you want glam and glitter, then I must mention the arrival of Jean-Paul Gaultier, the renowned fashion designer who stayed as guest of Sydney Gay Mardi Gras. He was there to open an art exhibition. I was hosting a small party of strait-laced American travel agents in The Galileo. Dinner was going well until I noticed a number of motorbikes pull up at the entrance of the hotel. They weren't the usual mode of transport for our guests. A limousine then pulled up, into which hopped Jean-Paul Gaultier. As the door closed, there was a deafening roar as the bikes all started up at once and revved their engines, so loudly that the windows rattled. I went outside and saw fifteen Harley Davidsons, ridden by somewhat terrifying women. They were the famous Dykes on Bikes, who had come to escort M. Gaultier to the exhibition. It was rather difficult to explain to my guests, none of whom were from San Francisco, and I doubt had ever heard of gay Mardi Gras. I am uncertain if they ever sent us any business. [165]

Yet another star I had loved since the 60s was Susannah York, since I saw her in *Tom Jones*, the bawdy and entertaining period comedy with Albert Finney. She was soft spoken, gentle and demure, with lovely blue eyes and a beautiful broad smile. She was the sort of girl that one wanted to shelter and protect. She was altogether delightful. She had played many roles, in *Battle of Britain, A Man for All Seasons* and *They Shoot Horses Don't They,* along with the *Superman* series, *Sands of the Kalahari* and *The Killing of Sister George.* I thought this last one was a great movie when she played the love interest of the character who plays in the film the pseudonymous George, who is about to be killed off in a soap opera, with repercussions that are both very funny yet poignant. I hosted a small media lunch for Susannah. She was now in her sixties but had not lost any of her beauty nor that smile and to me looked no different from the young star I had admired back in 1963.[166]

As I sat next to her, I told her how much I had enjoyed her films, hoping not to sound like some infatuated fan. Her only comment was "Oh surely not those ones, they were not my favourites, I have certainly made better". I was crestfallen that my attempt to impress had failed so miserably, and I think she noticed and felt a little sorry for me, as after that she was very warm and chatty. I was very sorry to hear, just as I was about to retire due to my own health concerns, that she had died at the age of 72 of leukemia. I was starting to learn a lot about this myself, and each time I heard such news it was a reminder of my own mortality, and the need to enjoy life to the full.

While most of our stars seemed very down to earth, one group of our guests were the opposite, having *boldly gone where no man has gone before*. For some reason we were the favourite place for the *Star Trek* actors, many of whom beamed down to stay with us, including Robert Picardo from *Voyager*, Brent Spiner, aka Data from *Next Generation*, and Alexander Siddig who played Dr. Bashir in *Deep Space Nine* and went on to portray Prince Doran Martell, ruler of Dorne in *Game of Thrones.* Nana Visitor (Major Kira) and Rene Auberjonois (Odo) stayed over as well; movie fans may remembere him as Father Mulcahy in the original MASH movie. I can only assume there must have been a 'Star Trek' convention in town. [167, 168]

The Observatory had become very popular with those stars who sought a quiet retreat, but we also saw our fair share of tantrums. Christine Whyte, Director of Revenue Management, reminded me twenty years later of the *Kilmer-Sizemore Incident* which had gone down as a legend in the hotel's memory.

In 1999, Val Kilmer and Tom Sizemore were staying at the hotel for several months whilst making the movie *The Red Planet*. Val Kilmer had developed a reputation for being a bit difficult on and off the set, and Tom Sizemore was having problems. The tension between the two was such that they would not speak to each other in the hotel and each expected that his suite should be bigger and better. If they ever met in the lobby, the ensuing language was colourful to say the least and, on several occasions, they were close to fisticuffs.

As Emil Bashay, Executive Housekeeper, recalls it, Val Kilmer rang down one Saturday morning to say his TV was not working and he wanted it fixed immediately. Emil asked the Maintenance Fitter, Ken Gurnett, to go to Suite 327 and see what the problem was.

Ken knocked on the door and on receiving no reply entered the lounge room and proceeded to work on the television set. Mr Kilmer, who was on the phone in his bedroom, belatedly realized someone else was in the suite on hearing a loud noise coming from the lounge room. He yelled out for Ken to get out of his room and come back when he was not on the phone. Ken did not hear him with the TV sound on and continued working. Believing the guest to be out, Ken turned the TV up even louder. It was at this point Mr Kilmer hung up the phone, and the swearing started, with explicit language flying at Ken. With the TV volume on high, Ken had to yell at Mr Kilmer in order to be heard.

Ken's appearance was somewhat like that of John Jarratt who plays Mick Taylor, the serial killer in the horror film *Wolf Creek*. Upon seeing Ken, yelling, with a screwdriver in his hand, Val Kilmer immediately believed he was going to be attacked. He screamed out for Ken to back off, and called the Duty Manager, in fear of his life, being threatened by a mad staff member with a screwdriver.

The Duty Manager arrived, escorted Ken from the suite, and spent the next hour placating Mr Kilmer who claimed he would be departing the hotel that evening. He was at Reception a bit later, demanding his personal manager find him another hotel. Tom Sizemore, on overhearing this, immediately asked to move to Mr Kilmer's suite (he still believed it was bigger!). This resulted in Mr Kilmer staying, as he would not give Tom Sizemore that satisfaction.

After that we not only had to keep Mr Sizemore and Mr Kilmer separated, but had to ensure that Ken was never again seen in or around Suite 327. When the press became aware of the difficulties between the two stars, they asked Val about The Observatory, but he claimed he had never been near the hotel. I was never sure as to the need for such an emphatic denial. [169, 170]

While this all sounds like an episode of *Fawlty Towers*, I'm pleased to say the hotel ran smoothly without a hiccup when

Basil Fawlty arrived in person to stay in the guise of John Cleese. I had first met him when he was promoting a series of training videos on customer service back in the 70s. These were the early days of such training aids and were a brilliant concept at the time.

We'd had the idea that we should write a book about the hotel and thought what a great *coup* it would be to have John Cleese write a 'Foreword'. We thought if he was easy going and approachable it might be worth sounding him out. I soon realised this was not going to happen. On meeting him I found a very tall and imposing man, very much a Hollywood star, polite, yet distant, like a CEO of a multinational company. He was far from the bumbling, inept hotel manager from Torquay.

Amongst all the famous and glamorous people who stayed with us, there was one who belonged in a category of her own. My cousin, Stephen Phillips, was the Director of the South Australian Opera Company, and had gained some fame for his production of Wagner's *Ring Cycle*. I was surprised when he told me they were putting on a very different opera based on the book that became the movie *Dead Man Walking*, which had starred Susan Sarandon and Sean Penn, the story of a nun who helps comfort a prisoner about to be executed. The guest my cousin was hosting was the real nun who had written the book, Sister Helen Prejean. I have met many actors, but this was the first time I had met a person on whom a role was based. She did not resemble Susan Sarandon one little bit, but was indeed a lovely woman with whom I had afternoon tea in the drawing room. A little more appropriate I thought than a beer in the bar.

Chapter 14

#prostateproblems #governmentapathy #australianorders

My hedonistic lifestyle was in danger. In a surgery in 2005 the doctor told me I had chronic lymphocytic leukemia (CLL). I was relieved when she kindly reassured me that of all the cancers this was probably the best one to have. Then followed the comforting news that there was nothing to do now but 'let's keep an eye on it'. I was not whisked into hospital nor pumped full of drugs, so I felt that there was nothing to worry about and returned to my work and my enjoyable lifestyle with little concern.

My life was going along fine after that little hiccup until, in 2008 on a sales trip to Japan with Robyn Poyntynen from Lilianfels, we were having a delightful dinner with Japanese guests in the Hotel Okura in Tokyo. In the middle of the meal I suddenly experienced a sharp pain in my lower abdomen. Upon seeing me stand, and bend over - not out of politeness but due to excruciating pain - they all stood up and bowed.

I made my escape to the bathroom, and tried to recover. I returned to the table, where a concerned head waiter quietly enquired if everything was alright with my meal, having seen me run in the direction of the bathroom. After extending my apologies and more bowing I excused myself and left a perplexed Robyn to see out the evening with our guests.

The hotel's doctor was very understanding and most helpful, but advised me that it might be better if I returned to Australia for treatment. Few countries are as efficient as Japan and by the morning the hotel staff had arranged with the doctor for a letter stating I was able to fly, rebooked my flights, and booked a car to take me to Narita Airport where a hotel representative would be waiting to assist me to the plane. Fortunately, having my 'Chairman's Lounge' card and being upgraded to first class (God bless you Kylie-Jane Menzies at Qantas), I was soon on my way after much enthusiastic bowing at the departure gate.

As I sat back and tried to relax for the flight back, I thought of the Japanese culture and their politeness. I wondered whether I should have explained my predicament to my guests, but thought it was best not to - rather too much information for a dinner chat. Plus, I had learned that, rather than cause you any embarrassment, they would ignore any misadventure. Once on the platform of a rail station, a Japanese man had slipped onto the tracks, which everyone appeared to ignore. A foreigner jumped down to assist him back onto the platform and to safety, where he simply nodded and walked off. It seemed that rather than embarrass the man by bringing his misadventure to everyone's attention, the Japanese thought best that they would simply ignore him. Possibly urban myth, but from my experience it is very believable.

In Sydney, I was referred to a leading urologist at St Vincent Hospital and some investigative surgery. One can always tell when something is not quite right when a specialist enters your room and closes the door behind him. They had taken a sample for biopsy whilst I was in surgery and found evidence of prostate cancer. This time it was not a case of 'don't worry it's not a major cancer, let's just wait and see'. This was the real thing. Over the next few weeks further investigative surgery was done, and due to the fact I had the complication of leukemia, it was thought better to save any chemo for later. The plan was to operate as soon as possible and remove the prostate. It was not something I was keen on as I had heard about the various possible side effects and - as a man of 62 - I was not pleased, but there was really no other option.

As it happened, I was exceedingly fortunate. With the wonders of modern technology they used what was called the daVinci Procedure. Not something inspired by Dan Brown, but a way of operating robotically with the surgeon sitting on the other side of the room. Magical stuff at the time. As a result, the operation went very well and a few months later I was in remission, if not cured. The other issues I just had to learn to manage.

This episode almost made me give thought to my health, but true to form, I did not dwell on it for long. For a start my job just didn't allow the time. Hotel management is not a 9 to 5 job. No hotelier around the world has ever worked an eight hour day, and I still felt that I should be involved in politics and industry development outside the four walls of my hotel, as these all have profound impacts on the hotel's success.

At this point, I would hate for readers to go away thinking I had spent my entire career on fun and frivolity. There was - and is - a more serious side to hospitality that would be wrong to ignore. I'll run through some of it now, so if you only want the lighter side, skip to Chapter 15.

Hospitality and tourism is a multifaceted sector, incorporating a wide range of businesses, and is interdependent on both local and international travellers. I read a definition that said the tourism and hospitality sector is 'a broad category of fields within the service industry that includes hotels, guest houses, event planning, theme parks, transportation, cruise line, travelling and additional fields within the tourism industry'. Even the dictionary could not specifically define it. At the end of the day this complexity is what motivated me to get involved in associations and organisations that had an impact on the hotel itself, and to support the growth of the industry at large.

In Kenilworth in the UK, I was involved with community programs, and whilst they did not contribute directly to the hotel's business, I made contact with city councillors, local businesses and the community, raising the hotel's profile. In Coventry, I served as chairman of the Hotel and Leisure Section of the District Chamber of Commerce, chairman of the Coventry and District Conference Association and served on the Tourism Task Force of the City of Coventry Department of Economic Development and Planning. Ultimately they would all have an influence on the business we did at the De Vere Hotel: by increasing tourism destination marketing budgets, promoting new infrastructure and opposing plans that might impact negatively on our business. Part of the purpose of this voluntary and unpaid work is not only that our hotel would benefit, but the hotels and tourist attractions in the area would also benefit. The rising river lifts all the boats, as we know. Instead of fighting over the small pie, we worked to ensure that the pie was bigger overall so that we all got a bigger share.

When I arrived in Australia, the tourism and hospitality sector seemed even more complex, with restaurants, pubs, caravan parks and more being included in the political and statistical analysis. The industry is so disparate and dispersed across this huge country, a close friend and colleague with whom I worked at the Australian Hotels Association once said to me '*it's like herding cats.*' And how right she was – with over twenty different business associations representing the different sectors that make up tourism and hospitality (and two competing associations fighting to represent the accommodation sector!) with mostly, but not always, common interests to align for the purposes of lobbying fractious politicians. I can say this: it was never boring.

In Australia in those years, if the car industry so much as sneezed, or the construction industry coughed, governments of all stripes would throw open their coffers to offer aid for recovery or industry development. For tourism and hospitality, the vast number of interests made it difficult to front up to the government with a clear message or a definitive ask. Add to that the view that tourism and hospitality was seen by governments as a cash cow to reap revenue from international tourists (who don't vote!). So rather than assist us, governments tended to increase taxes. We'd hear "let's put a bed tax on hotels" or "let's increase the passenger charge" that all people pay to fly out of Australia. To my mind the sector's biggest challenge was putting up a united front; often we focussed more on the differences rather than the common issues that would benefit the whole industry. We also did not have a heavily unionised workforce - even though the sector employed over 8% of the workforce - so there were no high-profile union leaders or strikes to get the government's attention. On the upside, these challenges made us even more determined to keep up a strong united group of associations, with links to the right Ministers and other influencers at all levels of government, and this is what motivated me to join the leading association to add my voice where it may be able to help support our industry.

I started as a voluntary member on the executive of the AHA NSW, and on the executive of the national Australian Hotels Association (Accommodation Division). These were the primary industry advocacy and lobbying bodies for the accommodation sector at the state and national levels. I soon found myself as National President, but thankfully I was fortunate to have an excellent manager (Juliana Payne, our National Manager

Accommodation Division and who has worked with me on this book) who ran the operations and did most of the work! There was a lot of politics involved, both inside the associations, and with the various governments we dealt with. Over the years we dealt with a huge range of issues from the ongoing skilled staff shortage, requiring governments to invest in training, the ever present threat of increased taxes and charges on business, tourism marketing, airport and other transport infrastructure challenges, the impact of the internet and online commerce on the industry, restrictive liquor licensing laws, increasing regulation on building, safety and insurance, the global financial crisis in 2008 and rising energy costs. And that's not a complete list.

It was almost impossible to get real cohesion across the industry; we'd win a few battles but it felt like we never really won the war to make our sector a big influential dealmaker with governments. It seemed to me that while we could get relatively easy access to Ministers and members of Parliament, I became rather cynical about it all as I think they were just there for the hospitality, which was always generous, and to meet the hotel managers who might give them an upgrade on their next visit. It never seemed to translate into hard policies that would really boost the industry. With the devastating impact of the coronavirus pandemic in 2020 on both international and domestic tourism in Australia, there may be some actual recognition that this industry is an economic powerhouse with $43 billion turnover a year, and not just have a junior 'Minister for Good Times' assigned to the sector. At least tourism and hospitality is now assigned to the Minister for Trade, which gives us some measure of clout in Canberra.

One of my early encounters in the Canbera 'bubble' was with Jackie Kelly, who rather unexpectedly won the seat of Lindsay for the Liberals in 1996 in an otherwise red band of Labor seats in

Sydney's west. She was appointed Minister for Sport and Tourism, having been a *blue* in rowing and therefore seen as a good fit in view of the up and coming Sydney Olympics. I can only assume her knowledge of sport was far greater than her knowledge of tourism. In one discussion over tourism, I was rather brushed off with the comment that unless I had all the figures and statistics she couldn't help. "Statistics are the only thing that matters." All I could think of was Mark Twain quoting Benjamin Disraeli: *There are three kinds of lies: lies, damned lies, and statistics*. It seemed the Minister just wanted to focus on the micro stats, whereas we were trying to provide a bigger picture narrative of the significance of the industry to the whole economy.

The Olympic Games of 2000 was seen as the panacea to all the woes of the tourism industry. Having staged the Games, then Premier of NSW, Bob Carr appeared to think there was nothing else to do but sit back and watch the industry boom. For a few months after the Games it did, and Sydney tried to ride this wave forever. Soon however things were back to normal; all of us in the lobbying area kept trying to get the Premier and the government to take up the opportunity to build on what Mr Juan Antonio Samaranch, the president of the IOC announced as *"the best Olympic Games ever".*

Insult was added to injury following the government's handling of difficult problems with its aviation policy in 2001. When Ansett Airlines collapsed in 2002 (one of only two airlines servicing the domestic market) the tourism industry was shocked that the Howard Government imposed a new airline ticket tax to help fund the unpaid entitlements of the company's employees. The Minister for Sport and Tourism rivalled Marie Antoinette in showing disdain for the tourism sector she was supposed to represent. Referring to the Ansett crisis, and it was a crisis believe me, she said it was *"about getting over a little blip and getting back into the very, very bright future that is ahead for tourism."* This seemed to demonstrate the government's limited understanding of the uphill battle the industry faced to recover. She might as well have said '*Let them eat cake*.'

Big, high-rise city hotels were an easy target for governments looking for revenue. One of my first press conferences that related to a proposal of then Premier Bob Carr to bring in a bed tax for hotels. I had learned little from my press encounters thirty years previously at The Castle Hotel in Norwich. I genuinely believed the press would be sympathetic to the industry's case, but instead I was suddenly confronted by hostile journalists asking me *why these wealthy foreign tourists who stay in our hotels could not afford a few dollars to build a hospital that would save children's lives*? The government had played its usual card that this money would provide new hospitals and schools: if I heard this once, I heard it a thousand times. Yet when the tax is imposed, we rarely see the actual schools or hospitals as the tax mysteriously gets absorbed into consolidated revenue.

In the UK, I had long been a fan of the industry mag, *The Caterer & Hotelkeeper*. It was a national publication, read by everyone in the hotel industry, not least for the jobs section. I found nothing like this existed in Australia, with a depth of topics and reach in readership, that covered issues for accommodation hotels nationwide.

My eyes lit up therefore when I found a new publication: Hotel Management Magazine (HM) published by The Intermedia Group, driven by a young entrepreneurial journalist James Wilkinson.

James and I would meet over coffee in the Globe Bar, to chat about issues of the day and what the industry needed. He had some great ideas, and I encouraged him, and two of them even came to fruition. In 2002 we had the first ever HM Awards Night to recognise excellence in service and operational areas, and it's still going strong. Then, in 2010, my personal favourite, we finally launched the Australasian Hotel Industry Conference and Exhibition (AHICE) in conjunction with the AHA. It was the first dedicated accommodation hotel conference in Australia, with leading industry executives and field specialists speaking and debating the issues of the day, at an event focussed squarely on the managers and supervisors who keep the many wheels of a hotel turning day and night. These events have grown enormously since then, and are pre-eminent hospitality industry events.

One of our industry's best stories to tell is that hospitality gives so many young people their first job; it teaches them great technical and interpersonal skills, and provides career paths for life as well – I mean, just look at me. Through the hotel and the AHA we would often be involved in training and job-start programs to encourage people into the industry and help young people in their first foray into the real-world job market. One such project in 2004 was called *Youth Matters*. It was an attempt to help young long-term unemployed people into work. Along with the AHA and Training Australia, we interviewed dozens of kids, some of whom had never worked in their lives. It was sad to listen to some of their stories; they had been simply cast on the scrap heap. The Observatory employed three such youngsters in a pilot program. They all started well but then dropped out. I was disappointed when the last young lad who had worked in concierge failed to show up one morning. When we eventually were able to contact him I was rather shocked to learn about his family. He lived at home with his siblings, mother, father and grandparents and not one of these family members had ever had a job in their lives. It was hard for me to understand. It showed that we needed to find different strategies and tactics with young people from these backgrounds. We were not deterred in our employment programs and kept trying over the years, with varied levels of success.

With my fellow hoteliers (all of us volunteers and on our own time) and the tireless staff of the AHA, we worked for years on myriad issues that three levels of governments seemed to endlessly inflict on our businesses. I loved the work and the engagement we had with the industry, the politicians, the journalists and the many other stakeholders who are involved in tourism and hospitality.

It was therefore wonderful to receive a Medal of the Order of Australia (OAM) in The Queen's Birthday Honours List in 2009 for services to hospitality; it was gratifying to know that at least all our hard work through the AHA was not going unnoticed, and I hope that it will encourage the young managers coming through to also invest some time in the wider industry and the personal and professional rewards it can bring. [171]

Without a strong united association to fight our political battles, the industry is left open to be taxed and regulated by governments who only see us as a source of easy revenue, and the associations need their members to represent the 'real face' of the sector in the never-ending battle.

Chapter 15

#timesarechanging #fondfarewells #endofthehighlife

By 2007 I had been with Orient-Express for sixteen years. I loved my job, the lifestyle and the travel - who wouldn't? But the company was changing. Simon Sherwood had departed for grander things, Jim Sherwood was taking a step back from the general hotel operations and a new President had been appointed. I was delighted when it was announced that my new boss was Paul White, the young man with whom I had started this journey. He had been sent from London to assist in setting up the finances when we were working on the opening of The Observatory Hotel. We'd sat watching my son Tim play cricket all those years ago. He was a great guy and we had shared many highs and a few lows both in work and within our domestic lives, so I was pleased with his success.

It was also a time of change for the industry. Orient-Express had listed on the New York Stock Exchange in August 2000 and since that time the share price had performed rather below expectations. Things became considerably worse when the financial crisis hit in 2008, the worst since the Great Depression of the 1930s. Luxury travel as always was the first to suffer. Paul had a tough task and not one I envied.

I had fought and won my battle against prostate cancer, but it had taken its toll. The company had become more focussed on financial matters than on the quality of service. It had probably always been the case to a certain extent, but it seemed to me that my service-oriented approach was now less of a priority. Managers were expected to spend more time sitting in front of their computers, poring over budgets and balance sheets, than out at front of house caring for the guests, which I had made a priority for nearly fifty years. I therefore felt this time of transition was possibly the right time for me to take my final bow. It was not an easy decision but I felt that I had achieved some great milestones in my career and that in the new online era it would be hard for me to continue to do so.

The biggest question I faced was *what should I do in retirement?* I had been shocked when I had mentioned to a colleague the name of Ted Wright, the elder statesman of our industry for many years. It had only been a couple of years since he retired, but the response was "Ted who?" My heart sank.

Things started to happen that confirmed my fears that The Observatory Hotel and Sydney were not high on the list of the company's priorities. The tyranny of distance still played a role; Australians don't bat an eyelid at a long flight, but even in the jet age Americans and Europeans baulk at a ten-hour journey. There was also the issue of profit. In our newly acquired Asian properties, profits were excellent, not least due to low labour costs. In Australia, the rank and file of the staff earned more than their counterparts in London, yet room rates in London were three times that of Sydney. We were a luxury hotel with limited room capacity, with service as the key offering. We were expensive. The result was that a discreet word went out in the industry that offers might be considered for the hotel.

One day I a friend who was involved in the very upmarket end of the aged care sector said he thought the hotel would transform into a great establishment for this market. I met the main guys involved and discussed the offer with head office, who quickly dispatched Philip Calvert, the company lawyer to follow up. I was delighted that it was Philip as he was an old and close friend of twenty years, and if someone were to sign the 'death certificate' on The Observatory, at least it would be him.

The negotiations went well. Paul White, the president, assured me that I would be looked after, as would the staff. Furthermore the contract required me to stay on for a year to oversee the transition from luxury hotel to a luxury aged care facility. I had come to terms with this, and with some trepidation and sadness we entered the offices to sign the papers. We all sat with piles of documents between us. The purchaser with pen in hand picked up a document, then hesitated and - to our surprise - he put the pen down and requested a private meeting aside with Philip. They were gone for no more than fifteen minutes. Philip returned to the conference table, obviously angry. He looked at me and quietly shook his head. The deal had fallen through. It is hard to describe my feelings at that moment. After much thought, consideration and eventual acceptance that this was likely to be the end of my career, cushioned by the financial settlement I would receive, my expectation burst like a bubble. I tried to remain positive, but I set out to plan my future after Orient-Express.

In March 2010 I attended my last general manager's conference at Charleston Place in Charleston, South Carolina. How things had changed from my first conference in New Orleans. We now had four times as many hotels represented and ten pin bowling was the team bonding activity. As I shuffled awkwardly down the bowling lane, to send a ball straight into the gutter, I made up my mind. [172]

I had always loved Thailand and I had many Thai friends. I didn't particularly want to leave Australia, but in Thailand

I could start on a new venture and build my own small luxury hotel. This would allow me to maintain my connection with the industry I loved, whilst setting up my own Fawlty Towers over which I could rule as a colonial Basil Fawlty. On the land I had purchased on the banks of the Mekong River, on the Laos border in the most picturesque part of northeast Thailand, I was to build my hotel, *Amoon on the Mekong*. A Sydney architect drew up the plans. I did my costings and it all looked very rosy. I put my concerns of developing leukemia behind me, confident in the knowledge I could monitor it and return to Australia if required.

People asked me worriedly, did I really know what I was doing? Are you sure you can survive in Thailand? I really thought I had everything covered when I made the acquaintance of Dr Kantathi, the Thai Foreign Minister in the government of Thaksin Shinawatra. With contacts like that, what could go wrong? My new friendship was short-lived however. There was a coup in Bangkok, Thaksin was sent packing and my friend disappeared to the USA. The eventual outcome of my Thai adventure would give me material for another book, but at the time my enthusiasm for my hotel in Thailand remained unabated and my plans for retirement proceeded apace.

With a degree of apprehension I announced my intentions to my family, but they gave me their support, so this opened the path to negotiate my resignation with the powers-that-were in London. I could then tell my *other* family: my friends and colleagues at The Observatory. Easier said than done.

I cannot recall exactly when and how my retirement reached them. I don't believe a formal notice went out but the hotel had an efficient grapevine that worked exceedingly well in such matters. Not long into the new year of 2011, people started to ask if I was really leaving. I had to explain that it was likely to happen in the second quarter by which time I would have reached the age of 65, but no actual date had been set.

I was deeply moved by the number of staff who approached me to ask 'why?' To be truthful I wasn't sure myself, except that I felt the time had come. It was hard to walk down to the staff canteen for lunch, as all along the corridor were photo boards of the teams past and present. Every year from opening in 1993, someone was tasked with going around the hotel and taking candid photos of all staff. It was quite an effort and as the years went by they became more intricate and creative. It was a fun exercise and there was often a buzz of excitement when each year at the staff party the board would be unveiled and staff would go searching for their photo - The Observatory version of *Where's Wally*. Woe betide the person who compiled it for that year, if it turned out that they had missed anyone. [173]

The photo-boards brought back so many memories of staff who had come and gone. I had watched many of them grow up in the hotel, like Steve Dodsworth, son of the chief engineer Charlie, who had joined us at the age of seventeen and was now grown up and settled down, and ran the department he first joined. There was Emil Bashay, the executive housekeeper who was with me when we opened. I had watched his daughters grow up and graduate. So many had started young, grown up, married and now had children of their own. There were those who had been my deputies and now ran international hotels. There was the face of a lovely young receptionist from when we first opened, called Cornelia Rau. We celebrated when she achieved her ambition and became a Qantas flight attendant, and were shocked years later at the terrible events in her life. The ABC made a drama series about her called *Stateless,* starring Cate Blanchett. There was another bright smiling face, Tori Johnson, who had been a porter and then a manager, only to be tragically killed in the Lindt Café siege in Sydney in 2014. I had shared a part of their lives, their trials and tribulations, and each and every one had helped to make The Observatory Hotel a success.[174]

When you work with people every day for nearly twenty years, walking, talking, eating and drinking with them, it's hard not to see them as family. I loved all the little interactions; quiet chats with Emil, Elsie and Soshilla, who for twenty years had run the laundry efficiently with rarely a sick day, or with Ernesto and his team who always started my day with a smile when I had my breakfast. In over a thousand staff over the years, I can only think of two or three people whom I regretted employing; I like to think that was a pretty good record for employee relations.

I always said to the staff *"if you have a problem, don't sit in the canteen and complain to other staff, as often they won't care and even if they do they are unlikely to help you with your problem. Speak to your boss and if they are unable to help then come and see me. If I can't resolve your problem, I will explain why"*, and many did. It helped that I ate in the staff canteen, so that people could see I was approachable.

My other favourite mantra was *"If you become unhappy with your work or your heart is no longer in it, then don't come to work, because if you don't like what you do, how can you expect to enjoy looking after the guests or your working colleagues, and the wrong attitude will always be noticed."*

I was determined to make a change. Much as I had done nearly twenty-five years ago in migrating to Australia, now was the time to start a new chapter in my life whilst I had the energy and drive to do so. I gave notice to the Board of my intentions to depart in the first half of 2011, as I was now officially a pensioner, allowing them several months to seek out and employ my replacement. Paul regretted my decision and JBS was disappointed writing me a personal note wishing me well, but they respected my reasons for leaving.

The last few months at The Observatory were a bit of a blur, with a lot of dinners and discussions. I recommended we appoint a very qualified young man with flair who understood what The Observatory was all about. Ralph Bruegger was charming and very urbane, and was also an active supporter of the work of the AHA.

Eventually the final day came. I had been busy sorting things out, again marvelling at how much bric a brac I had collected over twenty years. I knew we'd have a bit of a farewell party, as Kim Salt, Christine Whyte and others had been busy but I was utterly taken aback at what transpired. Around a hundred people turned up: staff past and present, together with a surprising number of our regular guests. Ian Smith had travelled from Adelaide, Peter Aloi from Melbourne who I had known since my Como days, Glen A Baker was there, who had been my companion as I had travelled the globe on Qantas listening to his playlist on the airline channel, *Reelin' in the Years*.

I was picked up and carried down memory lane. On stage in the midst of my well prepared 'final curtain' speech, I glimpsed someone onto the stage behind me. It was the well-known TV presenter John Mangos. He interrupted me mid speech at my great moment! Everyone started to murmur. When he started to speak, I was taken back to when Eamonn Andrews and Michael Aspel were on English TV years ago, but now it was me being surprised with the famous lines, *Excuse me interrupting, but tonight ...Patrick Griffin ...This Is Your Life!* John Mangos held aloft a large red book with those words inscribed on the front.[175]

It was the most surprising moment of my life, and the most emotional moment of my career; a group of people had done some extraordinary time-consuming research to pull it all together and - best of all - I had had no idea whatsoever what was going on! One after another, staff, friends and even guests came on stage and reminded me of some episode in my life, not only in Australia but back to childhood. There were video links with my brother Chris in France, Angela Clarke in the UK, and then my boss, and friend, Paul White in London. As the event drew to a close, there was another surprise telephone link up to an old friend and colleague who had worked with me at the hotel, Jeremy Goring. He called from his family's hotel, The Goring in London, that he was running very successfully, particularly these days following Prince William's party on the eve of his wedding. As we chatted over the link, I suddenly turned to find Jeremy standing right there, mic in hand! [176]

It was a wonderful event, laughing, crying, cringing, hearing reminiscences that not only meant something to me, but apparently also meant something to my colleagues, friends and staff, which to me made it all the more moving and memorable. I will always treasure my big red book.[177, 178, 179]

As I departed the hotel that night, I experienced so many emotions. This was really the last time I would exit the building as the boss, the leader of my team, an elder statesman in an industry that meant so much to me. My life was indeed flashing past my mind's eye, as I reflected on the past.

The writer L.P. Hartley opened his novel *The Go-Betweens* with a wonderful insight: "The past is a foreign country; they do things differently there." Many other writers and historians have drawn on this, and I am going to do so as well. I can't think of a more apt metaphor for just how different the hotel industry of the past looks today compared to when I entered it fifty years ago. What would Cesar Ritz think now? He was the imperator of hoteliers, who brought The Ritz to London and the world in

1906. That year may seem like the dark ages to some people, but my father was born in 1908 - only two generations ago.

Today's hospitality students would laugh in disbelief. When I started work in England, five star hotels were only just considering the need for all rooms to have *a bathroom*. Bedrooms were not equipped with shampoos and other amenities. At best, you might find a small bar of *Milk Soap* provided, and there were certainly no dressing-gowns or slippers. If you had a room with no bathroom, you would have brought your own dressing gown to walk down the corridor to wash or go to the lavatory. No rooms had televisions - I recall an old general manager bemoaning the idea as they might hold the guest back from spending money in the bar. If the hotel was 'forward thinking' they may have offered two television rooms: one with a TV tuned to BBC One (as there were no other BBC channels) and the other with a TV tuned to the single commercial channel, ITV, both black and white sets of course. The majority of the rooms would have been twin bedded, with very few doubles. There were no safes in the rooms. In a four or five star hotel room you might have had a dial up phone, but all calls were routed through the hotel switchboard.

Dress was required to be formal, of course; not simply a suit and tie when dining in the restaurant, but a *dinner* jacket. I recall one hotelier lamenting his disappointment that white tie and tails were no longer worn, except maybe at a ballroom dancing competition. Women were expected to wear skirts, and hotel staff uniforms reflected this. Even in the late 90s I read that Ted Wright at the Regent in Sydney (now the Four Seasons) would not allow his female staff to wear trousers as part of their uniform, feeling "that our customers are as yet not ready for this". Back in the 60s female staff did not work in restaurants or cocktail bars in luxury hotels, let alone in management roles. Women were confined to reception, housekeeping and serving afternoon tea in the lounge.

On payday all staff received a little brown envelope containing their wages in cash. No cheques or bank transfers. Health and insurance benefits were in the form of a stamp that was stuck on your card each week. Whence came the term when someone was sacked, they were 'given their cards'. There were no such things as credit cards; guests paid in cash or by way of a personal cheque, and no-one was asked for ID. It all related to the strict English social order; only the wealthy entered the portals of a five star hotel, and it was assumed that they would always pay. No-one from the working class would dream of going to such a fine establishment as a five star hotel.

Most bookings were made by letter, or occasionally by phone, but calls were timed and very expensive so usually this was avoided. Managers had female secretaries, to whom letters were dictated and taken down in Pitman shorthand then typed, at an average speed of 60 words per minute, then signed by the manager and posted. The postal service was very efficient at the time. A letter would arrive in the morning, and the reply would be in the post that afternoon, and the guest received confirmation of their reservation in the first post the following morning. We did not even have a telex machine (look it up on Wikipedia) which some other hotels had, and the *fluorescence-activated cell sorting,* or facsimile machine as you might know it, was not in common use until nearly thirty years later in the 1990s.

The sexual revolution of the 1960s and 70s had a major bearing on hotel operations. As a young assistant, I would be on the lookout for unmarried couples who were brazen enough to book a room, as it could have brought the hotel into disrepute. Up until this time the divorce laws were so draconian the only way to get one was to prove infidelity. This tended to be achieved by a man taking a woman other than his wife to a hotel and at the appropriate, or should I say inappropriate moment, be caught by a photographer *in flagrante delicto.* This would prove sufficient in court, the proceedings of which would be published in the scandal sheets, naming the hotel - it thus behoved us to keep this out of the papers.

Dress standards changed over the years with the levelling of social classes and a burgeoning wealthier middle class. A man could lawfully beat his wife but not his dog, and there was a growing feminist movement, much driven by a feisty Australian woman called Germain Greer, and around the world women were *burning their bras.* Homosexuality was illegal in Britain for males, and they were victimised and thrown in prison. Strangely enough, being a lesbian was not illegal. Employment laws were changing. I had just started work when the UK government introduced *The Contract of Employment Act 1963*, whereby the employer was required to actually give each member of staff their written working conditions such as hours and holidays. My boss thought it was the beginning of the end, not that they actually honoured anything in the contracts. So many antiquated rules and laws were being swept away, it was truly a revolutionary time.

I had to restructure the hotel's finance system to take into account decimalised currency in 1971. This was followed in 1973 by the change from numerous taxes to one, the Value Added Tax (VAT). While these were all welcomed as advances for the national finances, there were no computers for us to use, and everything had to be calculated in your head or, at best, with a calculator. Readers will know of my antipathy for maths; imagine the mental acrobatics needed when VAT started at 10%, then almost immediately dropped to 8% and then a higher rate of 12.5% for petrol and certain luxury goods. I had the responsibility of training all the staff to handle these changes, as it was far too complicated for my boss at the time. I was training him on the new machine called a 'photocopier'. It was a wet and dry type, requiring single sheets to be fed into a huge machine. Naturally being the young up and comer, I rather scoffed at his lack of understanding. Much as my staff must have done with me and computers many years later.

I had to manage our way through a number of financial crises, such as the devaluation of the British pound in 1967 right up until the crash of 2008. We had the miners' strikes which caused power blackouts, a major headache when you suddenly had no lifts or lights in a multistorey hotel. We ended up being forced to operate a three-day week. The IRA and its campaign of bombing public buildings meant that the London Hilton and our own Grand Hotel in Brighton were in the front line of their attack.

In fifty years I have witnessed and adapted to enormous changes in our industry across social, legal, commercial, and technological spheres. Through no fault of our own, the world threw any number of challenges at us: airline strikes, postal strikes, emergency service strikes, natural disasters, and threats of terrorism. As hoteliers, it was our job to handle it well and look after the guests as our first priority.

My career has been primarily with two companies, De Vere Hotels in England for over twenty years and Orient-Express Hotels, Trains & Cruises for a similar time here in Australia. Both groups comprised very distinctly unique hotels, with quality service front and centre. Managers ran them almost as owner-operators, retaining their responsibility, individuality and autonomy that rendered the hotels highly sought-after. Then the accountants started to call the shots, and uniformity was deemed to be more cost efficient. Unfortunately, this also led to blandness, which was anathema to me.

For some hotels there is pride in the fact that - no matter where you go in the world - the product is the same. To my mind this is all well and good for hamburgers, but not for the hospitality industry. Corporate rulebooks have made managers rather boring and timid. They simply look to the handbook and company policy - absolving themselves of any responsibility, like Party members in China in the sixties using Chairman Mao's Little Red Book.

Jim Sherwood summed it up. *In life today we are confronted with so much mediocrity. In an age when everyone is deluged with homogeneous brands, I have liked to create the special. There is a real unfulfilled need and desire to experience it.*

Creativity and individuality are what characterise a great hotel. Stifling this leads to unhappy and unfulfilled staff who become robots with little acceptance of responsibility. My thinking may be outdated but - as with many things in today's world - I would simply ask the question "have we gone too far?" in allowing systems to take over from humans.

Jim Sherwood had created a collection of unique hotels to which I, with others, had been privileged to belong. His beliefs were echoed by a fellow Board director, George Rafael, who had himself in 1986 developed another iconic brand of hotels under his name, eventually selling them in 2000 to the Mandarin Oriental Hotel Group. He was a passionate hotelier with a belief in service, and I always remembered his exhortation: *"Computers have a major place in our hotels, but as the manager - for God's sake, get out from behind them, and out in the front of your hotel and meet your guests. Without them you wouldn't have a hotel!"*

Wise words but sadly ignored by many nowadays. The computer has become rather a security blanket for some people. I fear I will now offend many: there are reported to be more than 2,500,000 chartered accountants in the world, probably more, and at times most of them appear to be in the hospitality sector!

When I first started, 90% of the staff were involved in delivering service to the guest, with the remaining few in administration. I would hazard a guess that today this balance would be 50-50 at best. The industry seems to have lost sight of the fact that front of house staff look after the customer interaction and have the responsibility to provide the excellence of service that persuades the guest to return. Accountants just add up the figures! By now some people who have invested in this book may well be tossing it in the bin! I cannot emphasise enough the importance of the relationship between the General Managers, the staff and the guests: don't become a robot! Hospitality is all about human interaction. I am a case in point: it was my personal contact and positive interaction with guests over the years that brought me the many great experiences I've been writing about. Guests love and appreciate being recognised and acknowledged: that's what brings them back.

Of course, it helps if they can tell who the General Manager is! I see people walk into a restaurant in jeans and a T-shirt, or at best an open neck shirt, and I imagine Charlton the butler at The Grand Eastbourne, or Johnny Johnson and Cliff Edwards from The Cavendish, spinning in their graves. This change in style came home to me most clearly in the form of Ralf Bruegger who replaced me as GM at The Observatory in 2011. He was very suave and charming but had a penchant for the tie-free look, a matter that concerned me in this rather traditional luxury city hotel. When asked by head office if there were any issues of concern I might have with Ralf's appointment, I replied none, but said as an aside, "Well he rarely wears a tie, which he may need to change."

The response said it all. "I see nothing wrong in managers not wearing a tie, it's about time we got rid of the stuffy atmosphere at The Observatory." I knew then that I'd picked the right time to go.

All GMs at Orient-Express had *always* worn ties and suits. It seemed strange to dress staff up in uniforms with bow ties or ties, yet the GM looked like he was off to play golf.

The London office had developed a well-staffed Human Resource department; rather overkill I thought, as we employed two exceedingly professional and competent HR staff at the hotel itself, who after all did all the employment, training, and staff relations. Our staff turnover was one of the lowest of any Sydney hotel, we'd only had one legal issue in 20 years, yet we were bombarded with emails about compliance and regulations, requesting forms be completed and new procedures implemented. We actually needed more staff to deal with the head office paperwork!

Gradually all decision making, independent thinking, and responsibility was being taken away from the hotel manager. We wouldn't be able to create a magical experience unless authorised to do so; we wouldn't be able to add some special magic for the guest, or make amends or rectify a guest's problem without authority, especially if it involved spending any money. I know some hotels have strategies in place for this, but I think they are still far too limited.

Over the years I have found extraordinary talent amongst staff at all levels who have come up with brilliant new ideas. Why? Because they have been encouraged to do so, and on seeing one of their ideas implemented they have gained confidence and a great source of pride in their work, making them a more enthused, happier and committed employee, and loyal to the hotel where they have been appreciated. The management team that supported me believed in this and it flowed through to staff in all departments.

Was this successful? Yes indeed it was! The proof was in the low staff turnover, the plethora of local and global awards and the recognition staff of The Observatory Hotel. The proof of the pudding is truly in the eating, as you can see by just some of the awards listed in Appendix B [180, 181, 182, 183, 184].

I pondered on the night of my retirement about how much had changed during my career, and why I had stayed in hospitality. So many people are stuck in a job they hate, but I had loved every minute of mine. I had been able to choose where to work and where to travel, and met remarkable and interesting people along the way. My job was *fun* and I realised how spoilt I had been. I was fortunate to have been part of the boom times in our industry. I had arrived in a career almost by accident, with modest talents. I remembered how the nurse at my birth had said I had *bags of personality.* I recalled those musty old school reports so carefully preserved by my father, dismayed at my lack of academic achievement.

1958 - Headmaster's Report – His good character and charm of manners will help him out one day.

We shall miss his cheerful and genial personality, but he must come to terms with the fact he cannot get through life with a smile and these attributes alone. W.T.Bryant

I was twelve at the time he wrote that. I am now seventy-four. Would my father be proud of what I achieved? I would like to think do. I think of my father when I listen to one of my favourite artists, James Blunt, singing *Monsters.* I wish I could have said those words to my father. (https://www.youtube.com/watch?v=DTFbGcnl0po)

I mused on human mortality. I thought of all the things said, and unsaid over the years, and how people pass away unexpectedly. I had missed my gentle father's demise, but fortunately had been able to say a proper good-bye to my dear mother. These were the thoughts that inspired me to write of how my family and the hotel industry have indeed provided me with a *very* Grand Life.

Epilogue

#what'sbeen #survivingthegrandlife #howgoodwasthat

All through our lives we have people to tell us what to do - parents, relatives, teachers, colleagues, friends, bosses. Our careers often follow planned paths. We marry (in my case a little too often, until I got it right), raise a family, and suddenly we are talking of retirement. My parents' retirement was very different to mine, both financially and culturally. My father had accepted the inevitability of aging in the conservative way his father had before him, sitting back reading a book and smoking a pipe. He never owned casual sportswear or jeans. He was still wearing a collar, tie and jacket every day at eighty.

I didn't want to be told what to do, so following my retirement, I set off to Thailand to pursue the hotel dream I had been developing over the previous few years. At sixty five I set off to build and operate a small luxury hotel on five acres of land I had purchased on the banks of the Mekong River. It did not work out. A mixture of naivety and on my part, with unscrupulous developers in a country where corruption is a way of life, meant that I eventually succumbed to ill health with cancer and my dreams were not fulfilled. That is another story and maybe another book.

Through my twenty years with Orient-Express I had served under three extraordinary presidents of the company, Jim Sherwood, his son Simon Sherwood and Paul White.[185, 186, 187] Somewhat to my surprise, Paul resigned from Orient-Express in 2011, and tragically died in a car accident a few years later. The Observatory Hotel was sold to Langham Hotels, who had long sought a suitable and - I would like to think - special hotel in Sydney upon whose reputation they might build. The hotel operated for a short time under the Langham banner before closing and setting out on a $30 million renovation. This was a much-needed investment and one that Orient-Express Hotels had not been prepared to do. I was however pleased to read a press comment that "The Observatory's notable collection of Australian art has been extended under the loving watch of Sotheby's", but I gather Sidney Nolan's morbid 'Billy Budd' did not survive the renovation.[76]

The hotel was totally renovated and rebranded. A few years later when I visited I found, with a twinge of regret, it was unrecognisable from the hotel that I had known. It had become modern and minimalist, in line with so many other hotels of today. Its individuality had gone; I had to accept that this was what younger customers wanted. There is no question that The Langham is a very stylish contemporary hotel, and this helped me to appreciate that The Observatory Hotel I had helped to build and develop no longer existed. A page in history had turned and all that remained were my affectionate memories, which I was delighted to discover were shared by many of my old staff and colleagues.

Even more change was on the horizon for the parent company of Orient-Express Hotels, Trains & Cruises. In 2015 they discarded the iconic brand, and rebranded its portfolio of hotels, river cruises, trains, safaris and restaurants as Belmond Hotels.

In place of the classic, elegant and stylish logo, a new logo appeared, looking like, what a number of wags referred to as *a knock off of a Krispy Kreme.*

Along with this rebranding, all the properties were renamed with Belmond as a prefix to the more venerable names, so well-known in their own right. This was inevitable as it is very difficult to promote a hotel globally without a recognisable corporate banner. As a result, Philip Carruthers' famed Copacabana Palace Hotel in Rio became the 'Belmond' Copacabana Palace, as did Natale Rusconi's hotel become the 'Belmond' Hotel Cipriani in Venice, and my dear friend Nick Seewer's hotel in Cape Town become 'Belmond' Mount Nelson Hotel. Only The Venice Simplon-Orient-Express Train appears to have escaped, for which I am grateful, but there was little left in the name or culture of the Orient-Express Hotels as I had known them.

I was heartened by the news in 2018 that luxury goods maker Louis Vuitton Moet Hennessy had agreed to buy the Belmond hotels group for an estimated $3.2 billion. I hope that under such a prestigious banner we will see this incredibly unique and special portfolio created by Jim Sherwood enhance its presence in upscale hospitality, and re-establish itself as one of the world's most distinctive collections of hotels.

As for my 'home' The Observatory, it is wonderful to see that the spirit and the culture we developed was not lost. In 2017 a Facebook page appeared: *The Observatory Hotel and Orient-Express Australia.* It rapidly attracted nearly 250 members of the hotels' teams from both The Observatory and our sister hotel Lilianfels in The Blue Mountains. Members post updates, social events and news and we stay connected. I have enjoyed a number of reunions with those who still live and work in Australia. I'm always touched to hear of their fond memories for the time we spent at the hotel together.

Along with The Observatory, other hotels in which I had spent many years of my career have also passed into mere memories. Back in Britain, The Manor House Hotel in Leamington Spa is now self-catering apartments. The Castle Hotel in Norwich was demolished and replaced by The Castle Mall shopping centre. The Cavendish Hotel in Eastbourne was "sold to a group dubbed 'the worst hotel chain in the UK'". The De Montfort Hotel in Kenilworth is now a Holiday Inn and sports a Starbucks whilst the De Vere in Coventry is now The Britannia Hotel.

The one constant remains The Grand Hotel in Eastbourne where my career first started. Now owned by Elite Hotels, they have tastefully renovated the hotel so that it is still a much-respected luxury hotel under the management of my old friend and colleague, Jonathan Webley. He has overseen and maintained the high standards and long traditions of service for over twenty-five years and for this he has my admiration and thanks for keeping safe a little haven of my memories.

I subtitled this book *'Confessions of an Old School Hotelier in the Digital Age'.* I thought I'd be talking about hotels, but I see I have also painted a picture of evolving social values, standards, culture and technology throughout my journey. Many of the names that so impressed and influenced me mean little or nothing today. I meet young people who have never heard of Charlie Chaplin and look blank at the mention of *Gone With The Wind*. I grew up in a world when homes weren't locked, where children played outside in woods and parks without fear. There were few televisions and many homes did not have a telephone. Mobile phones were only seen in science fiction programs.

Now I have trouble keeping up with views on gender equality, sexuality, race and what is deemed *political correctness*. Was this the same for my parents? Will it be like this for my children?

To show that I have tried to keep up with the times, I can use internet and I am active on social media (!). There is a blog that I like, Dennis Byrne's "The Barbershop" on which he posted an essay by Randy McDaniel. I quote:

> *You know ...time has a way of moving quickly and catching you unaware of the passing years. It seems just yesterday I was young, starting out on my career, getting married and embarking on my new life. Yet in a way, it seems like eons ago, and I wonder where all the years went. I know that I lived them all, (as this book tells). I have glimpses of how it was back then and of all my hopes and dreams. But, here it is...retirement ... and it catches me by surprise...How did I get here so fast? Where did the years go and where did my youth go?*
>
> *I remember well, seeing older people through the years and thinking that those old people were years away from me and were so much older that I could not fathom it or imagine fully what it would be like. But, here it is...my friends are retired and getting gray...they move slower and I see an older person now. Some are in better, and some worse shape than me...but, I see the great change...Not like the ones that I remember who were young and vibrant...but, like me, their age is beginning to show and we are now those older folks that we used to see and never thought we'd become....*
>
> *http://www.chicagonow.com/dennis-byrnes-barbershop/*

I hope you have enjoyed reading my book as much as I have enjoyed writing it... and indeed living it.

As my mother would counsel me: "This is no rehearsal, life is a gift to you. The way you live your life is your gift to those who come after." And so I say dear readers, make your life a *Grand* one, live it well and enjoy its every minute.

Afterword

As we do the final edit during the 2020 Covid-19 pandemic, I fear that the world will consign my style of management to the pages of history. Nothing has been seen like this since the influenza pandemic of 1918 when an estimated 500 million people or one-third of the world's population became infected. Countries now are closing borders, airlines are grounded and hotels stand empty. Seventy-five years ago, at the end of World War II, the hotel industry also stood devastated. My early mentors like Dick Beattie and Reg Constable, staff like Morris and Charleston at the Grand, set about rebuilding what was left. By the time I started my career much of the hard work had been done - I rode a wave of development that led to the thriving global industry that existed up to 2020. I grew up with tales of pre-war and post-war times; will my children grow up telling their children of the pre and post Covid-19 times?

I do not know how the industry will recover and evolve. I recall Hilton's early mission statement 'To cater for Americans abroad'. They ended up serving all travellers, but with the changes brought about by lockdowns and technology, will there be any need to travel? I know that the hospitality industry will in future be very different to what it was in my lifetime. I've always said that hospitality can rightly claim to be the oldest profession. It has survived and adapted through the ages, and

I'm sure it will again. There may even be a silver lining: for the first time I am hearing governments making positive statements of the importance of the industry. Maybe at last they will recognise the value of the sector to the economy and our global society and culture. I'm certain that hospitality will continue to offer young people an exciting career, and a taste - in whatever form it may take - of 'The Grand Life'.

o0O0o

THE END

Appendix A

Jim Sherwood (1933 - 2020) and Orient-Express

(This chapter is based on conversations I had with Jim Sherwood over twenty years and his book 'Orient-Express - A Personal Journey', a book I would commend as an excellent read.)

I didn't know it at the time, but I was to spend the next twenty years, nearly half of my entire working life, with this company. I'd like to expand a little about Orient-Express and especially about the remarkable man and founder of the company, whose vision, charisma, direction and mentoring I was to admire and commit to from my first day to my last in his employ.

James B. Sherwood was known to us as JBS. No matter how friendly or warm he might have been, I only ever called him Mr. Sherwood to his face. To call him anything more familiar just didn't seem appropriate. There was a warm smile yet it came with icy blue eyes.

JBS was born in Kentucky, USA. His father was a prominent patent lawyer and his mother was a homemaker and a talented musician. His ancestors had arrived in North America from England a few centuries before and, as early settlers, had become tobacco plantation owners.

He attended the elite Ivy League university of Yale where he read economics, and whilst there, during the Korean War, his uncle, Vice-Admiral William A Glassford, steered him into joining the Naval Reserve Officer Training Corps. He signed up to be a Naval Officer and served much of his time in Southeast Asia, including Japan and the Philippines.

He was an exceptional bridge player, a skill not common amongst many of his fellow officers. This came to the notice of his commanding officer, with whom he was invited to 'make up a four'. To quote from his book "My reputation as a reasonable hand at bridge proved to be of considerable benefit to me in the Navy and led afterwards to my career in shipping - without which I could never have bought Orient-Express."

As a deck officer involved in transportation, he was posted to Subic Bay, a major American naval base in the Philippines. He told me it was here that he was given the command of a number of Japanese named and flagged LSTs - Landing Ship Tanks - for 'special duties'. He explained that, at the time, the Americans were not keen on being overtly involved with the problems in Indonesia. President Sukarno was battling the communists for control, having recently gained independence from the Dutch. It was the start of what was called the 'domino effect' and so JBS found himself shipping arms and materials under a foreign flag to support Sukarno, a man not particularly liked but the better of two evils.

I had not pictured my boss as a swashbuckling adventurer, a gun runner, but it added to his charisma and my respect for the man.

In 1959, following his Navy days, he joined the United States Lines shipping company who ran luxury liners such as the *SS America* and the *SS United States*, as well as cargo freighters. He was based in Europe and it was there that he saw and developed cargo handling which would dramatically change the way the shipping industry operated.

On a business trip to Switzerland, he learned that there was a major export market in high-value goods such as watches and cameras. Most goods were generally flown to the USA at great cost, as there were fears of pilferage, an endemic problem at the time with normal cargo handling. There were also frequent delays at wharves with loading and unloading. JBS realised that high speed ocean liners could be used for cargo. At the time these liners were losing business due to the growing popularity of flying. The challenge was that when these liners came into port, such as at Le Havre, they required a very fast turn around due to schedules and port charges.

JBS's question was how could valuable cargo be safely, quickly and economically loaded and unloaded? Necessity is the mother of invention, and JBS wanted this business. An idea emerged of building a number of steel containers that could be safely sealed and loaded onto a train in Basel, delivered to the dockside at Le Havre the following evening. They would be lifted by crane into the liner's hold and be on their way within the limited allotted time in port. No risk of pilferage, no issues of go-slow dockers, and delivery at their destination almost as fast as by air services at less cost.

JBS admitted this idea was not totally new, as a fellow American, Malcolm McLean, was pioneering it in the US, but it was in its infancy. It was JBS's visionary concept of buying containers and leasing them to shipping companies to meet the demand of an ever expanding concept of moving cargo in this way. His company, *Sea Containers* is what led to JBS becoming a multimillionaire by the age of thirty five.

His entry into the hotel industry came almost by chance. One of his favourite hotels was quietly rumoured to be for sale. The Hotel Cipriani in Venice was opened in 1958 by Giuseppe Cipriani. He was the entrepreneur behind the famed Harry's

Bar, a favourite of Ernest Hemingway, amongst other celebrities. Hemingway's novel *Across the River and Into the Trees* features Harry's Bar often. The Guinness brewing and banking family had been the main investors at the time and the hotel quickly established itself as the finest in Venice. The story goes that Giuseppe wanted to outshine all the competition in Venice and be the only hotel with a swimming pool. To fund this he asked the Guinness sisters, who although wary, agreed subject to London architects designing it. The pool was built according to the plans, however some confusion arose when the Imperial measurements were interpreted by the Italian builder in metric terms. As a result, the Hotel Cipriani not only had the only swimming pool in Venice but the *largest* at 25 by 50 *metres* rather than 25 by 50 *feet*.

The hotel was an unrivalled success, however, Italy was in a downward economic spiral. A period of social and political turmoil that started in the late 1960s, marked by a wave of both left-wing and right wing terrorism. In this climate the hotel's fortunes declined, and as a result the Guinness family sought to sell while they could. JBS received an urgent call one day from Enzio Cecconi, who ran the hotel, informing him that Arrigo Cipriani, son of the founder, was about to buy the hotel and had made it clear that when he did Enzio's services would no longer be required. His call, as JBS writes, *got me at a good moment*. Sea Containers was looking to diversify, as JBS saw competition growing with major, well funded, international companies entering the container market. He believed that hotels as a business could be managed side by side with marine containers, which was not a view shared with his board. To convince them, and to arrange company funding for such an investment, was not an easy or speedy one. Therefore in 1976 JBS bought the Hotel Cipriani himself. This was to be the first hotel in a string of acquisitions that were to carry the JBS trademark of style and individuality.

As I got to know the company in the years ahead I noted that the hotels were all unique. They were the grandest and most traditional of hotels, bearing their legendary marques established over many years, but having seen better days. JBS took them in and brought them back to life, reviving the reputations of their illustrious pasts.

There was no 'hotel format' like so many chain hotel companies. JBS reminded me of another American entrepreneur, also ex-Navy and a Yale graduate, Victor Kiam. He had become famous as the spokesman for the Remington shaver. His catchphrase on the TV commercials was, "I liked the shaver so much, I bought the company!" Substitute 'hotel' for 'shaver' and it could have been JBS speaking. The hotels that JBS acquired were due to their personal appeal, were the best in their regions, and close to his major shipping interests.

His entrepreneurial style could be seen when he attended a Sotheby's auction in Monte Carlo in 1977. A number of rather shabby sleeping carriages were to be auctioned, which had been part of the fabled Orient-Express, a name which had been etched in romantic history, not least due to Agatha Christie's novel *Murder on The Orient-Express*. Having bought The Cipriani in Venice, JBS thought of reviving it and operating it on its original route from Paris to Venice. With his friends, Sir Bill McAlpine and Lord David Garnock, fellow train enthusiasts, JBS purchased the carriages.

As he writes:

> They were to launch me on an entirely new phase of my life that would not only see the resurrection of The Orient-Express, which had first carried passengers across Europe in 1883, but the

creation of the luxury hotel group I would develop over the next thirty years.

This was the man whose vision over those twenty years I was to share. It was also a period when I would experience a level of hedonism hitherto only dreamed about. Thank you JBS.

Appendix B

As I was in the process of signing off on this third and final book, I received an email from Simon Sherwood advising me that his father had died following a serious illness. I was deeply saddened by his passing as he was truly a great man, a mentor to many, respected and admired by all in our industry. JBS was buried in the burial plot attached to Hinton Waldrist church, Faringdon, Oxfordshire, in the gardens of the manor that he loved so much.

I have included his obituary as it appeared in *The Times* newspaper Wednesday 20th May 2020.

Obituary

James B Sherwood

Tenacious yet jovial anglophile American tycoon and bon viveur who recreated the Orient-Express and owned The Cipriani in Venice

In October 1977 Jim Sherwood bought two shabby prewar sleeping carriages at a Sotheby's sale held in a freight yard of Monte Carlo's railway station. They were not any old carriages, however: they were all that remained of the fabled 1920s Orient-Express train and had featured in the film Murder on the Orient-Express. He paid $72,800 for the first one and $41,000 for the second.

Sherwood's plan was to use them to recreate the Orient-Express train and operate it between Paris and Venice, where he had bought The Cipriani hotel the year before. He had budgeted $5 million for the project that he reckoned would take two years; in fact it cost $30 million and took five years.

He and his wife Shirley tracked down another 23 carriages, sad, decommissioned hulks of LX (super-luxury) sleeping and restaurant cars, their windows smashed and their beautiful marquetry covered by linoleum, ignominiously pensioned off when they could no longer meet the rigorous requirements of the high-speed French railways. The train, when it was finished, was half a kilometre long.

The original prewar route of the Orient-Express actually started in London, where British-built Pullman cars ran to Folkestone and passengers continued by ferry, joining the Dutch-built Wagon-Lits cars in Boulogne. Halfway through the project, Sherwood decided to recreate the entire London-Venice journey. That involved acquiring authentic carriages, built in the 1920s or 1930s, which he located in the most unlikely places, including one that was being used as a high-class brothel in Germany and another being lived in by a master at Eton. He even tracked down the private car used by General de Gaulle in Britain during the war and two cars from the special Pullman train that carried the body of Winston Churchill from Waterloo Station to Oxfordshire in 1965. He bought the original baggage car in the north of England from a pigeon fancier who had fitted it out to transport his racing birds.

In May 1982, Sherwood finally launched the new Orient-Express service from platform 8 in Victoria Station, 99 years after its first journey, and over the next two decades it became the centrepiece for a five-star luxury hotel chain that would eventually include some of the best-known properties in the world. The Cipriani, acquired by Sherwood for a mere £900,000 from the Guinness family in 1976 (its value today is in the hundreds of millions), remained the flagship. It had the distinction of being the only hotel in Venice to have a swimming pool; Sherwood rescued it from genteel dilapidation and turned it into the playground for the jet set. He added another 43 hotels, including The Splendido in Portofino, the Copacabana Palace in Rio de Janeiro, the Grand Hotel Europe in St Petersburg, the Ritz in Madrid, and The Mount Nelson in Cape Town, where he spent his last summer.

A multimillionaire by the time he was 36, Sherwood favoured a robust exchange of views in the boardroom and liked to go through every document meticulously, but he was also a jovial man who was always laughing and never boastful. Stout of build and ruddy of complexion, he was a bon viveur who over the years acquired or opened three of the most highly rated restaurants in the world: the Le Manoir aux Quat'Saisons in Oxfordshire, created by the chef Raymond Blanc, the 21 Club in Manhattan and Harry's Bar in Mayfair, co-owned with Mark Birley. Birley was best known for his clubs including Annabel's in Berkeley Square. When Mark died Sherwood fell out with his son Robin over the ownership and eventually sold Birley junior his share for £10 million. The row split London's high society into two camps; Sir Evelyn de Rothschild attempted to mediate and Taki wrote a furious defence of Birley's case in his Spectator column. Vanity Fair meanwhile devoted seven pages to the spat.

Sherwood was something of a food critic and in the mid-1960s he became so frustrated with the quality and price of food and wine in London restaurants that he set up his own Discriminating Guide to London and engaged a group of men-about-town including Sir Simon Jenkins and Anthony Sampson to sample the more expensive restaurants. The guide included a category "Not For Us", which he described as "a list of places whose fame might lead you to their tables but you will get a god-awful meal". He shocked the culinary establishment by including some of the most highly rated restaurants of the day, among them Bentley's, the Ritz, the Ivy, J Sheekey and even Wiltons. "My intention was to create a guide for busy, well-off people who did not want their time and money wasted," he said. The first edition sold 10,000 copies, the second 50,000.

Sherwood made his first fortune from containers, building his world-wide Sea Containers group, which specialised in leasing containers to other shipping companies, into one of the most successful in the shipping and transport world. In the late

1970s he moved his head office into Sea Containers House at Blackfriars Bridge, which he bought as an unfinished building from a bankrupt developer.

One of his favourite stories was the appearance in his office, soon after he had finished the property, of a hulking Australian who introduced himself as Kerry Packer. "You know Mr Sherwood, the way I spend my weekends is I walk around London and look at buildings. I like yours. I'm offering you £85 million for it."

When Sherwood responded that he rather liked his new accommodation himself, Packer became threatening. "Mr Sherwood, when I make an offer and you don't accept it, my next offer is always going to be lower. I think you should accept it."

He did not and it later became the headquarters of the Orient-Express group. Renamed Belmond after Sherwood's retirement, it was bought last year by LVMH, the French luxury goods company, for $3.2 billion. Sea Containers fared less well, running into stiff competition in the 1990s and eventually, after some bitter board-room battles, Sherwood left in 2006 and the company filed for Chapter 11 bankruptcy.

In 1984 he had paid £50 million to acquire Sealink, which operated ferries across the Channel, and also became a train operator, but in the last years of his business life Orient-Express became his all-consuming passion.

James Blair Sherwood was born in Kentucky in 1933 into a family that had farmed tobacco for nearly 300 years. His father, William (Bill), inherited tobacco farms but never farmed them and practised as a patent lawyer in New York, where Jim, an only child, grew up. His mother, Florence, was a pianist.

Sherwood went to Bronxville Senior School and then Yale, where he studied, but did not enjoy economics and developed a lifelong passion for bridge, which he played for money.

Under the influence of his favourite uncle, a rear-admiral, he served as a naval cadet while still at college, allowing him to do his national service as a commissioned officer. In the summer of 1955 he graduated with a BA and served four years in the navy, mostly in the Far East, and was often drafted by his superior officers as a fourth at bridge. One day his squadron of landing craft was assigned to spend the Christmas of 1956 in the "godforsaken" island of postwar Okinawa, only to be mysteriously rerouted to the much more agreeable Sasebo, where the admiral of the fleet summoned Sherwood aboard the flagship to play bridge.

His naval experience proved invaluable when he left to work for United States Lines, a US government-sponsored shipping company that owned what were claimed to be the two largest and fastest passenger ships in the world, the America and the United States. He then set up his own container company, based in Paris, in 1965, taking advantage of a huge boom in container traffic, where he was seen as one of the pioneers. Five years later, he listed it on the New York stock exchange, realising enough cash to live in comfort for the rest of his life.

In 1977 he married Shirley Cross, a widow whose husband had died in an aircraft crash. She was a botanist and scientist who worked on the Nobel prizewinning team that developed the drug Tagamet. It was she who oversaw most of the work on the Orient-Express train and was heavily involved in building up the hotel group, travelling everywhere with him.

He is survived by Shirley and her two sons: Simon, who took over as president of Orient-Express in 1994, leaving to chair Elegant Hotels, based in the Bahamas, in 2007, and is now retired, and Charles, a partner in the Permira private equity company.

In later years, Sherwood had his own vineyard, Capannelle, in Chianti. He also, sybarite to the end, retained two private suites in The Cipriani.

Jim Sherwood, businessman, was born on August 8, 1933. He died of complications after abdominal surgery on May 18, 2020, aged 86

Appendix C

"HOTELS DON'T WIN AWARDS - PEOPLE DO!"

Just a few of the team's awards : [180, 181, 182, 183, 184]

The Observatory Hotel and its team were recognised by many magazines, associations and organisations from around the world. Whilst I stood up there and received these awards, the accolades were due to the efforts, skill, dedication and professionalism of every member of the staff at The Observatory who worked with me over the years. I always felt a little uncomfortable that it was I alone who walked on stage as the recipient, and I took the applause. So to all of you for allowing me this honour on your behalf, as the manager, I thank you.

* Gold List - Condé Nast Traveler (U.S.)
* Best Five Star Accommodation - Hotel & Accommodation Management magazine (Australia)
* Best Overall Accommodation in Australia - Hotel & Accommodation Management Magazine
* Best Worldwide City Hotel, Andrew Harper 1997
* Best Townhouse Hotel in World - Tatler Magazine UK, 1998
* 4th Best Holiday Hotel in the World - Zagat Survey of International Hotels
* 6th Best Hotel in the World - (all categories) Conde Nast Traveller Magazine UK 1999

* 5 Diamond Five Star Diamond Award - American Academy of Hospitality Sciences
* Asia Pacific's Leading Hotel, 1998, 1999, 2000 - World Travel Awards
* Best Australian Hotel - Australian Hotel Association Awards 1997, 1998, 1999, 2000
* 20th Best Australasia and South Pacific Overseas Leisure Hotel - Condé Nast Traveller (U.K.)
* 11th Best Pacific Rim Hotel- Condé Nast Traveler (U.S.)
* Australasia's Leading Hotel 2003 - World Travel Awards
* Galileo Restaurant - 1998, 1999, 2000, 2001, 2002 SMH Good Food Guide - 1 Chefs Hat
* Tourism Australia Platinum Award
* HM Awards 2010 - Hotel of the Year
* HM Awards 2011 - Luxury Hotel - Highly Commended

And due to the team's support...

* 'World Independent Hotelier' Nominee - Hotels Magazine 1998
* 'Quintessential Hotelier Award 2004' Tourism Task Force
* 'Australian Manager of the Year' HM Awards 2005
* 'Life Member Award' by AHA NSW
* 'The Industry Hall of Fame' HM Magazine (Inaugural member)
* AHA Johnnie Walker's 'Hall of Fame'
* 'Honorary Life Member' *Les Clefs d'Or*
* 'The Medal of the Order of Australia' (OAM) - Queen's Birthday Honours List, 2009

THE PEOPLE - THE CAST AND CREW OF THE OBSERVATORY HOTEL

I have always maintained that hotels are in the people business and throughout these books I have regularly repeated my mantra: it's not bricks and mortar that bring the guests back time and again. It's the experience: the concierge, the reception, the restaurant, the service, the smiles, and most importantly it's the people who deliver all this to the guests. From those who greet you and check you in smoothly after a long journey, the room attendant who looks after your room, the friendly bartender who remembers your favourite drink; these and the many staff behind the scenes are the ones who really make the difference to your stay at the hotel.

I cannot claim to have been solely responsible for the success of The Observatory or for that matter any other hotel over the past fifty years. The success has been due to the staff around me, whether working with me or for me. They are the people who've made my career so exciting and enjoyable. I give my thanks to them and dedicate these books to them.

Throughout my life, as you have read in the books, I have found great bonds of friendship with many but in particular some from Ireland, who for some reason showed me kindness. Maureen who took me under her wing at the Isles Hotel where I had my very first job as a nervous sixteen year old; Murphy at the Manor House; Hanna Griffin at The Grand; Jimmy O'Shae at The Cavendish and then the irrepressible Frank McGann at The de Montfort in Kenilworth. At The Observatory, it was Ken Ward and Christine Whyte. She always made me laugh and was never afraid to put me in my place if she felt I was wrong. All have been wonderful colleagues and friends along the way. *"Bail ó Dhia do na hÉireannaigh!"*

I've listed here as many of those as I can recall from The Observatory cast and crew, where I spent half of my working career. This roll call is as orderly as I can manage but in no order of priority; thanks to Kirsty Peters and Christine Whyte for coming to my aid. For those in my distant past in England and

Melbourne, you are not forgotten and I am just as grateful for your hard work and friendship over the years.

This may well resemble a telephone directory, and to those whose names have been incorrectly spelt or omitted, and who cry *'Not happy Jan'* - my apologies in advance, please forgive me! I am getting a little older and the grey cells are in retreat.

In no particular order...

Management: Guntha Buhosluv, Russell Bullen (IT), Paul Walters, Andrew Drumond, Ali Ulus, Jeremy Goring, Alfonso Maccioni, Eddie Teh, Phil Musgrove, Grant Raubenheimer and Timo Bures

PA's: Anne-Maree Greeny, Tessa Cooper, Kate Baker, Vanessa Musgrove, Marina Seeto and Pauline Sidhom

Financial Controllers: David Campbell, Scott Downes, Stacy Gurrie, Elsie Vharghese

Accounts: Tina Barrington, Refat Jamil, Smith Zahang, Steve Walters, Benjamin Lee, Richard Mahar, Soe Naing

Purchasing: Richard Werner, Steve Dodsworth, Sam Wu

Security: Robert Elvin.

IT: Jay Polwaththe

Human Resources: Wendy Sawyer, Clodagh Cahill, Karl Wood, Julie Goodwin, Kate McKay, Kirsty Peters, Sam Swan, Marrisa Darris, Lucy Travaskis, Nicole McInerny, Stephanie Jones, Jodi Budd, Lucinda Kay, Samatha Walder, Judy Gomez, Micheline Kazzi

Front Office Management: Kristen Bashir, Matthew Elliot, Keiran Malthouse, Ken Ward, Mario Marangoni, Christine Whyte, Ron

Morris, Andrew Davis, Ben Steele, David Stanton, Craig Scott, Jenny Milner

Guest Service Managers: Phillipa Healy, Susanne North, Tania Reypert, Pascaline Legros, Virginia Maene, Noella Merrick, Polly Maitland, Archana Acharekar, Melissa, Ursula Castillo, Karishma & Rixma Shrestha (Identical twins), Lea Seguir, Elodie Artozoul, Simone Bryan, Tasmeen Kirkby, Vanessa Montiveros

Signature Boutique: Vera Gowling

Florist: Penny from Flowers on Norton

Front Office: Cornelia Rau, Bill Cheung, Isabella Della Cioppa, Muhammad Arif, Brendan Fellows, Michelle Goh, Edward Horman, Bhaskar Nivaskar, Poly Maitland, Amit Peshawaria, Melissa Owsron, Kaitlin Roche, Sam Roche, Mareike Shellenberg, Tin Sein, Cassandra Seow, Louis Sokota, Adrian Pedra, David Stanton, Locky Sutherland, Charlie Griffin, An Avima, Sacha Ubiparipovic, Jerome Wertz, Cassandra Martinenko, Johnny Liu, Robert Shipton, Samantha, Derek

Reservations: Angel Chan, Caroline Elmassian, Kim Roach, James Tsui, Natalie O'Brien, Julie, Kevin Miller, Julie, Pete Boddy, Maria, Jennifer Jones, Daniela Castro, Wendy Wilson, Anna Huntley, Dewi Woen, Yvonne Yau.

Concierge: Basil Cole, Guy, Michael Anderson, Damien Irvine, David Sutherland, Simon Matthews, Tori Johnson, Deo Zagami, Simon Bestre, David Metcalfe, Martin Bray, Michael Balaik, Ryan Gavin, Quercy Jouannes, Brian Hennessy, Simon Xian, Richard Bell, Toby Young,

Executive Housekeeper and his team: Emil Bashay, Simon Pawson, Kylie Williamson, Brendon Wood, Buddy Gamboa, Carol Hegarty, Elsie (Leng Choo Tan) & Soshilla (Liu Yuk ChingYeung)

Executive Chefs: Kit Chan, Mark Clayton, Anthony Musarra, Randal St Clare, Steve Grein, Haru Inukai, Masahiko Yomoda

The Brigade: Francesco Zonta, Ryo Seita, Stephen Tseng, Ewa Goralewski, Melissa McGeoch , Elsa Li, Hanif Muhammad, Malissa Au, Yamund Christiansen, Hideaki Matsumoto, Eduardo Almeida, Seiji Hayashi, Chou Chou Shuhei Nitta, Stephan Kaptain, Shimon Hanakura, Nick Honeyman, Andrew Naudi, Kevin Nguyen, Karl Reyes, Victor Liong, Michael .?, Penchan Siriwatna

Food and Beverage Team: Alberto Tita, Glen Boyland, Stuart MacKenzie, Stuart Port, Paulus den Haan, Alex Jacks, John Gunn, Mahen Guneratne, Grandee Hui, Mario Britti, Simon Doughty, Chris Culver, David Cocker, David Griffiths, Jan Barth, Gabbi Williams, Simon Jeffries, Ernesto Faundez , Sinim Ha, Christian Baeppler, Nicholas Cleradin, Nicholas Clapton, Ankur Sharma, Nevitta Dodds, Magno De Silva, Lyn Nattiya, Richard Brack, Shelby Rejoice, Bennie Gill, Apurpa Gomez, John Gunn, Jessica Kanerva, Mary Mouawad, Dani Krieke, Corrine Newson, Heman Pullut, Rizaldi Radityo, Selina So, Prapaporn Soda, Sumeet Nathan, Charmaine Stieger, Jake Boyd, Nitin Maithani, Bjoern Wenner, Sudhir Acharya, Nathan Sumeet, Rosie?, Insuke Pae, Adam McCarron, Sakul Tapa.

Globe Bar: Walter Lasses, Stuart Mackenzie, Trent Morson, Mohan Deheragoda

Directors of Sales & Marketing: John Verhelst, Angela Clarke, Vicky Legg, Marianna Luno, Yvonne Dolphin, Julian Haggar

Directors of PR: Angela Clarke, Joyce De Mascio, Megan Staal, Kim Salt

The Sales & Marketing Team: Erica Sue, Rhonda Valpato, Justine Mainwaring, Vivian Voultiantis, Donald Wong, Karen Karakashian,

Julie Adams, Sally McIntosh, Shane Arrold, Evelina Conti, Michelle Neilsen, Annalisa Gray, Cassandra Barter, Chriscelle Capito, Grethel Sanchez, Rebecca Cooper, Rita Gil, Suzan Griffin, Emma Jenkins, Dirk Loeb, Jenny Milner, Kylie Eilliamson, Johnathan Giles, Amanada Patience, Christine Haddad, Angela Purnell, Cassandra Barter, Ashley Jade, Stephen Arnold, Max Rodella, Maya Wetering de Roo, Mark Wilson, Birgette Winther, Verity Kitto, Grethel Sanchez, Ashley Hucker.

Health and Leisure Club: Kendra, Nicky Hucker

Day Spa: Deborah Manghum, Tania Specht, Nik Pappas, Svetlana Strbac, Karrie Allen, Malthi, Samantha Swan, Psyche Wong, Rebbeca Barlow, Dominic Borel, Jerry Jaroslav Thorovsky, Jodie Chin, Samantha Clitheroe, Rodney de Andrade, Vanessa Wood, Deborah Melloy, Kerrie Allen, Jodie Chin

Chief Engineer and the Team: Charlie Dodsworth, Janusz Zaklikowski, Dick Graham, Bichara Hawwa, Ken Gurnett, Mihailo Jankovic, Luke Werner, Barry Rose.

...and all the other unsung heroes, wherever you are.

Finally, where it began at The Observatory Hotel: Michael was with me from the beginning and we ensured he was no longer the 'face of the unemployed'... lest he forget:

https://www.facebook.com/dods77/videos/10204543607698156

Photographs

1. Hotel Como's discreet entrance.

2. The Como foyer, granite, chrome, birds eye maple walls and the 'The Aurora Australis' tapestry

3. The Bedroom, minimalist, with lots of 5° angles, looked good but not the most comfortable

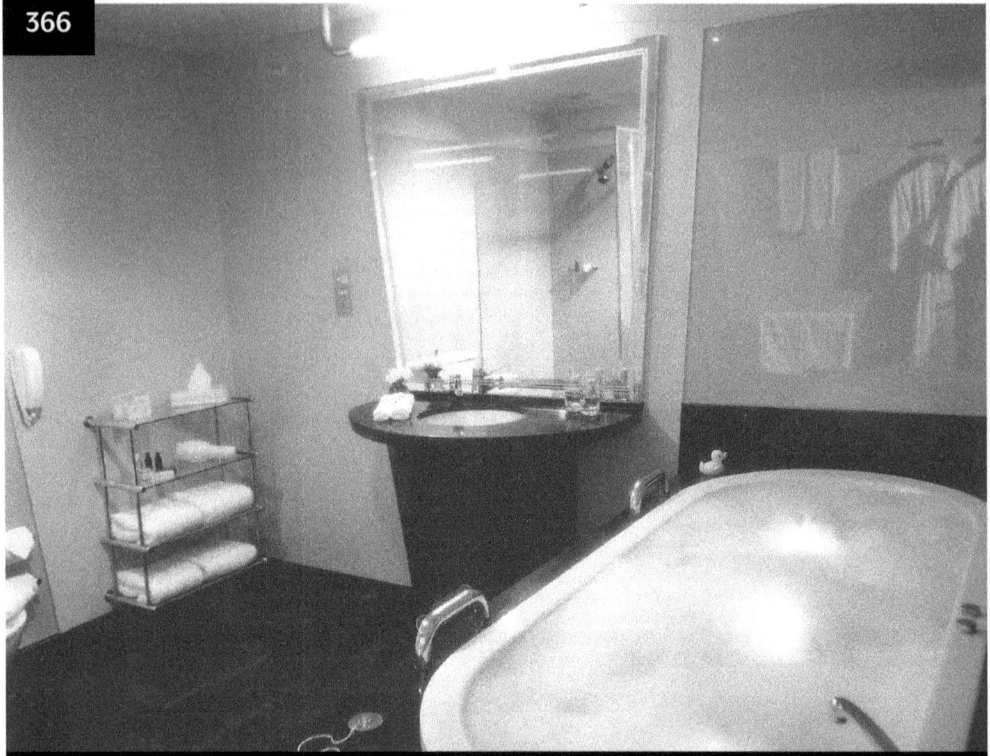

4. The Bathroom, with the deep Japanese spa tub - we had to build steps.

5. The famous Art Ducko, The Como Duck

6. Como's Japanese rooftop gardens

7. *Barry Everingham, Lady Clarke & Lady Sonia McMahon*

8. *My wife Bina & I at the 'Bird Cage' for The Melbourne Cup*

9. *The Team, first year winners at the Australian Tourism Awards*

TOP AUSTRALIAN BUSINESS HOTELS

	All travellers		
Hotel Como Melbourne	(1)	85.00	11.1
Mirage Gold Coast	(2)	83.64	27.8
Mirage Port Douglas	(3)	82.64	19.0
Regent Sydney	(4)	80.94	65.9
Rockmans Regency Melb.	(5)	80.71	44.4
Hyatt Regency Adelaide	(6)	80.64	38.9
Hyatt Melbourne	(7)	79.29	68.3
Intercontinental Sydney	(8)	78.23	63.5
Burswood Perth	(9)	76.89	22.2
Gold Coast International	(10)	76.32	17.5
Sebel Sydney	(11)	76.18	38.1
Ramada Sydney	(12)	75.43	18.3
Hyatt Perth	(13)	73.24	23.0
Sheraton W'worth Sydney	(14)	71.16	57.9
Parramatta ParkRoyal	(15)	71.15	16.7
Jupiters Gold Coast	(16)	71.02	46.0
Hilton Adelaide	(17)	70.27	58.7
Observation City Perth	(18)	70.00	18.3
Windsor Melbourne	(19)	69.96	46.8
Sheraton Perth	(20)	69.52	54.0
Menzies Melbourne	(21)	69.13	50.0
Hilton Brisbane	(22)	67.58	48.4

10. *Hotel Como - Voted 1# in Australian Business Magazine*

11. *Don Neilson & two of the team & another award*

12. *Shirley MacLean without Charlemagne*

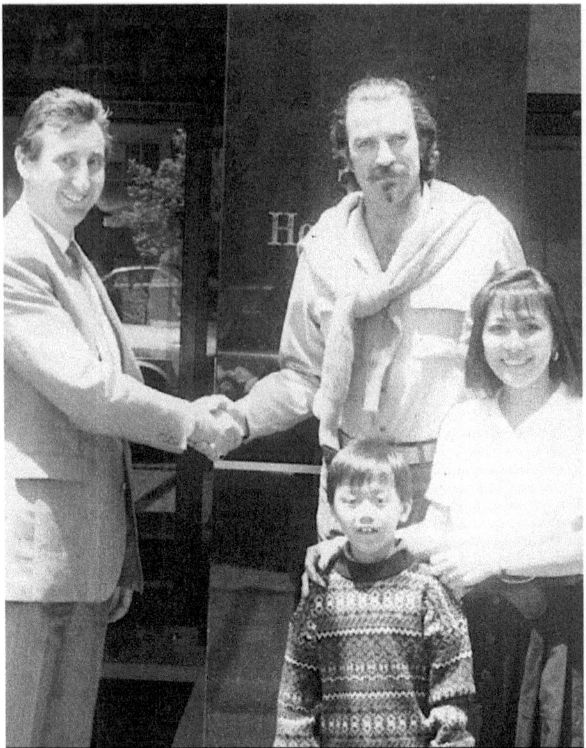

13. *Magnum PI, Tom Selleck - with son Tim, Bina & I*

14. *My son Tim, with Mission Impossible Team (TV)*

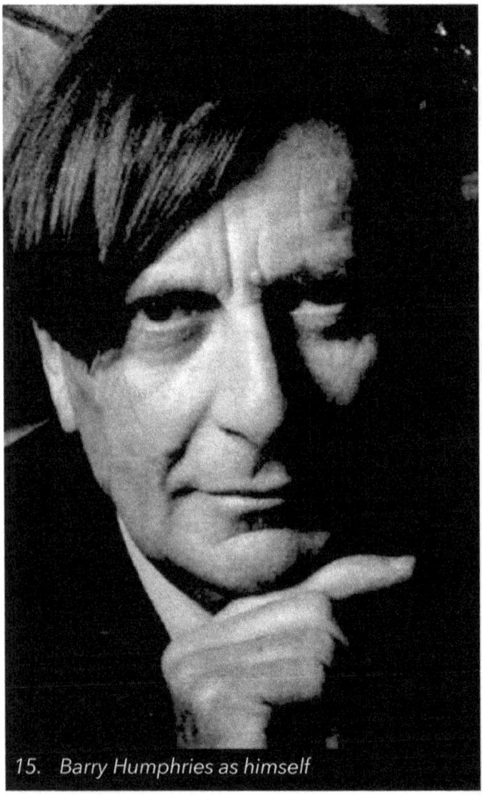

15. *Barry Humphries as himself*

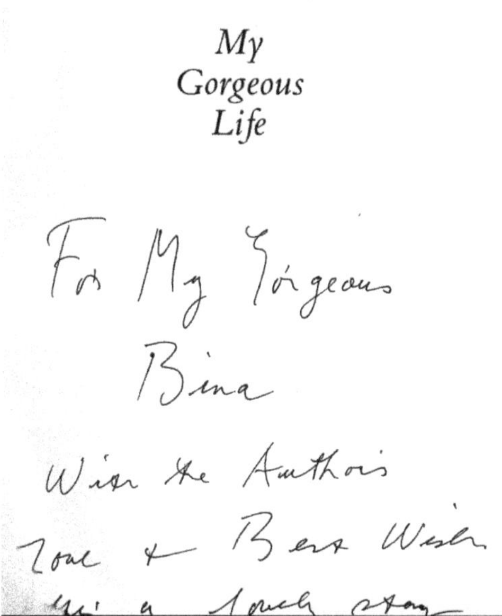

16. His alter ego Dame Edna's kind note to my wife

17. "The Mole" first appears at Como with Maurice & Barry Gibb of The Bee Gees

18. The Mole: unofficial paparazzo with Simon Le Bon and Nick Rhodes of Duran Duran

19. The lovely Lulu who gave Bina, Tim & I a 'spiritual experience'

20. The Mole is back with Mick Fleetwood of Fleetwood Mac

21. ...with Stevie Nicks

22. ...with Melissa Etheridge

23. ...with Eric Clapton

24. ...and again with BB King

25. ...and yet again with Bono of U2

26. ...and with Edge of U2

27. My Father's funeral, Chris, me, Bob, Ginny, to be the last photo with Mum who died the following year, and Bob who was to die shortly after of AIDS which we only found out about afterwards.

28. Good friends in a time of need, the affable Terry Holmes of Ritz, London & Michael Hall of the Sebel, Sydney

29. Charlie, our Aussie born son arrives just in time for our move to Sydney 1991

30. Meeting in Yokohama with Jim & Simon Sherwood, Jean Paul Foerster and Mr Nara, Mr Seigo & Mr Matsamura.

31. *The Observatory Hotel under construction*

32. *Millers Point Residents Committee 1993*

33. *Defects, a question of reflections in the mirror, all in the detail*

34. *Our leading Chefs Kit Chan ,Francisco Zonta, with food critic Leo Schofield*

35. *First Orient-Express Conference, Windsor Court, New Orleans, 1992, then 14 Hotels & Trains*

36. *Enjoying a night out in New Orleans with colleagues, before Katrina*

38. *Giving comfort to New Orleans Saints cheerleaders after Hurricane Katrina*

37. *Gordon Campbell Gray (One Aldwych, London) & Raymond Bickson (The Mark Hotel NY)*

39. *New York to London and an invitation to the flight deck on Concorde*

40. *Sharing a joke with London restauranteurs Roy Ackerman (The Gay Hussar and L'Etoile) & Richard Shepherd (Langan's,)*

41. *My future Orient-Express Journey all mapped out*

42. *Travelling London to Venice on The Orient-Express*

43. *My new creature comforts of my cabin, so different from my last train journey*

44. *My dining experience, an improvement on the British rail buffet car*

45. *The Observatory Hotel, Sydney now open*

46. *President, James B Sherwood at the opening*

47. *Our first 'royal' the very interesting Prince Tomislav of Yugoslavia*

48. *The Observatory Hotel opening team, 1992*

49. John Farnham with team members Archana and Simon 1993

50. Australia's own, Ernie Dingo & John Wood

51. Members of Metallica with chief concierge Michael

52. Lars Ulrich of Metallica & son Tim looking

very pleased having just beaten him at tennis
53. TV icon, presenter Ray Martin

54. Greeting Vietnam PM, Vo Van Kiet, unexpectedly with local resident Joyce

55. Michael Crawford & a young Richard Wilkins

56. Movie Director Sir David & Lady Putnam with Noella

57. HRH Prince Charles having been dragged into a photo with AHA Sydney hoteliers

58. HRH Prince Michael of Kent & staff member Justine

59. HRH Prince Michael of Kent on his 2nd visit, the 'impoverished peer'

60. The charming and urbane King Tupou V of Tonga

61. Sarah Duchess of York, with a sparkle in her eye, a kind comment & a nice gift

62. Gabriel Byrne who impressed the Duchess

63. *President Ramos of the Philippines, his wife, with only the shoes she wore and my wife and I.*

64. *Archbishop Desmond Tutu, activist, Nobel Prize winner with a great sense of humour*

65. *Another colony lost, Anson Chan, the new Chief Secretary of Hong Kong*

66. *UK Labour Leader Tony Blair (soon to be PM) cast off the cloth cap Labour image*

67. *Paul Keating, a very talented PM, or The Lizard of Oz as the British press refer to him.*

68. *A rather feisty Bronwyn Bishop (Speaker of the House of Reps) and Lady Sonia McMahon*

69. *Gough Whitlam who radically changed Australia's economic, legal and cultural landscape*

70. *John Howard, second-longest serving Prime Minister, behind Sir Robert Menzies*

71. *Tevin Campbell, not the Scotsman I thought.*

72. *Nicky of Westlife with my deputy Grant Raubenheimer*

73. *Lovely siblings, Kylie & Dannii Minogue speaking with press in the Globe Bar*

74. *A regular favourite Olivia Newton-John*

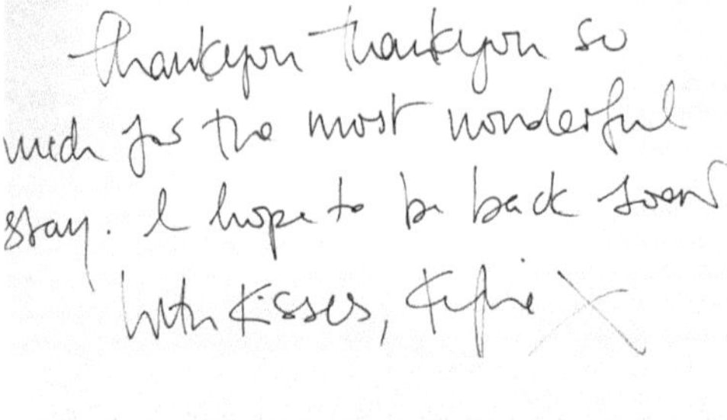

Thankyou thankyou so
much for the most wonderful
stay. I hope to be back soon
With Kisses, Kylie X

75. *The nice note left by Kylie*

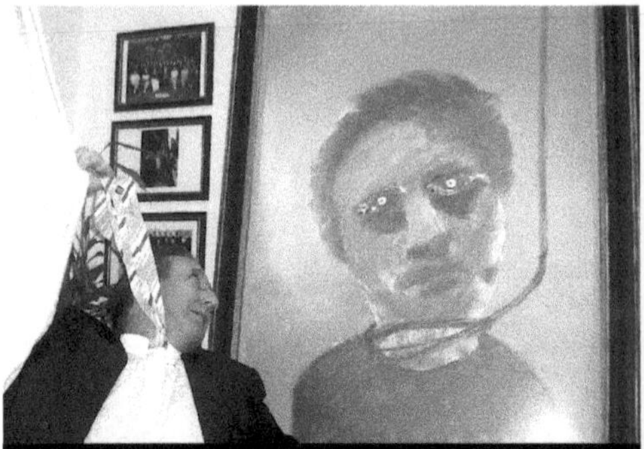

76. *The infamous Sidney Nolan's Billy Budd, my first Sotheby's purchase, not with my money*

77. *Andrea Tennant, wife of the likeable Christopher with Michael, ex-concierge, in 2019*

78. *Sir Richard Branson, the high flyer with Phillipa Healy*

79. *Phil Collins, one of my favourite musicians.*

80. *Randy Crawford, an all time favourite*

81. Chaka Kahn - R&B, soul, funk, pop, disco, she did it all

82. Tom Jones & son Tim in his Scots College kilt, educated by Tom as to the clan

83. Thelma Houston, Queen of Motown

84. Nigel Kennedy, violin prodigy and oh what a party boy

85. Who had an embarrassing moment, locked out and nowhere to go?

86. Maybe a little under the weather: down & out

87. ...But the staff came to the rescue

88. Our tennis court, where some 'greats' were to play

89. The dynamic duo of tennis, the Two Woody's with Susanne North.

90. Swim star, Hayley Lewis and the Team, still unsure of what they were promoting

91. Sachin Tendulkar, a king in his sport, also known as God of Cricket

92. David Coulthard. F1 racing driver, won 13 Grand Prix, with Susanna North

93. Torvill & Dean. Ice skaters as famous as their signature tune, Bolero

94. Sir Edmund Hillary, a man of few words

95. Buzz Aldrin, the astronaut who left an impression on me as well as the moon

96. Sally K Ride - First American woman in space

97. K Megan-McArthur - No longer just astronaut but 'Space Shuttle Capsule Communicator'

98. *Patrick, Lord Litchfield, he loved expression & hated botox*

99. *Alan Whicker an expressive gentleman who even shocked me.*

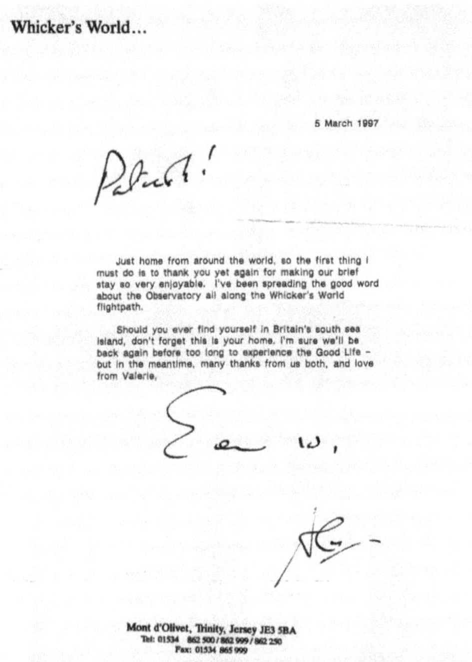

Whicker's World...

5 March 1997

Patrick!

Just home from around the world, so the first thing I must do is to thank you yet again for making our brief stay so very enjoyable. I've been spreading the good word about the Observatory all along the Whicker's World flightpath.

Should you ever find yourself in Britain's south sea island, don't forget this is your home. I'm sure we'll be back again before too long to experience the Good Life – but in the meantime, many thanks from us both, and love from Valerie,

Mont d'Olivet, Trinity, Jersey JE3 5BA
Tel: 01534 862 500 / 862 999 / 862 250
Fax: 01534 865 999

100. *A personal invitation to stay at the Whicker's residence in Jersey, sadly not taken up.*

101. *Michael Palin left Monty Python to travel & remained just as amusing*

102. *Sir David Frost who wanted to laugh in every photo*

103. *David Suzuki, who predicted global warming, with staff yet to be convinced*

104. *Sir David Attenborough sensitive to nature and to me it seemed*

105. *Seeking guidance in Rio de Janeiro, machine guns at the ready.*

106. *Keeping fit on Copacabana Beach*

107. OBS team experiencing the full Atkin's Diet at La Cabana, Buenos Ares

108. Our company meeting in London, growing larger in 1999

109. Nick Seewer & I enjoy some elegant transport in Charleston, South Carolina

110. Flying out to a meeting in Botswana to join the Big Five

111. Meeting at the famed 21 Club, New York, an old speakeasy, and life was looking up

112. Getting 'fortified' for our meeting in Reid's Palace, Madeira

113. Gathering at our newly acquired hotel The Ritz, Madrid - a religious experience

114. By 2004 our meetings had grown even further, here at the Inn at Perry Cabin on The Chesapeake Bay, to be the location for the movie 'Wedding Crashers'

115. 'My chum' Nick Seewer' and I, jovially referred to as OEH's Statler & Waldorf

116. Nick & I in customary style in Siem Reap, Cambodia with John Rogers, his wife & Sven Gevers

117. Keeping cool in Cambodia

118. US Travel Agents boarding The E&O Express, for an adventure in Thailand

119. A trip to buy Lizard Island on the Great Barrier Reef with Simon and Paul but no luck; instead we found a treasure in Robin Pontynen, new GM at Lilianfels.

120. Friends on The Great South Pacific Express, truly a great Australian experience, sadly short lived.

121. Never too many cooks - The first - Chef Kit Chan

122. An Englishman - Chef Mark Clayton

123. Home grown Aussie - Chef Anthony Musarra

124. Our American from Portland - Chef Randell St Clare

125. Chef Steve Grein a well travelled Aussie.

126. From Japan - Chef Haru Inukai, a master of creativity.

127. From a Tokyo Michelin Star restaurant - Chef Masahiko Yomoda

128. Chef Renato Piccoloto of The Cipriani, Venice

129. Guest Chef Christian Bodiguel, of The Venice Simplon Orient-Express Train, who enjoyed the adventure at the launch of Australia's own GSPE

130. From our sister property - Chef Garth Stroebel of Mount Nelson, Cape Town

131. No broth spoiled by these visiting Chefs - Tetsuya Wakuda, Yanni Kyritsis, Stefano Manfredi, Randal St Clare, Luke Mangan & Charlie Trotter

132. The extraordinarily talented guest Chef Charlie Trotter of Trotter's, Chicago

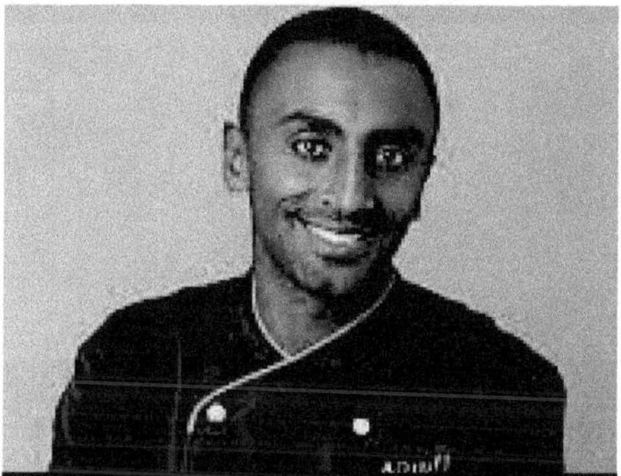

133. Chef Marcus Samuelson of Aquavit, New York, arrived just before '9-11' yet the show went on

134. The entertaining Ainsley Harriott from UK TV

135. Iron Chef, Eddie Teh & Manager of La Rochelle, Tokyo.

136. Iron Chef Team of 2008

137. Iron Chef Team face off, Haru, Yomo, Sakai & Chen

138. Iron Chef Chen & Sakai with host the delightful Tomo Ishikawa

139. Host John Mangos (TV Presenter) following the traditional of biting into the capsicum

IRON CHEF DINNER
MENU 2008

WELCOME COCKTAIL
GUAVATINI

CANAPÉS
1996 DUVAL-LEROY BRUT, VERTUS, CHAMPAGNE, FRANCE

SEASONAL CRAB MEAT WITH AVOCADO, TOMATO COULIS
BY GALILEO'S CHEF YOMODA
2007 FRANZ KÜNSTLER 'ESTATE' RIESLING, RHEINGAU, GERMANY

CONSOMMÉ OF LAMB & CHINESE DUMPLINGS
BY FRENCH IRON CHEF SAKAI
10 YEAR OLD MADEIRA, HENRIQUES & HENRIQUES, MADEIRA, PORTUGAL

STEAMED SNAPPER AND LENTIL PUREE, SHELLFISH BUTTER SAUCE
BY FRENCH IRON CHEF SAKAI
2006 HOWARD PARK CHARDONNAY, GREAT SOUTHERN, WESTERN AUSTRALIA

MOUKA SHARK'S FIN WITH SOYA SAUCE GRAVY
BY CHINESE IRON CHEF CHEN
2007 KILTYNANE ESTATE 'PRELIMINAIRE' BLANC DE NOIR, YARRA VALLEY, VICTORIA

ROASTED TAJIMA WAGYU BEEF À LA BLANCHARU
BY CHEF HARU
2006 AMISFIELD PINOT NOIR, CENTRAL OTAGO, SOUTH ISLAND, NEW ZEALAND

SZECHWAN TAN TAN NOODLES
BY CHINESE IRON CHEF CHEN
'MYSTERY WINE'

APPLE TARTE TATIN WITH MANGO SAUCE
BY GALILEO'S CHEF YOMODA
2006 NIGL GRÜNER VELTLINER EISWEIN, KAMPTAL, AUSTRIA

140. The Menu served on the night

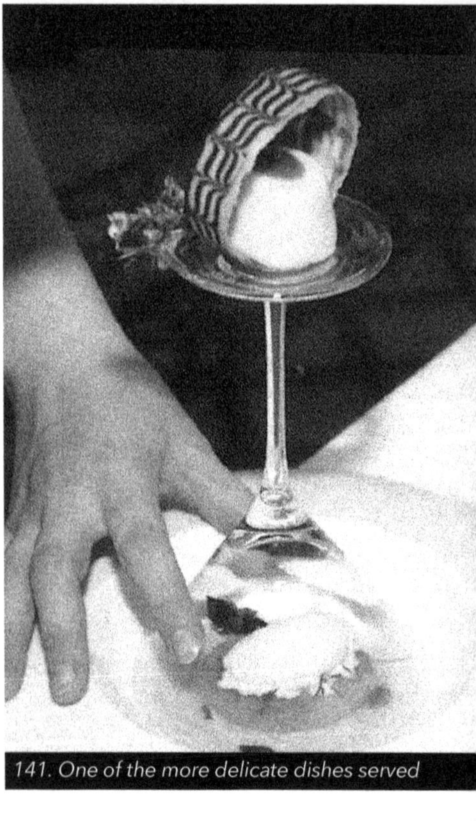

141. One of the more delicate dishes served

142. Even a tray of empty glasses can sometimes be a challenge

143. Some of the Iron Chef Team admiring their handiwork

144. Jan Barth, the multi talented photographer of the event

145. Lady Sonia McMahon & Lady Susan Renouf, such lovely smiles

146. Victoria Mather & Carol Thatcher - Tatler Award, Best Townhouse Hotel in World at The Ritz, London 1998

147. All smiles with the real Priscilla Presley

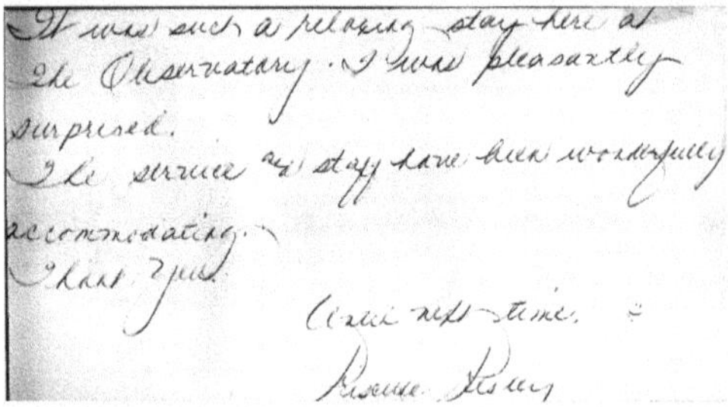

It was such a relaxing stay here at the Observatory. I was pleasantly surprised.
The service and staff have been wonderfully accommodating.
Thank you.
Until next time.
Priscilla Presley

148. …The nice note left by Prescilla.

149. Australia's own, Cate Blanchett

150. Glenn Close, none the worse for wear after her prison camp ordeal

151. *English actress Elizabeth Spriggs who shared the prison experience*

152. *Kim Cattrall of Sex in the City made David's day in the lift*

153. *Stephanie Powers, of Hart to Hart fame, with Marianne Lunoe*

154. *Hollywood great Cyd Charisse, undervalued by the local celeb snipper*

155. *With the lovely Ruth Cracknell, shortly before her death*

156. *Burlesque star, the very ebullient Dita von Teese*

157. *…The extravagant 'Thank you' from Dita.*

158. Geoffrey Rush went on to win the Triple Crown of Acting

159. Charming Ralph Fiennes with Phil Musgrove

160. Rowan Atkinson aka Mr Bean

161. Matthew Perry, a staff heartthrob.

162. Carrie Fisher, Princess Leia was nowhere to be seen

163. Charles Dance, not as villainous as the parts he played

164. Dudley Moore encroaches on Alex the hotel pianist's turf

165. Jean-Paul Gaultier, with his signature as unique as his designs

166. Susannah York, whom I had adored since my teens

167. Robert Picardo, The Doctor from Star Trek consults with Simon Matthew

168. Rene Auberjonois- An original with MASH left 'to boldly go where no man has gone before'

169. Val Kilmer all smiles but not a happy chappie

170. Tom Sizemore not a great fan of Val his co-star

171. Sons, Tim & Charlie at my investiture for an Order of Australia

172. My last OEH Conference, Charleston, South Carolina, from 14 to 60 Hotels & Trains by 2010; times they were a'changing.

173. One of the annual 'Where's Wally' team photo boards that appeared from 1992-2011

174. Cornelia Rau, who appeared on our photo board, and sadly later became the subject of a TV drama, staring Cate Blanchett

175. *This Is Your Life - My big surprise by TV Host John Mangos*

176. *Glenn E Baker, whose voice and music on Qantas had travelled the world with me for almost 20 years*

178. *Wonderful plotters and colleagues, Kim Salt, Maya de Royta, & Christine Whyte*

177. *Another surprise, not a proposal, old friend and colleague Jeremy Goring flew in from The Goring in London*

179. *Guests & good friends, John Mangos, Peter Aloi & Ian Smith*

180. Collecting The AHA Best Hotel Trophy which needed its own seat on the return flight

181. Hotel Team AHA Awards 1998

182. Hotel Team AHA Awards 2001

183. Hotel Team HM Awards 2005

184. Hotel Team HM Awards 2007

185. Under whom we served - The Presidents of Orient-Express - James B Sherwood

186. Simon Sherwood

187. Paul White

INDEX

C

G

H

I

J

K

L

M

N

O

P

Q

R

S

T

U

V

W

Y

Z

Milton Keynes UK
Ingram Content Group UK Ltd.
UKHW021818201123
432921UK00014B/999

9 780645 055924